Jagannath Basu & Jayjit Sarkar (eds.)

Geographia Literaria

Studies in Earth, Ethics, and Literature

Jagannath Basu & Jayjit Sarkar (eds.)

GEOGRAPHIA LITERARIA

Studies in Earth, Ethics, and Literature

Bibliografische Information der Deutschen Nationalbibliothek

Die Deutsche Nationalbibliothek verzeichnet diese Publikation in der Deutschen Nationalbibliografie; detaillierte bibliografische Daten sind im Internet über http://dnb.d-nb.de abrufbar.

Bibliographic information published by the Deutsche Nationalbibliothek

Die Deutsche Nationalbibliothek lists this publication in the Deutsche Nationalbibliografie; detailed bibliographic data are available in the Internet at http://dnb.d-nb.de.

ISBN-13: 978-3-8382-1580-6

© *ibidem*-Verlag, Stuttgart 2021

In the hope for ~~a~~ better ~~Earth~~ Earthians.

Table of Contents

Preface

Geographia Literaria is the result of our humble effort to bring forth a complete volume on the varied existing studies on the intrinsic relationship between earth, ethics and art. It seeks to understand the ethical involvement of art in general and literature in particular with the planet and vice-versa, the way the geo-materiality of the planet influences art and the *poiesis* of art. In doing so, the volume makes a distinction between the socio-political, cultural and economic aspects of the "world" and the physical geography of the "earth". It focuses on the latter, especially the vital materialism of the natural world, instead of the anthropomorphism of the former. Each chapter in this volume deals with mankind's involvement with the natural world and the different ways such "involvementality" is represented in world literature.

A catalogue of speediness and slowness, relations of motion and rest, in a Deleuzian manner, molded the making of this book. The world was still battling the second wave of Covid 19 pandemic; hence it was emotionally challenging for every one of us, be it in any part of the world. It is worth recounting that this riveting experience of putting these longitudes and latitudes of emotions together was only made possible because of our mutual understanding and collaborative mentality. The contributions by Jayson Althofer, Mario Bosincu, Ratul Nandi, Pavlína Flajšarová, Ankita Sharma, Oriol Batalla, Rachel L. Carazo and Debnita Chakravarti really make the reading of this volume a rich experience. We are extremely indebted to all of them for bearing with us and showing their tremendous patience throughout the project. We also thank Prof. Douglas Vakoch, Professor Emeritus, Department of Clinical Psychology, California Institute of Integral Studies and President of METI International and Prof. Lauri Scheyer, Xiaoxiang Distinguished Professor at Hunan Normal University and Professor Emeritus of English and Creative Writing at California State University, Los Angeles, USA for their incredible support and encouragement. Finally, we would like to offer our sincere gratitude to all the staffs at ibidem Press for being extremely cooperative and accommodating throughout this journey.

Jagannath Basu

Jayjit Sarkar

India

5 April 2021

Introduction

"I think *where* I am not, therefore I am *where* I do not think."
—Jacques Lacan, *Écrits: A Selection*

Give me a place to stand on and I can move the earth: thus affirms the third century BC Sicilian mathematician Archimedes. What is this *place* that Archimedes is suggesting here and how is that different from *space*? Is it an island, an archipelago or a continent? And moreover, is it a geographical or an epistemological assertion? Or both? If we account and go on to explain the different reverberations of this statement, will that be considered as geography (from the Greek, *gē* + *-graphia* meaning "earth-writing"): a form of writing done on the earth or writings on Earth or "writing-earth"? Is it at all possible to have such a disciplined understanding on the "topic" (from the Greek *topos* meaning "place")? And, if space, time and causality are pure *a priori* intuitions, why then is Archimedes asking for one? How can one ask for a place until and unless one has one already? Because in order to ask *for* a place one has to ask *from* a place. What kind of place does he wants—real, imagined or real-imagined? Is it an imperative to ask for place? Is asking for a place a "hypothetical imperative" for moving the earth or is it a "categorical imperative"? And is it an obligation to "give" place? Who will give whom and to what extent? Am I only asking for place or, "place" is only a mode by which I am trying to get other things? Does a place assure anything? And is its assurance based on condition/s?

Understanding a place is overtly a complex phenomenon constituting processes which are psychic, somatic, psychosomatic, historical, geographical, literary, cultural, ecological, racial, and, most importantly, temporal. The space-time continuum does not allow us to understand place/space in its unconditioned or "pure" form. A place is where time is made tangible, and at the same time, one cannot *be* at the same place twice. There is a certain kind of *pace* (distance covered by time) to p(l)ace and/or (s)pace. What Heraclitus thinks about time is even analogous to place: "No man ever steps onto the same [place] twice, for it's not the same [place] and he's not the same man" (our insertion). Although, we have been using "place" and "space" interchangeably so far, they are very different from each other: "space appears to be the more general term; it implies a certain expansion and is therefore to certain extent unknowable"; in contrast, "place" is "considered to be smaller, more specific and local area that is characterized by its familiarity, the possibility of orientation and manageability" (Schröder 2006, 45). "Space" has no value attached to it and is more or less abstract; "place" on the other hand is created by human experience, "[w]hat begins as undifferentiated space becomes 'place' as we get to know it better and endow it with value" (Tuan 2001, 6). In the daily humdrum of our existence we do not experience this difference: place and space are dialectically intertwined as they derive meaning from each other. But as Yi-Fu Tuan observes lyrically, "place is security, space is freedom" (3). The subtlety with which Tuan distinguishes place and space is unprecedented in the western metaphysics.

Does space or place exist in itself? The question is overwhelming and it has overwhelmed the twentieth-century, science and aesthetics equally, to a great extent or what we now call "the spatial turn." The "turn" is characterized by a renewed understanding of territorial knowledge or earth-knowledge — a sort of geographical consciousness. This geographical consciousness or "conscience géographique" — "the intimate and subjective Geography" — eventually led to the establishment of categories like "Geopoetics" and many others such as Bertrand Westphal's "geocriticism", Geopolitics, Geohistoire and Geophilosophy (Italiano 2008, 2). The influence of the "turn" can also be observed in critical understandings in Edward Said's "imaginative geography", Deleuze and Guattari's "de/territorialisation", Gloria Anzaldua's "the borderland", Gaston Bachelard's "topophilia", Edward Soja's "the postmodern geographies", Frederic Jameson's "cognitive mapping", Henri Lefebvre and Michel Foucault's the "production of spaces", Robert T. Tally's "literary cartography", James Lovelock's "Gaia", Marc Shell's "islandology" and Kenneth White's "Geopoetics", to name only a few. The fundamental ideas of place and space on the earth and how we negotiate with and react to them is the underlying semasiological or psycho-geographical principle which cuts across all these varied and at times conflicting schools. How are we on/with the earth? Isn't our body and psyche integral parts of the earth-thought? Isn't art, taking a cue from Hölderlin, a symptom of the way "man lives poetically on the *earth*"? — are some of the pivotal questions which this geo-turn puts forward.

On Geopoet(h)ics

As one of the major movements, Kenneth White's "Geopoetics" tries to *create* E(art)h, an eclectic (in)fusion of art and earth, so that the world of the art always remain in touch with the earth of the world. White, while writing for the Institute of Geopoetics in 1989, lays bare the fundamentals of "Geopoetics" in the following manner:

> If, around 1978, I began to talk of "geopoetics", it was for two reasons. On the one hand, it was becoming more and more obvious that the earth (the biosphere) was in danger and that ways, both deep and efficient, would have to be worked out in order to protect it. On the other hand, I had always been of the persuasion that the richest poetics came from contact with the earth, from a plunge into biospheric space, from an attempt to read the lines of the world.

> [...] In the fundamental geopoetic field come together poets and thinkers of all times and of all countries. To quote only a few examples, in the West, one can think of Heraclitus ("man is separated from what is closest to him"), Holderlin ("man lives poetically on the earth"), or Wallace Stevens (the poems of heaven and hell have been written, it remains to write the poem of the earth"). In the East, there is the Taoist Tchuang-tzu, the man of the ancient pool, Matsuo Basho, and beautiful world-meditations such as one can find in the Hwa Yen Sutra. (White 1989)

This sounds less in the manner of a manifesto and more a passionate outburst towards a *creation* of E(art)h: the word "Geopoetics" comes from *gē* (meaning, "earth") and *poiesis* (meaning, "to create"). The *poiesis* in Geo-poetics has a sort of Heideggerian "bringing-forth", herein case bringing forth of the earth, not as something which was hitherto not there but by bringing something from concealment into unconcealment and from darkness to light. The earth is "brought into the light (or clearing) opened up by the created work itself" (Whitehead 2003, 3). The phenomenon, as Murray Cox and Alice Theilgaard remark in their discussion of *poiesis* as "poetry without poets — the blooming of the blossom, the coming-out of a butterfly from a cocoon, the plummeting of a waterfall when the snow begins to melt" and then go on to point out that, "the last two analogies underline the fact that Heidegger's example is a threshold occasion, a moment of ecstasis when something moves away from its standing as one thing to become another" (1997, 23) The "Geopoetics" as "thinking" (*noein*) "always, already" constitutes not only the idea of the earth but the earth itself (*gē-*) and also, not only the poetry but the very process of creation (*poiesis*). The "Geopoetics" is "poetry" of the earth and "poetry" with the earth in the etymological sense of the word.

And as one would expect, "Geopoetics" is not only the task of the poets and philosophers but rather interests or *should* interest a whole gamut of thinkers whether scientists or aesthetes. Kenneth White writes:

> ... [G]eopoetics is not the exclusive domain of poets and thinkers. Henry Thoreau was as much an ornithologist and a meteorologist ("inspector of storms") as he was a poet, or rather, we might say, he included the sciences in his poetics. The link with biology is just as necessary, and with an ecology (including mind-ecology) well-grounded and well-developed. In fact geopoetics provides not only a place, and this is proving more and more necessary, where poetry, thought and science can come together, in a climate of reciprocal inspiration, but a place where all kinds of specific disciplines can converge, once they are ready to leave over-restricted frameworks and enter into global (cosmological, cosmopoetic) space. One question is paramount: how is it with life on earth, how is it with the world? (White 1989)

More than the "on" what is being emphasized here is "with": the "with-the-place", the "with-the-earth" poetics and hermeneutics. The place ceases to remain merely the background but rather foregrounds itself, at the forefront of our understanding showcasing how our pre/consciousness is always intertwined and shaped by the *Umwelten* (the "environs"). "The Geopoetics" as

Italiano points out, "of an author is to be understood as his territorial intelligence, poetic and imagining ability for producing and constructing [*poiesis*] a world, his characteristic determination and presentation of the relation Man-Earth" (Italiano 2008, 6). The literature as heterocosm is here understood in terms of more earth-ly geocosm and biocosm. Let us un-earth this deep-rooted spatiality in the two major (and very disparate) works of literature: Joseph Conrad's *Heart of Darkness* and Kālidāsa's *Meghaduta*, and compare their "Geopoetics".

***

The choice of the texts here might look very eclectic and erratic, and certainly not naïve; as a matter of fact, it is eclectic and erratic. The choice is also not a routine postcolonial discursive practice either. The subject-position of Kālidāsa's *Meghaduta* is not as the postcolonial *other* or br*other* of Joseph Conrad's *Heart of Darkness*. The former stands in the capacity of its own merit as a text which is geographically conscious. On the other hand, Conrad is the favourite child of all dealing with the intersection between literature and geography and his *Heart of Darkness* is the productive meeting ground of the two. The underlying principle behind the choice of *Meghaduta* and *Heart of Darkness* is quite simply the fact that they are so much different from each other — spatially, temporally, culturally and socially — but what binds them together is some sort of what Albert Einstein would call *spooky action at a distance*. In both these works we find *writing* as a mode of *earthing*, and that is precisely what this book also aims at. The eerie connection between the two: Conrad and Kālidāsa, apart from the similar consonant sound, is the "earth" or the earth-consciousness. Both the authors and their respective works encourage and propel a dialogue between the consciousnesses of the narrators (Marlow and *yakṣa*) and the topoi "they" traverse: Marlow travels from the Company's Outer Station to the Central Station of Congo Free State and yakṣa travels in mind from Rāmagiri in Vindhya mountains of central India to Alakā in some distant Himālayas. They travel from one place to another in search — Marlow for Kurtz and yakṣa for yakṣi—and with them travel their geographie imaginaire, not the scientific geography of commensurable nature but what Jean-Mac Besse would call in French *un autre savoir de la Terre*, that is, "another knowledge of the Earth" (Italiano 2008, 3). *Meghaduta* and *Heart of Darkness* although worlds apart, in Conrad's own words, are "welded together without a joint."

What Conrad is doing in this novella is "a kind of geographical inquiry into historical experience" by postulating Charles Marlow not only as the narrator but the interpreter of the deep, dark territorial complexities of the heart of Africa (Said 1993, 7). And in doing so, what constitutes the narrative-within-a-narrative is Marlow's and in a way Conrad's "cognitive mapping" of the unknown, uncanny, and unrepresentable landscape and eventually the cartographical anxiety it leads to. This is in sharp contrast to the known, canny, representable, and indeed "mappable" certainty that Europe begets. A map yields a sense of "totality" and concomitantly an assurance of some sort: an assurance of the blurring distinction between *poiesis* of cartography and *praxis* of geography and between the boyish fantasies (or even "phantasies") and real-life geographical expeditions. Marlow reminiscences:

> Now when I was little chap I had a passion for maps. I would look for hours at South America, or Africa, or Australia and lose myself in all the glories of exploration. At that time there were many blank spaces on the earth and when I saw one that looked particularly inviting on a map (but they all look that) I would put my finger on it and say, "When I grow up I will go there." (Conrad 1899, 9-10)

The blank spaces are metaphors of those white fantasies which often tend to create desires of filling-in those so-called voids on the surface of the earth: the scathing *terra nullius* or *tabula rasa* of colonial cartography. In an effort of homing-the-unknown, Marlow falls into the deep abyss between the metropolitan centre or what Tally would call the "privileged zone of civilization" on the one hand and the unfamiliar, exotic and primitive "periphery" on the other—with no promise of a firm ground underneath. The contours of a Eurocentric map get blurred at, what Maya Jasanoff (2005) calls, the "edges of the empire." These edges of the empire are where Conrad sets off and dramatizes most of his (Geo)poetics and (Geo)politics and while doing so problematizes the ideas of adventure and departure. Unlike other late nineteenth-century travel writers like Rudyard Kipling and H. Rider Haggard who made efforts to reduce and "assimilate" the periphery into the centre, in Conrad we find adventure as a tool to interrogate and problematize the very binary between centre and periphery. At times, he brings centre to the periphery only to showcase that centre is not the centre rather, as peripheral as it can be. There is no "assimilation" in Conrad; he diagnoses how centre becomes volatile and unstable the moment it come into the contact of the periphery. The "edges" are also the contours (read, limits of the "cognitive mapping") of the Enlightenment (*Aufklärung*) — of reason, logic and understanding — where light ends and darkness begins. Marlow in *Heart of Darkness* is tightrope walking along the contour (literally meaning, "with the turn") — wobbling, tensed and confused — so that he does not fall on the other side. This "other side" is the side of Kurtz ("all Europe contributed to the making of Kurtz", writes Conrad), of savagery, violence and corruption. Conrad is here building up a tension by meticulously dramatizing the "cartographical anxiety" with the idea of (advent)ure and (depart)ure. Marlow, the narrator/interpreter/ adventurer is cusped in-between two spatial impulses: "advent" which is coming-to-a-place or "to depart" which is moving-away-from-a-place.

Robert T. Tally calls the word "adventure" a paradox. The etymological origin of the word and as we understand it in common parlance are very different: almost diametrically opposite to each other. Tally notes:

> For the word, "adventure" denotes, simply enough, an arrival, an "advent", or "coming to" a place or event.... However, in common parlance, the word *adventure* has long carried the sense of a "setting forth", a departure, or a venturing outwards. To go adventuring is to leave one's home. True, any "setting forth" from one place leads to an "arrival" somewhere, whether at another place entirely or a return to the original point of departure, but in common parlance, an adventure is not generally associated with the arrival

at the destination.... When someone is said to be going on an adventure, it
is normally understood that he or she is not arriving, but rather departing,
notwithstanding the etymology. A paradox, perhaps. (Tally 2018, 21)

The word "adventure" captures this inherent dichotomy: an arrival
to a place entails departure from another place and vice-versa, that
is, departure from a place entails arrival at someplace (even that
"someplace" can also mean the point of departure). The word in a
way embodies both the senses of the term: "adventure" means
"advent" which is coming-to-a-place and "to depart" which is
moving-away-from-a-place, at the same time. Marlow's advent at
the Congo basin also marks his departure from London. When
someone encounters an unknown and uncanny space, he/she tries
to understand the space with the place of belonging ("home"), the
place from where h/she is coming. Marlow's journey from the
Outer Station to the Central Station and also, Conrad's journey
from Kinshasa to Kisangani through the River Congo is a journey
of this continuous fluctuation or vacillation between fleeting
moments of "advent" and "depart", and which finally culminates
with his encounter of Kurtz. This last encounter can be read as the
encounter with the Other, the un-assimilable "other" where Conrad
qua Marlow finally is able to bring the centre to the contour. The
centre of the psycho-geographical map gets dis-placed and replaced with the contour. The "contour" here is a "counter" —
counter to everything which Marlow's "place" stands for. The word
"adventure, therefore, is as paradoxical as the "Free" in Congo Free
State.

The hitherto blank, white spaces and now the "impressionist"
topography of the river expedition is far away from the
meticulously drawn Enlightenment maps of the "Columbian
epoch". The "Columbian epoch" as Janice Ho points out, "arguably
ended by 1911 when the last frontiers of the world were breached,
Robert Peary having arrived at the North Pole in 1909 and Roald
Amundsen at the South Pole two years later" and with that came to
an end the centuries of expeditions and explorations (Ho 2007, 3).
There were no more blank spaces on the earth. The politics of
geography and cartography overwhelmed the romance of

adventure, the romance with the unknown and the untrodden. Marlow says: "The glamour's off... by this time [Africa] was not a blank space any more. It had got filled since my boyhood with rivers and lakes and names. It had ceased to be a blank space of delightful mystery" (Conrad 1899, 10). Marlow laments the "delightful mystery" which once used to reign the kingdom of map-making. But the way with which (or rather, the romance with which) Conrad describes and even at times abstains himself from describing the places and spaces reminds us of not only the romance of maps but also the maps of romance populated with different mythistorical animated objects with creatures like dragons and sea-monsters — the examples of which are the Borgia map, the Fra Mauro map and even maps in Ptolemy's *Geographia*. The obscurity with which Conrad constructs his narrative also sips into the way Marlow draws on geography and cartography with his "here-be-dragon" genre of attitude. Marlow describes the river on the map (which we now know as the Congo River joining the two cities, Kinshasa and Kisangani) as "an immense snake uncoiled, with its head in the sea, its body at rest curving afar over a vast country, and its tail lost in the depths of the land", going against the tradition of the "Columbian epoch" and maintaining that "delightful mystery" of the maps which he thinks is a thing of the past now (10). Obscurity and "delightful mystery" are the hallmark of Conrad's Geo/poetics. It, as Ho points out "is intended to re-mystify a world whose secrets have been relentlessly exposed" (Ho 2007, 7).

Marlow is neither "at home" in the West nor is he at home in the East (here in case, Africa). As opposed to Conrad's dramatization of the "cartographical anxiety" or what Georg Lukács calls "transcendental homelessness" which "translates into a bewilderment in space," Kālidāsa's *Meghadūta* is inherently "mappable" in mandākrāntā metre. In the latter, there is a sense of "a perceived wholeness that [has] made it inherently 'mappable' in the minds of its people, whether through metaphysics, politics, or geography; [the poem has] what Joseph Frank called a spatial form, as the organization of events depend less on chronology than on locations within a fixed universe" (Tally 2011). The emphasis on map and spatiality becomes evidently important (at times more than the message itself) as we find the yakṣa instructing the cloud-messenger:

> So listen as I tell you your journey's right route
>
> Later, water-giver, you'll hear
> my message with your eager ears. (Kalidasa 10)

Kālidāsa's *Meghadūta,* an ancient poem on the themes of *viccheda* ("separation") and *viraha* ("the pangs of separation") is one of the best known *dūtakāvya* and *sandeśkāvya* in the world. The *vichheda* and *viraha* in the narration are not only in terms of "then" and "now" but also "there" and "here": that is, not only in terms of past and present but also in terms of home and exile. This is not simple nostalgia (from the Greek nostos meaning "return home" and algos meaning "pain") but rather an epiphenomenon of South Asian lived reality: a more layered, subtle and at times poetic sensibility which ensues centering around a place and longing for that place in this part of the world. While pointing at different ways of thinking about place, Ananya Jahanara Kabir writes in her *Partition's Post-Amnesias*:

> Moonjh (Siraiki: 'longing), ishq (Urdu,Punjabi, Hindi: 'desire'), viraha/biroho (Hindi/ Bengali: 'seperation'), yaad (Urdu, Hindi: remembering), mone pora (Bengali: to fall into the mind, to remember), vatan (Urdu, Hindi: homeland), bhita (Bengali: homestead), and the multivalent desh/des (multiple languages: nation, country where one's roots lie, rural hinterland) are just few of the words in different South Asian languages for place and ways of thinking about place. (Kabir 2013, 22)

A yakṣa (a semi-divine creature) has been banished for a year to live on the mountains of Rāmagiri in the Vindhyas by the god of wealth Kubera. Lovelorn-ed and intimidated, he catches hold of a patch of cloud, a "tumble of vapour, heat, water [and] wind/ To deliver a message" to his beloved living in the city of Alakā in the distant mountains of Himalayas. The cloud-messenger, therefore, will have to traverse the major part of the sacred and sensuous geography of the Indian subcontinent and deliver the message to the yakṣi; but before all of that, the cloud will have to understand the "right route". The latter will need appropriate geographical data and evolve a Geographic Information System (GIS), "a system designed to capture, store, manipulate, analyze, manage, and present all types of geographical data." And, thus begins the first part of the poem, the *pūrvamegha*, where the narrator is trying to create a "map" for the cloud with all the relevant information on the topography and the demography required to position the cloud in relation to the dharma of the "right route". The map of narration (of the yakṣa) in the *pūrvamegha* posits a narration of map and blurs the distinction between narration and map and also, between reading and mapping (of the cloud). The GIS of the cloud here, with the help of which it is going to navigate through the topoi laid down by the yakṣa, is what Frederic Jameson would call "cognitive mapping". What constitutes the *pūrvamegha* of *Meghadūta* is the underlying tension between the yakṣa's *cartographie et imaginaire* and the cloud's cognitive mapping.

In *Meghadūta*, we find cartographical certainty, whether physical or imaginary, especially the way yakṣa describes it to the cloud. Even at an exile, we find, in yakṣa a sense of "at home" with the geography of the sub-continent. He describes the events and the places, especially between Rāmagiri and Daśapura, with a finesse of a geographer and the experience of everyday life with a tinge of realism: as opposed to the Impressionist portraits of Marlow. It is only in the uttarmegha, the second half of the poem that the narrative takes a mythical turn; although in the Indian context, as opposed to the west, it is very difficult to establish a distance between myths and realism. The realism in the Indian subcontinent is peculiarly mythical and it is the mythical, as it happens quite often, becomes more "real" than the real itself. Concomitantly, our understanding of geography, just like our understanding of history, politics and people, is somewhere between the mythic and the real. So, the geography in the uttarmegha is as "geo/historical" as in the pūrvamegha, if not more. Kālidāsa cannot be, thus, held accountable solely for this mythical turn. Even the very origin and development of Kālidāsa as the greatest of all poets" is mythical in the strictest sense of the term. "The place" as Ananya Vajpeyi points out, "produced into presence by Kālidāsa's poiesis, [...] is neither the space of history, nor the space of power, nor epic space. It is rather the space of Indic imagination, the space of poetry and of an Indic poetic tradition [...]" (Vajpeyi 2012, 107-8).

The events and places are "described" in *Meghadūta* and "hinted at" in *Heart of Darkness*. There is no trace of obscurity in the yakṣa's narration/map. The cartographical certainty in the latter's narration/map can also be observed in the fact that he not only charts the route for the cloud but also goes onto chart the root of the cloud to the reader. He describes the origin of the cloud in the following manner:

> I know you—
>
> You're born in the world-famous family of
> Puṣkara and Āvartaka clouds
>
> You're Indra's main aide
> You take any shape you please. (Kalidasa 7)

In the yakṣa's narrative, we find an ethics towards not only the cloud (which can easily be deemed as utilitarian in nature) but also toward other beings of the biosphere, animate and inanimate alike. This ecological consciousness in Kālidāsa's poiesis is a kind of "Geopoethics" (earth+poetry+ethics), rare in *Heart of Darkness*. A poet and a lover do not make any distinction between different phenomena of the ecosystem, as is evident from the following lines:

> The lovelorns' nature is such—poor things—
> They cannot discriminate
> between animate and inanimate. (7)

Although it was very harsh on the part of Chinua Achebe to call Conrad, a "bloody racist", the latter was not hospitable and open to the "other" either. Marlow's transcendental cynicism is an embodiment of the spirit-of-the-age, same is true of Kālidāsa's pantheism. The Indic poetic tradition of Kālidāsa's age is replete with such examples of connected-ness in the sphere of geopolitics and geopoetics. In the map of *Meghadūta*, there is not much of a difference between a "tumble of vapour, heat, water, wind" and a lump of flesh and blood, between yakṣa's craving and Cātaka bird's thirst, between mountains and a woman's breasts, between the scent of hill's grottoes and prostitutes and most importantly, between a cloud and a messenger. The peoples, the hills, the clouds, the strangers, the cities, the rivers, the flora, the fauna and the topoi are all connected by the "being-with" of Geopoethics, an indispensable component at the heart of Geopoetics.

In Conrad's *Heart of Darkness* and Kālidāsa's *Meghadūta*, there is no now-often used/misused/abused/overused/underused colonial/postcolonial transaction but rather an attempt towards understanding the underlying principle of Geopoetics—that is the principle of E(art)h. Both these texts are geo-ethically connected to their respective worlds. They are also connected with each other geo-ethically. There is no centre and periphery here: one is not a centre, the other periphery. There is no geodesy (from the Greek *geōdaisia*, from *gē* "earth" + *daiein* "divide") here: it is an earth with no longitude, no latitude and no equator; no North/South and no West/East either; where every geographical location on the earth is a centre and where every cultural location on the surface is equidistant from the inner core of the earth. As Robert Frost says:

> Earth's the right place for love:
> I don't know where it's likely to go better. (Frost, "Birches")

Studies in Earth, Ethics and Literature

The nine chapters in this volume seek to understand this experience through a diverse choice of topics ranging from Marx and Engels to Alexander von Humboldt, from the poetry of Sarah Maguire to Wordsworth and Keats, from Yoko Ogawa's *Memory Police* and Priya Sarukkai Chabria's *Clone* to Louis Sachar's *Holes*, from Jibanananda Das' "Banalata Sen of Natore" to *Tintin in Tibet*. The book also, in one of its chapters, tries to analyse how through "Reef Thinking", one is able to comprehend the present predicament of the Anthropocene and the consequent Sixth Mass-Extinction. Literature exemplifies a geographical consciousness—an intimate and individual experience of the earth, since "*Earth's* the right place for love" (Frost, "Birches", italics our emphasis). This book is an attempt to conceive *the* heterogenous distillation of art and earth, so that we are able to ensure that the biosphere of art always remains in touch with the geosphere of earth. And by doing so, we intend to pave a journey where literature would cease to remain a mere heterocosm and move towards being more earthly, biological and ecological. This book therefore, intends to un-earth this *limitless* spatiality in literature. More than the world of the art, the book is concerned with the earth of the art. It is an imitation of earth through art, as this is the only place where we can live.

The first chapter "Marx, Engels and Literature from the Depths of the Earth" by Jayson Althofer analyses how, in a fundamentally poetic language, Karl Marx and Friedrich Engels envisioned sustainable human development coevolving with the earth. Their chthonian vision to bring-forth and re-create the earth through social revolution was anticipated in their youthful poetry and elaborated by their communist literature. Before their collaboration in 1844, Engels versified Marx's Promethean call not just to philosophise upon but to poetically enrapture the earth: "As if to seize and then pull down / To Earth the spacious tent of Heaven" (Marx and Engels, 336). Marx's own early literary works found art in, and forged it from, geological forces — "volcanic Earth" — and decried any god or power that "hacks the happiness of the earth to pieces" (598, 619). As Franklin Rosemont perceived, it was "under the sign of *poetry*" that Marx identified himself "as an enemy of the bourgeois order" — an abysmal system based on robbing, enclosing and huckstering the earth unto its very end(s) (Rosemont 1989, 203). It analyses some ecological, ethical and corporeal facets of the poetics of the katabasis that Marx and Engels undertook into the bowels of the earth to expose the planetary violence of capitalist accumulation and its inherent tendencies that will culminate into capitalism's death-throes. It discusses the rapacity, immorality and monstrosity of capitalist accumulation, as opposed to their vision of dwelling sparingly and sustainably with the earth. It connects their youthful writing of poetry, expressive of intimate, subjective experiences of the earth, to the chthonic poetics of their objective, communist critique of the robbing of the world and the working-class. The chapter thus, foregrounds a pair of interfused tropes vital to their subterranean imaginary: the *cave* as archetypal space wherein proletariats dwell, work and are buried alive, and the bourgeoisie's production of its own *gravediggers*. Out of the depths of the earth, the communist literature of Marx and Engels demonstrated that violent accumulation, cave-dwelling and bourgeois society's creation of its own gravediggers must necessarily remain as the core tendencies of capitalism until its blessed end.

The next chapter "A Glance at the Whole: Nature, Earth and Subjectivity in Alexander von Humboldt's *Cosmos* and *Views of Nature*" by Mario Bosincu examines *Cosmos* and *Views of Nature* in terms of the subjectivity formed at the constitution of which these texts were aimed. Particular attention is paid to the *topos* of the view of the Earth from above, which found expression in the ancient spiritual exercise of the imaginative overflight, allowing the practitioner to become aware of the despicable tininess of the Earth and thereby to attain high-mindedness. Taking up the *topos* of the view of the Earth from above, Humboldt modernised it by focusing not on the tininess of the Earth but on the fullness of being of nature and, as a result, wrote down *ekphraseis* so that the readers might imaginatively reconstruct the places portrayed and experience a sense of wonder at the "plenitude of life that flows throughout creation" (Humboldt 1845, 6). Accordingly, the feeling of wonder replaced the high-mindedness that ancient philosophers thought of as the goal of the contemplation of nature, which, in turn, was resacralized into a metaphysical power. As a consequence, Humboldt's *ekphrastic* exercises bear a striking resemblance to the Jesuit meditative technique of the composition of place, with the important difference that the reader of the *Views of Nature* is now faced not with the Christian God but with all-living nature. In this sense, Humboldt's text documents the shift from the spiritual exercise of the view of the Earth from above, typical of the ancient *culture de soi* (Foucault), to an inner-oriented practice granting access to a lived experience in accordance with the Romantic subject code, which made a strong case for deepening one's inner world through imagination. At the same time, the German naturalist writer reframed the ancient spiritual exercise consisting in resituating each event within the perspective of universal nature in terms of the scientific subject culture. Consequently, the expansion of the self into the infinite was no longer related to the constitution of a subject impervious to the blows of fortune but led to a new holistic consciousness of the interconnected web of life and of man's dependence on a violence-ridden and wild nature.

Ratul Nandi's chapter "Romantic Earth/Art? Impossible: Re-Locating Romantic Inheritance in the Contemporary Critical Thought" addresses the question of how very few literary epochs have been as sensitive to and self-reflectively aware of man's poetic dwelling on earth as the English Romantics. The aesthetic topography of romantic poetry, especially in William Wordsworth, environs a space which is "inherently green" as it claims to forge harmony between the earth and the art. The promise of such harmony, however, overlooks a veiled aspiration to construct an *interior self* alienated from the earth, inadvertently effecting a rupture between earth and the art, between the earth and the man. In a move opposite to Wordsworthian "egotistical sublime," the poetry of John Keats inspires a fundamental thinking of earth-art dialogue based on the "impossibility" of knowing earthly beings or objects in their entirety. The force of such impossibility is to raise doubts about the *usefulness* of the aesthetic form and the metaphorical language to truthfully re-present or "copy" the world external to itself. Exposing the readers to the radical finitude of the literary language, the *a-human* environment of literature facilitates a "negatively capable" experience of an inescapable irony wherein the literary art concurrently aspires to capture the earth, yet realizes painfully how such endeavour is doomed to remain incomplete, anticipating, as it does, the contemporary deconstructive criticism of environment and climate change. In what follows, the chapter claims that these two modes of romantic thought eventually culminate into two distinct strands of green literary criticism today finding strong theoretical voices in both sides with their distinct reading ethics and capacities to recast the earth/art question in the context of current widespread ecological concerns with the earth.

Geopoetry has a long tradition within Anglophone literature. In the modern history of Great Britain, it has been stimulated by a deep interest in nature, as pioneered by the English Romantic poets Samuel Taylor Coleridge and William Wordsworth, who perceived nature as the primary source of humanity and inspiration. Building on their manifesto, Pavlína Flajšarová's chapter "Green Thumbs: Floral Geopoetics in the Poetry of Sarah Maguire" studies the nature of language used in the "Preface" to *Lyrical Ballads*, the theories of nature proposed in *Biographia Literaria*, and furthermore, the sensitivity towards nature connected with the poets of Lake District as well as German philosophers such as Schlegel, Schelling, and Herder. The chapter intends to look in details into the floral geopoetics as practiced by the trained horticulturalist and distinguished 20th-century British poet Sarah Maguire, who is well aware of the tradition of her British and German predecessors. Maguire's poetry collections *Spilt Milk*, *The Invisible Mender* and *The Florist's at Midnight* foreground various landscapes that are filled with human emotions within the historic and political context. Her editorial works *A Green Thought in a Green Shade* and *Flora Poetica* are based on her close relationship with flowers and her interest in the relationship between human beings and the natural world. Many of her own poems are linked with artistic works by poets, composers or sculptors. Maguire gained an interesting insight into horticulture, culture and medicine during her stay at the famous *Chelsea Physic Garden* (founded in 1673), where she served as its first poet in residence. *The Garden* was the place that led Maguire to contemplate human nature and the ways in which humans interact with wilderness. In her poetry, the author discusses through metaphors of nature the influence of urban culture upon the natural order of things. In addition, the chapter also looks into Maguire's mature collection *Pomegranates of Kandahar*, in which she utilises a view of Western civilisation in comparison to the culture and nature of Asia.

Fiction explores multiverses, alternate realities and the depths of the human mind. Literary imagination dilates to sense even "that which we're probably not going to see." The contemporary fiction is characterized by an understanding of spatiality as a dimension of being. The workings of the creative imagination, to represent a historical experience in time and reality, challenge the theoretical boundaries of space consciousness in interesting ways. Ankita Sharma's chapter "The Memory of Here and Elsewhere: Geopoetics and Literary Fiction" proposes to juxtapose the memory of disappearance with the memory of perception vis-à-vis space, through a close scrutiny of Yoko Ogawa's *Memory Police* and Priya Sarukkai Chabria's *Clone*. The distinct philosophical reflections of the two authors, on the embodiment of humanness within geographical spaces mediated through memory, generate unique understanding of human history outside the immediate locality and historicity. While Ogawa obliterates the memory of the islanders through systematic disappearances, Chabria refurbishes the memory of her clones with artificial intelligence. The resistance to adhere to specific genre and non-linear timelines in the narratives facilitate a fluid transition through the literary landscape. On one hand, this movement suggests continuity in spatial-temporal dynamics with a sense-of-being directed towards the future. On the other hand, it implicates shifts in the meaning-making process of humans in the projected future highlighting a history of loss. Convergences in the two narratives, to emblematize the brave attempts of language and poetry in retrieving the displaced human-ness through writing and remembering, mark the narratives with an intimate experience of what it means to be a human in changing physical surroundings.

Seen through an Environmental Humanities and New Materialist lens and relying on posthuman and beyond-human theoretical grounds, Oriol Batalla's chapter "Reef Thinking: Coral Reefs, Materialism and Ecology at the End of Nature" portrays a milieu-specific analysis of the politics, semiotics and aesthetics of the coral reef bleaching processes that have taken part in the last few years. The general aim of this chapter is to reflect how thinking through these specific milieus can be fruitful in order to come to terms with the current crisis of the Anthropocene and the subsequent Sixth Mass-Extinction. This, in turn, can steer philosophical and political understandings of such catastrophic events towards an ecological, inclusive rationality that challenges the established truths.

The next chapter "Asia and Asia*bodh*: Historicality, Ethics and Jibanananda Das' 'Banalata Sen of Natore'" by Jayjit Sarkar explores the question of Asia as not being free from the question of historiography. The "Asia," as we understand it today, is a result of narratological ploy: as it has been narrated *from* and narrated *by*, to us. "It has had", Ranajit Guha writes in the context of the Raj, "the effect of replacing the indigenous narratologies of precolonial times by ones that are typically modern and western" (Guha 2002, 5). It becomes then, an imperative, in Guha's own phrase, to look "over the fence" for other possible narratologies different from that of historiography and the way the latter arranges itself with historicality. One such alternative or possibility can be found in literary narratives and that it is the poet who can help us in our doing of history of Asia, significantly different from that of an academic historian (or what Rabindranath Tagore would call "*aitihasik pandit*"). It is the poet's *sense* of history which is going to give us a possible Asia — the poet's Asia — as it is lived: as an Asia we have been living and experiencing as an everyday reality. In the search for Asia as lived-experience in literature, the chapter looks into "Banalata Sen of Natore" (1942) as a text replete with various and often contradictory experiences of being concrete and obscure, exotic and mundane, spatial and temporal, familiar and exotic, all at the same time. The poem presents us with an Asia*bodh* or Asia consciousness which is ontologically different from the "Asia" we find in historiography — an Asia as lived-experience — as we have been living for aeons and will do so for aeons. This is different from the Asia in academic histories — histories which were written when we were "inside" those histories. This is the being-in-the-asia and being-with-the-asia which becomes fundamental here and need to be taken into consideration in any possible discussion on the idea of Asia, whether modern or pre-/post-modern, whether colonial or pre-/post-colonial, whether historical or pre-/post-historical. With the help of thinkers such as Tagore, Okakura and Kuan-Hsing

Chen, this chapter, therefore, tries to understand the lived-history and lived-geography of Asia.

Children's literature often provides a social commentary about gender, ethnic, or environmental issues through the eyes of a group of young men or women who are struggling to find themselves and their places in the world. In Rachel L. Carazo's chapter "Filling the "Empty" Space between the Natural World and Humans: Environmentalism, Non-Human Animal Rights, and Broken Promises in *Holes*" a similar phenomenon occurs. A group of boys, which includes Stanley Yelnats and Zero, finds themselves digging holes at Camp Green Lake looking for a lost treasure. As these young men learn how to get along with one another and appreciate the families that they have lost, the truth about what happened to the environment begins to emerge. Kissin' Kate Barlow curses the land when discord over her interracial romance occurs and, after the promises between Stanley's (Elya Yelnats's) and Zero's (Madame Zeroni's) families are broken, the environment degenerates. The landscape becomes dry and marked by *holes*; animals, like the donkey Mary Lou, that were once loved, turn into dangerous representations (the venomous yellow-spotted lizards). Only when the good intentions between humans, nature, and the environment are re-recognized, does the earth recover — making the connection between human and the environment both significant and problematic.

The last chapter "The Adventures of Tintin in Heterotopia" by Debnita Chakravarti is a fascinating study of how the world is a book, and how we travel our planet mostly through pages. For many of us, one of the earliest passports to the remotest corners of the world — and even beyond, to the moon — has been the Tintin albums. Their creator, the Belgian artist Georges Remi or Hergé, took his young journalist and his little dog Snowy on adventures to faraway exotic places, and for the last nine decades readers from seven to seventy have been accompanying him delightedly. The *Tintin in* […] format of many of the album titles signal their strong connect with particular places. While the locations serve several functions apart from furnishing fascinating settings, there is one album *Tintin in Tibet* where the site of the narrative is of unique importance.

This chapter is a Foucauldian reading of the above mentioned album. It argues that the Himalayan terrain portrayed here may be analysed as a heterotopia of crisis following the French thinker's theory of "other places." The chapter considers the Tibetan peaks, where Tintin ventures against all rational advice to search for his planewrecked friend, as unique among all the spaces into which the intrepid boy reporter has ever ventured. In what is undoubtedly his most difficult expedition ever, Tintin finds himself in a landscape more desolate than even the barren surface of the moon. The severity of the snow-capped peaks throws into stark relief the very sense of identity of the usually-confident protagonist. Personal bonds are appraised and moral fiber tested as one's existence hangs precariously over ravines as unplumbed as one's doubts.

The chapter reads this twentieth volume in the series, one of the later albums, against Hergé's personal crisis which found resolution in creating this "white volume." His psychoanalytic therapy, his snow-drowned nightmares, his failing marriage and his lost liaisons all find poignant representation in the unremitting blanched expanse of this text. The chapter thus, examines how Tibet functions as a heterotopia of crisis for both Tintin and his creator. And in doing so, it provides a uniquely "grounded" perspective never before accorded to a work otherwise the subject of such "mountainous" commentary.

Bibliography

Baig, Ahmed and Elias Kahraman. *Environmentalism: Environmental Strategies and Environmental Sustainability*. New York: Nova Science Publishers, 2010.

Bauer, Joanne R. *Forging Environmentalism: Justice, Livelihood, and Contested Environments*. New York: Routledge, 2006.

Conrad, Joseph. *Heart of Darkness*. 1899. Planetebook.com. https://www.planetebook.com/free-ebooks/heart-of-darkness.pdf

Cox, Murray and Alice Theilgaard. *Mutative Metaphors in Psychotherapy: The Aeolian Mode*. Pennsylvania: Jessica Kingsley Publishers, 1997.

Das, Jibanananda. *Jibanananda Das: Selected Poems*. Translated by C. D. Gupta. Gurgaon: Penguin Books, 2006.

Enenkel, Karl. "Meditative Frames as Reader's Guide in Neo-Latin Texts." In *Meditatio — Refashioning the Self. Theory and Practice in Late Medieval and Early Modern Intellectual Culture*, edited by Karl Enenkel and Walter Melion. Leiden-Boston: Brill, 2011.

Federico Italiano, "Defining Geopoetics", *TRANS* [Online] 6, 2008. http:// journals.openedition.org/trans/299. DOI: https://doi.org/10.4000/ trans.299

Frost, Robert. "Birches." Poetry Foundation. https://www.poetryfounda tion.org/poems/44260/birches

Graczyk, Annette. *Das literarische Tableau zwischen Kunst und Wissenschaft*. München: Wilhelm Fink Verlag, 2004.

Guha, Ranajit. *History at the Limit of World History*. New York: Columbia University Press, 2002.

Ho, Janice. "The Spatial Imagination and Literary form of Conrad's Colonial Fictions." *Journal of Modern Literature* 30, no. 4 (Summer 2007): pp. 1-19.

Humboldt, Alexander von. *Cosmos: A Survey of the General Physical History of the Universe*. New York: Harper & Brothers, 1845.

Kabir, Ananya Jahanara. *Partition's Post-Amnesias: 1947, 1971 and Modern South Asia*. New Delhi: Women Unlimited, 2013.

Kalidasa. *Kalidasa for the 21st Century Reader*. Translated by Mani Rao. New Delhi: Aleph Book Company, 2014.

Kraft, Tobias. *Figuren des Wissens bei Alexander von Humboldt: Essai, Tableau und Atlas im amerikanischen Reisewerk*. Berlin-Boston: De Gruyter, 2014.

Macherey, Pierre. *The Object of Literature*. 1990. Translated by David Macey. Cambridge: Cambridge University Press, 1995.

Marx, Karl and Frederick Engels. *Collected Works. 50 Vols*. London: Lawrence and Wishart, 1975-2004.

Møllegaard, Kirsten. "Haunting and history in Louis Sachar's Holes." *Western American Literature* 45, no. 2 (Summer 2010): pp. 139-161.

Ritter, Joachim. *Subjektivität: Sechs Aufsätze*. Frankfurt am Main: Suhrkamp, 1974.

Rosemont, Franklin. "Karl Marx and the Iroquois." *Arsenal: Surrealist Subversion* 4 (1989): pp. 201-213.

Sachar, Louis. *Holes*. New York: Scholastic Paperbacks, 1998.

Said, Edward. *Culture and Imperialism*. New York: Vintage, 1993.

Schröder, Nicole. *Spaces and Places in Motion: Spatial Concepts in Contemporary American Literature*. Tubingen: Gunter Narr Verlag, 2006.

Tally, Robert T. "On Literary Cartography: Narrative as a Spatially Symbolic Act." NANO, 1. (2011). https://nanocrit.com/issues/issue 1/literary-cartography-narrative-spatially- symbolic-act

____. *Topophrenia: Place, Narrative, and the Spatial Imagination*. Indiana: Indiana University Press, 2018.

Tuan, Yi-Fu. *Space and Place: The Perspective of Experience*. Minneapolis: University of Minnesota Press, 2001.

Vajpeyi, Ananya. *Righteous Republic: The Political Foundations of Modern India*. Cambridge, MA: Harvard University Press, 2012.

Walls, Laura Dassow, Stephen Jackson and Mark Person. "Reclaiming Consilience." In *Views of Nature*. Chicago: The University of Chicago Press, 2014.

White, Kenneth. "For the Institute of Geopoetics." 28 April 1989. https://www.institut-geopoetique.org/en/presentation-of-the-institute.

Whitehead, Derek H. "Poiesis and Art-Making: A Way of Letting-Be." Contemporary Aesthetics 1, 2003. http://hdl.handle.net/2027/spo. 7523862.0001.005

1

Marx, Engels and Literature from the Depths of the Earth

Jayson Althofer

The earth is the mother of material wealth, labour its father. This axiom of the economist William Petty was two hundred years old when Karl Marx (1818-1883) referenced it in *Capital*, Volume 1 (1867).[1] By then, Marx could cite abundant evidence that under the capitalist mode of production the accumulation of wealth creates continuous havoc for the earth and labourers. "Accumulation for accumulation's sake, production for production's sake: by this formula classical economy expressed the historical mission of the bourgeoisie, and did not for a single instant deceive itself over the birth-throes of wealth."[2] So Marx aphorized the bourgeoisie's mission on the basis of the extensive exploration of capitalism's ramifying underworld of penetrative and extractive violence that he and Friedrich Engels (1820-1895) had made since the early 1840s. This chapter follows up some ecological, ethical and corporeal facets of the poetics of their katabasis (literally, a "down-going") into the bowels of the earth, or "nature's heart, underground,"[3] to expose the planetary violence of capitalist accumulation and its inherent tendencies that will culminate in capitalism's open-eyed death-throes.

Before Marx and Engels became friends and collaborators in 1844, they independently remarked the acquisitive drives and environmental destructiveness of capital's regime of accumulation. Percy Bysshe Shelley's attack on bourgeois society's commodification of all the fruits of human art, the heart and earth influenced their earliest critiques of political economy. Engels translated Shelley into German in 1839-40 and Marx regarded the poet as "essentially a revolutionist."[4] In "Landscapes" (1840), Engels appreciated "a tenderness and originality in the depiction of nature such as only Shelley can achieve."[5] He was also touched by

Shelley's tough, terse rendering of the alienation of humanity from nature in poems such as "Queen Mab" (1813): "All things are sold: the very light of heaven / Is venal; earth's unsparing gifts of love, / The smallest and most despicable things / That lurk in the abysses of the deep, / All objects of our life, even life itself … / Are bought and sold as in a public mart."[6] Inspired by the likes of Shelley, "Engels saw the deep need for the reconciliation of humanity with nature, which only a revolution could bring."[7]

Universal venality indicated that capitalist huckstering, denounced by Engels and Marx in 1843, was hegemonic. Engels' "Outlines of a Critique of Political Economy" (1843) apprehended the separation of direct producers from natural conditions of production, that is, expulsion from "the land which is our one and all, the first condition of our existence," as fundamental to capitalism; yet "the original appropriation—the monopolisation of the land by a few, the exclusion of the rest from that which is the condition of their life—yields nothing in immorality to the subsequent huckstering of the land."[8] Marx's "On the Jewish Question" (1843) argued the need to negate the capitalist negation of nature: "The view of nature attained under the dominion of private property and money is a real contempt for and practical debasement of nature."[9] Marx affirmed both an older ecological ethics by quoting a German peasant revolutionary's opposition in 1524 to the commodification of non-human nature—"Thomas Münzer declares it intolerable 'that all creatures have been turned into property, the fishes in the water, the birds in the air, the plants on the earth; the creatures, too, must become free'"—and a contemporary revolutionary ecology by endorsing communism: "An organisation of society which would abolish the preconditions for huckstering, and therefore the possibility of huckstering."[10]

From scores of sources besides Münzer and "Queen Mab"— "Hence commerce springs, the venal interchange / Of all that human art or nature yield"[11]—Marx and Engels unfolded their youthful anti-capitalist invective into full-blown theories of exploitation and expropriation that exposed capitalism's structural tendency to expanding ecological catastrophe (literally, a "downwards turn"). Capitalist production, Marx wrote in *Capital*,

Volume 1, "violates the conditions necessary to lasting fertility of the soil" by disturbing the circulation of matter, or metabolic interaction, between humanity and the soil and "moreover, all progress in capitalistic agriculture is a progress in the art, not only of robbing the labourer, but of robbing the soil".[12] Marx and Engels' theory of exploitation, involving capital's expropriation of surplus labour, is invoked by "robbing the labourer" and "robbing the soil" refers to their theory that the expropriation of the earth has engendered a *metabolic rift* between human beings and the earth.[13] *Capital*, Volume 3 (1894), edited by Engels from drafts left by Marx, capped their lifelong ecological, ethical and corporeal critique of capitalist production for creating "conditions which cause an irreparable break [or *rift*] in the coherence of social interchange prescribed by the natural laws of life."[14] Capitalism does not spare earth's unsparing but not unlimited gifts. Its derangement of the natural laws of life—"venal interchange" culminates in unnatural, anthropogenic disruption of metabolic interchanges between organic and inorganic nature—entails a crisis-ridden global ecology and bourgeois society's progress in corruption and ruination. Without the abolition of earth-mongering, the bourgeoisie's wanton accumulation will continue to engender what John Bellamy Foster has called "the accumulation of catastrophe on a truly planetary level."[15]

"That lurk in the abysses of the deep": Shelley's words reverberate in Marx and Engels' delving into capital's chaos of accumulation and their uncovering of tendencies that could lead to the abolition of capital's robbery of the earth. The next section of this chapter amplifies the foregoing identification of capitalist accumulation's immanent rapacity and, in the young Engels' term, "immorality," as well as his and Marx's alternative vision for dwelling sparingly and sustainably with the earth. The chapter's central section connects their youthful poetry, expressive of reverential, subjective experience of the earth, to the chthonic poetics of their objective, communist critique of the robbing of the world and the working-class. The last two sections foreground a pair of interfused tropes vital to their subterranean imaginary: *cave* dwellings for workers and the bourgeoisie's *gravediggers*. These tropes, which suffused their writings from the 1840s until their deaths, can be read as recurring "moments in an ongoing chthonian revolution," to borrow from Ned Lukacher's analysis of Walter Benjamin's "revolutionary chthonianism."[16]

"Accumulate, accumulate!"

"A secret correspondence seems to have been established between theoretical analysis and poetic vision," Pierre Macherey has surmised apropos "the birth of a literature of the depths" and "the development of visionary theories about the man [sic] from below" — a development that involved "a downwards displacement of theoretical interest".[17] Alexander Kluge's identification of Marx's use of the term *accumulation* as a metaphor illuminated such a correspondence: "'Accumulation' is a 'pileup,' as in a pile of earth one shovels. This is an image. We no longer realize this because it is a Latin word, so we see it only as a concept."[18] The concept-image of pileups can turn the conceptual-poetic gaze upwards to vast sierras of commodities — as implied by *Capital*'s opening sentence: "The wealth of those societies in which the capitalist mode of production prevails, presents itself as 'an immense accumulation of commodities'"[19] — and also to the catastrophic tempest arising from commodity production: "onwards the history of capital goes … the perils mounting … and, with [Walter] Benjamin, the debris growing 'towards the sky. What we call progress is *this* storm.'"[20]

Marx gazed downwards too, into the bowels of the earth and the proletarians sapped under the bourgeoisie's monomaniacal commandment "Accumulate, accumulate!"[21] Across Great Britain, he witnessed "the passion of capital for a limitless draining of labour power," tearing up "by the roots the living force of the nation," as part of the "same blind eagerness for plunder" whereby industrial agriculture "exhausted the soil" and then "spread guano over the English fields."[22] Trying to compensate for the spoliation of the soil, British capitalists imported immense piles of guano, for even accumulated, nutrient-rich bird excrement was not free but commodified and controlled by bourgeois competition.[23] Caring only to maximize the labour power "that can be rendered fluent in a working day" — profit being churned through "a productive expenditure of human brains, nerves, and muscles" — capital depletes and deletes "the labourer's life, as a greedy farmer snatches increased produce from the soil by robbing it of its fertility."[24] Marx called capital an *Auspumper*: "literally a pumper-out, that performs the *Aussaugung* of the worker, literally the sucking out, or sucking hollow, of a 'stunted, short-lived and rapidly replaced human being;'" meaning that capital is "a hideous dredging into vacuousness."[25] And as disposable, replaceable workers are dredged to death, an irreplaceable world — the earth — is ravaged into uninhabitableness.

Détourning Gothic literature like Shelley's "Song to Men of England" (1819) — "Those ungrateful drones who would / Drain your sweat — nay, drink your blood" — Marx conceptualized, and darkly poeticized, capital as "dead labour, that, vampire-like, only lives by sucking living labour, and lives the more, the more labour it sucks."[26] He was especially influenced by the chemist Justus von Liebig, whose notions of the "robbery system" and "robbery economy" of industrialized agriculture nourished his recognition of capital's anti-ecological monstrosity in general and its vampirism in particular.[27] Agents of British capital not only stockpiled guano from Peru, but also plundered mountains of human remains from across Europe, to use as fertiliser. "Great Britain," Liebig accused, "robs all countries of the conditions of their fertility; she has already ransacked the battle-fields of Leipzig, Waterloo, and the Crimea for bones, and consumed the accumulated skeletons of many generations in the Sicilian catacombs." Thus, "she hangs like a vampire on the neck of Europe, and seeks out its hearts-blood."[28]

Marx's image of an *ungeheure Warensammlung*, which was first translated as an "immense accumulation of commodities," also connotes a *monstrous* collection of goods. Elsewhere in *Capital*, his Industrial-Gothic epithet for a Frankenstein-assemblage of machines, *ein mechanisches Ungeheuer*, was translated as "a mechanical monster."[29] Likewise, his dissection of bourgeois wealth creation avers to the systemic monstrosity of its pleonexia: "Modern society, which, soon after its birth, pulled Plutus by the hair of his head from the bowels of the earth, greets gold as its Holy Grail, as the glittering incarnation of the very principle of its own life."[30] Capitalist modernity's profane evisceration and exhaustion of natural resources reaches around the planet and beyond the present, as Hans Martin Enzensberger reckoned in "A Critique of Political Ecology" (1973): "The 'wealth' of the overdeveloped consumer societies of the West, insofar as it is not a mere mirage for the bulk of the population, is the result of a wave of plunder and pillage unparalleled in history; its victims are, on the one hand, the peoples of the Third World and, on the other, the men and women of the future."[31] The worship of vacuousness swells the capitalist world.

Dialectically united with their earthy anatomy of the original and ongoing accumulation of capitalism's genesis and gigantism, Marx and Engels envisioned an end to capitalism's robbery of nature—in Marx's prolepsis, "The knell of capitalist private property sounds"—and the emergence of human development sustainably coevolving with the earth, or non-human nature, all articulated in their coruscating literary and ethical idiolects.[32] From sustained analysis of the crisis of the earth, or soil, they developed a concept of sustainability that was central to their ideas about communist society.[33] This prescient passage from *Capital*, Volume 3, encapsulates their radical vision and lifelong fight for sustainable development and care of the earth for future generations:

> From the standpoint of a higher economic form of society, private ownership of the globe by single individuals will appear quite as absurd as private ownership of one man by another. Even a whole society, a nation, or even all simultaneously existing societies taken together, are not the owners of the globe. They are only its possessors, its usufructuaries, and, like *boni patres familias* [good heads of the household], they must hand it down to succeeding generations in an improved condition.[34]

The springs of ecological consciousness and solicitude coursed deeply through Marx and Engels' ruthless criticism and mordant mockery of bourgeois wealth-creation. They often paraphrased Epicurus, as in *The German Ideology* (1845–46): "the world must be *disillusioned*, and especially freed from fear of gods, for the world is my *friend*."[35] In his doctoral dissertation (1841), Marx had portrayed

Epicurus as the great enlightener of antiquity and associated him with the mythical revolutionary figure Prometheus, as depicted by Aeschylus in *Prometheus Bound*, who defied the gods of Olympus and brought fire—light, enlightenment—to human beings.[36] Marx and Engels pulled Prometheus, not Plutus, *from below* to figurehead their struggle for sustainable human being, becoming and dwelling with the earth as a beloved, well-maintained home.

Poetry in Brutal Detail

Marx and Engels' consciousness of the intrinsic value of the earth and of its estrangement under capitalism found expression in their youthful poetry and impelled them beyond poetry to practical-critical activity against capitalist accumulation. "Marx came to recognize himself as an enemy of the bourgeois order," as Franklin Rosemont perceived, "under the sign of *poetry*"—yet he stopped writing his own in the late 1830s.[37] Engels too had poetic aspirations but abandoned poetry in the early 1840s. In each case, however, "poetry was not passively let go, but actively sublated, that is, at once negated and kept hold of."[38] Their collected works are, to adapt   Keston   Sutherland,   "poetic   throughout   and fundamentally."[39] "References to poetry, often revolutionary in nature," stand in Engels "for an irrepressible, luminous natural and social reality outside and opposed to the bleak world and degraded existence imposed by industrial capitalism."[40] Beneath the relatively superficial deployment of poetic quotation and allusion to catalyse or deepen their arguments, something essential was at stake: "Marx"—*and* Engels, it should be added—"sought a new language, literary as well as theoretical, a radical poetics through which to read capitalism" *and* to revolt against it.[41] With accumulation presenting itself as the brute appearance and real brutality of piled-up earth, bones and entrails, signifying the vitals of land and labourers being sucked hollow, their critique of political economy was, inexorably, chthonian. Sutherland's precept that "Marxist critical thinking has a poetics" underpins the following overview of Marx and Engels' transformation of their versified expressions of reverence for the earth into the radical register of chthonic communism.[42]

Adducing S.S. Prawer's *Karl Marx and World Literature* (1976), Paul Hamilton has stated "Marx was steeped in literature and history to an extraordinary degree" and noted Prawer "has him virtually fulfilling Goethe's prophecy of an age of *Weltliteratur* single-handed."[43] Multilingual polymath Engels was also fabulously erudite. Marx and Engels' interventions against capital's accumulation of the earth, and visions of social revolution, sustainable development and classless society, plumbed a remarkable range of chthonic imagery, mythology and narrative, most notably Dante's *Inferno*,[44] as well as contemporary earth sciences and social studies. For instance, the anthropology of Johann Bachofen could have provided Engels "a historical basis for a chthonian, matriarchal, classless society."[45] Based only on Marx and Engels' assiduous reading of Goethe, Byron and Shelley, a book could be written about their visionary recycling of geogenic, geographical and seismological symbols and stories, including their ventriloquy of volcanos' voices.[46]

From the sublime to the small and seemingly despicable: another book could be written about Marx's adoption of an animal that digs and dwells in the earth, the mole, as a revolutionary figure. Borrowed from Shakespeare, via Kant, Hegel and Heinrich Heine, "the old mole" surfaces in Marx to symbolize the seismic stealth, slowness and suddenness of social revolution. Esther Leslie has noted that, "in the early 1850s, Marx drew on the term 'geological formation' to name his notion of a 'social formation.'"[47] In the same period, his old mole made its subsequently celebrated appearances in *The Eighteenth Brumaire of Louis Bonaparte* (1851-52) and "Speech at the Anniversary of The People's Paper" (delivered in London, April 14, 1856). As George Bataille argued, the old mole "must be understood in relation to the notion of a geological uprising as expressed in the *Communist Manifesto* [1848]. Marx's point of departure has nothing to do with the heavens". For Bataille, "He begins in the bowels of the earth, as in the materialist bowels of proletarians."[48]

Marx's juvenilia of 1835-37 decried any power that "hacks the happiness of the earth to pieces" and he found art in, and forged it from, natural forces, including "volcanic Earth."[49] Also from the streets and other elements of capital's "natural" or "naturalized" social formation, which he came to read as the debasement and denaturalization of the underlying geological formation: "Kant and Fichte soar to heavens blue / Seeking for some distant land, / I but seek to grasp profound and true / That which—in the street I find."[50] In this stanza from "On Hegel" (c. 1837), Marx's desublimation of the flights of idealist philosophy indicated his comic-intellectual debt to Heine's *umheimlich* irony and his personal-political streetwise ambition "to live in the present."[51] The stanza also foreshadowed Marx's appreciation of Thomas Carlyle's phantasmagorical streetscapes and his own *Theses on Feuerbach* (1845), in which he contended that Feuerbach "does not grasp" the significance of revolutionary praxis and famously concluded: "The philosophers have only *interpreted* the world in various ways; the point, however, is to *change* it."[52]

In the mid-1840s, first Engels, then Marx emulated the Dantean katabasis of Carlyle's *Past and Present* (1843)—"Sooty Manchester, it too is built on the infinite Abysses"[53]—and thereby demystified German Romanticism's "poetry of coal."[54] The climax of Marx's journey into the underworld, following both capitalist and labourer "into the hidden abode of production," was a nekyia in "The Working Day" chapter of *Capital*, Volume 1: "the motley crowd of labourers of all callings, ages, sexes," Marx the necromancer reveals, "press on us more busily than the souls of the slain on Ulysses."[55] In that chapter, his "confrontational use of direct speech"[56] told of past, present and prospective working-class struggles against the "vampires," "werewolves" and other "flesh agents" of capital who thirst to suck and steal surplus-value from labour "during all the 24 hours of the day."[57] For Marx and Engels, capital's abysmal mechanisms of hacking and heaping up the earth's riches are finite, possessing natural and human limits, beyond which capitalism cannot exist. In *Economic Manuscripts of 1857-58*, Marx got a geomantic grip on the dangerous precarity and opportunity that he found beneath capital's fetishized street-front and public mart: "within bourgeois society, based as it is upon *exchange value*, relationships of exchange and production are generated which are just so many mines to blow it to pieces."[58] *Sous les pavés, les abîmes!*

Shortly before November 1837, when he announced to his father that he had stopped writing poetry, Marx penned "The First Elegy of Ovid's *Tristia* Freely Rendered" (1837): "For poetry's magic fullness flows / Out of a breast stirred with elation, / But oh, a pall of darkest woes / Covers the brow, kills inspiration."[59] Marx's translation effectively elegized his imminent abandonment of poetry. His sense of poetic vocation had been undermined by "the urge to wrestle with philosophy" and to fathom the modern street.[60] Engaging with contemporary philosophy—"If previously the gods had dwelt above the earth, now they became its centre" — gave Marx the impetus to dig deeper into Hegel, breaking down his negative first impression: "I had read fragments of Hegel's philosophy, the grotesque craggy melody of which did not appeal to me."[61] Now, however, Hegel's "grotesque and rocky melody" — Sutherland's translation of Marx's *groteske Felsenmelodie*—"was beginning to exercise an unshakeable grip on Marx's mind," even being "conspicuous in the style and substance" of the momentous letter to his father.[62] Marx's "Afterword to the Second German Edition" (1873) of *Capital*, Volume 1, recalled that he had "here and there ... coquetted with the modes of expression peculiar to [Hegel]."[63] This suggestion of a merely casual textual relationship with Hegel was itself coquettish, for "Hegel's *style*, the dissonantly wrought 'melody' [and] rocky approximations to poetry,"[64] had become part of the bedrock of Marx's communist literature, not least in *Capital*, with its craggy beauty, "internal generic disintegration" and "difficult collage of the poetic."[65] Through intensive study of Hegel, Marx broached a materialist understanding of Germany's political, industrial and environmental conditions. In *Notebooks on Epicurean Philosophy* (1839), he wrote: "as Prometheus, having stolen fire from heaven, begins to build houses and to settle upon the earth, so philosophy, expanded to be the whole world, turns against the world of appearance. The same now with the philosophy of Hegel."[66]

Also in 1839, the precocious Engels was discovering appalling conditions in the homes, streets and worksites of his native region. His "Letters from Wuppertal" (1839) reported that factory workers were forced to respire dark woes that enclouded them: "Work in low rooms where people breathe in more coal fumes and dust than oxygen—and in the majority of cases beginning already at the age of six—is bound to deprive them of all strength and joy in life."[67] Blakean vignettes of innocence violated are everywhere in Engels. Stanley Edgar Hyman's statement about Marx's critical sensationalism is readily applicable to Engels: "Like a poet, Marx strives to summon up an immediacy of sensation, to make the reader feel the experience itself."[68] In the early 1840s, Marx's Promethean call not only to philosophize upon but also to poetically and critically grasp, and bring together, heaven, earth and street attracted Engels. He and Edgar Bauer co-authored a poem about the Young Hegelians, "The Insolently Threatened Yet Miraculously Rescued Bible" (1842), which parodies yet exalts Marx, who "moves in leaps and bounds, / Raving aloud. As if to seize and then pull down / To Earth the spacious tent of Heaven up on high, / He opens wide his arms and reaches for the sky."[69]

Engels became, as Foster has detailed, "an early exponent of an ecological worldview, particularly of the dialectical relationship between human beings and nature."[70] The dialectic of nature-ecology grounded his life's work. His 1843 article "Outlines of a Critique of Political Economy" positioned his study of actually-existing capitalism and its consequences, such as deepening degradation of natural resources and environmental immiseration of humanity, within a profound attentiveness to the earth. In this vanguard critique, which moved Marx to join critical arms with him, Engels argued that "two elements of production in operation—nature and man"—were severed by the alienation inherent to capital's privatization of the means of production: "The immediate consequence of private property was the split of production into two opposing sides—the natural and the human sides, the soil which without fertilisation by man is [soon] dead and sterile, and human activity, the first condition of which is that very soil."[71] His argument implied that, ultimately, if private property is not abolished, it will dig a global grave for humanity. This foreshadowed "the gravedigger thesis" discussed below. From his first book, *The Condition of the Working-Class in England* (1845) — "a foundational environmental work" — to his last, *Can Europe Disarm?* (1893), Engels addressed "the robbery of the earth" as "a governing principle of accumulation."[72] His last book outlined, among other things, the "chronic process of ruination" of forests, subsoil water and crops in Russia: "not only are the human beings ruined, but in many areas so is the land itself for at least a generation."[73]

Engels' preternatural understanding of the value of nature and of its tragic estrangement under capitalism was fired by his reading of Shelley and Lord Byron, who he praised in *Condition*: "the prophet, Shelley, and Byron, with his glowing sensuality and his bitter satire upon our existing society, find most of their readers in the proletariat."[74] As these poets helped to strike up anti-capitalist activism amongst those proletarians "cherishing the most glowing hatred, the most unbroken inward rebellion against the bourgeoisie in power," so Engels' love of their poetry had been a factor that drove him to abandon his own poetry and devote himself to revolutionary criticism, working-class struggle and a communist vision of human beings and the earth reunited in glowing sensuality.[75] In their first collaborative publication, *The Holy Family* (1845), Marx and Engels evoked "matter, surrounded by a sensuous, poetic glamour."[76] They sought, as Esther Leslie observed, "to reassert materialism in which knowledge of the material world or 'science' stems from sense perception, has 'poetic blossom' and values human perspectives."[77]

"For poetry's magic fullness flows / Out of a breast stirred with elation": the breast as a lofty, noble, blooming object-symbol in Marx's translation of Ovid epitomized the figuration of sublime anatomy in his poetry. As Sutherland has elucidated, Marx did not dispense with "sublime anatomy and concentrate exclusively on real anatomy" when he renounced his writing of poetry.[78] In Sutherland's words, he simultaneously satirized the capitalist's "sublime" *Hochbrust*, or "high, convex, swollen breast" — "The passion for accumulation prevails in the swollen capitalist breast" — and undertook a forensic analysis, often a social autopsy, of working-class bodies malformed or mutilated by their immediate work and wider social-environmental conditions: "The proletarian has a concave chest from obstructed infantile respiration or a depressed sternum."[79] In Sutherland's argument, Marx figured the "opposition between life and capital within the unity of the 'capital-relation'" as the "opposition between a concave fragmented body with no poetry in it and a convex breast swelling with grotesque poetic afflatus."[80] Poetry, in Marx's materialist critique of political economy, "is intensification pressed to the point of absolute impotence against the real limit of capitalist social reality, where abstract relations reveal their abhorrent imperviousness to poetry in 'brutal' detail."[81]

This unity of opposites, of high, swollen capitalist and depressed, concave proletarian, expresses a general law of movement of the capital-relation charted by Marx: "in proportion as capital accumulates, the lot of the labourer … must grow worse."[82] This law "rivets the labourer to capital more firmly than the wedges of Vulcan did Prometheus to the rock. It establishes an accumulation of misery, corresponding with accumulation of capital. Accumulation of wealth at one pole is, therefore, at the same time accumulation of misery, agony of toil, slavery, ignorance, brutality, mental degradation, at the opposite pole."[83] Marx's attention to proletarian humanity "enabled him to expose the corporeal depths of capitalist immiseration"[84] — in other words, to detect bourgeois society's culpability for murder inside a concave chest. As Engels repeatedly demonstrated in *Condition*, "society in England daily and hourly commits what the working-men's organs … characterise as social murder": "it has placed the workers under conditions in which they can neither retain health nor live long [and] it undermines the vital force of these workers gradually, little by little, and so hurries them to the grave before their time."[85] The condition of housing for workers presented a chthonian correlation to the concavity of their fragmented bodies. Their small, obstructed and poorly-ventilated dwellings recalled caves partly buried in the earth and even sodden graves wholly in the earth — whereas the typical bourgeois hearth and home swelled with grandeur within what Marx called "the heaven of wealth."[86]

"(unter den Troglodyten)"

The Holy Family lampooned Platonism, and idealist philosophy generally, for clinging to a poetic illusion of the sublime *soul*: "Since the 'Truth,' like history, is an ethereal subject separate from the material mass, it addresses itself not to the empirical man but to the *'innermost depths of the soul'*; in order to be *'truly apprehended'* it does not act on his vulgar body, which may live deep down in an English cellar or at the top of a French block of flats."[87] Marx and Engels' own apprehension and reconstruction of truth was based in historical time and space, and emerged, as Bataille suggested, from the bowels of human beings and the earth.

Indeed, from the mid-1840s, they were making the innermost revelation later proposed by Bataille: "By excavating the fetid ditch of bourgeois culture, perhaps we will see open up in the depths of the earth immense and even sinister caves where force and human liberty will establish themselves."[88] For Marx and Engels regarded the *cave* as recursively (re)produced by the accumulation of misery and as the archetypal space in which proletarians dwell, work and are buried alive. Simultaneously, they foresaw revolutionary force and human liberty, in the form of proletarian self-emancipation, as an irruption from so many caves, blowing to pieces the social crust, the apparent second "nature," of bourgeois society.[89] In the *Communist Manifesto*, their image of the upspringing movement of the proletariat—a Promethean anabasis, or geological-troglodytic uprising, of "the lowest stratum of our present society"—was indebted to Heine.[90] In Paris in 1842, Heine had unearthed a "powerful academy," which taught "revolution and overthrow." That academy preserved its "terrible incognito" and lived "like a poor pretender in that ground-floor or cellar of official society"—but he publicized its identity: "Communism is the name of the terrible antagonist [of] the *bourgeois regime*."[91] After the 1848 revolutions, Heine justifiably commended his own foresight: "Many a time and oft did I depict the demons"—*titans troglodytes* in the French edition—"who lurked in the lower depths of society, and who would come bursting up out of their darkness when the destined day should come. These monsters, to whom the future belongs."[92]

Besides Heine's investigative journalism and ironic jeremiads, Marx and Engels' caving journeys grappled with Plato's allegory of the cave and German Romantic literature. The latter "is crawling with so many miners," spelunkers and ecstatic visions of underground riches.[93] Although Marx's *Economic and Philosophic Manuscripts of 1844* "echoed Novalis's image of the miner, under the earth's crust, digging out beautiful gems for their aesthetic value alone," he and Engels vulgarly displaced theoretical interest from allegorical and Romantic caves and cavers to the cave-spaces manifested by the factory, the cellar-dwelling and even the dark, smoke-shrouded industrial city itself.[94] According to David McNally, when Marx, in the first volume of *Capital*, turned to the sphere of production, "the underworld that harbours essential truths about capitalism," and entered "the cave, the domain of darkness, the space of invisible forces," he reversed "the whole trajectory of Western philosophy which, since Plato, has sought truth by means of an ascent from the cave, a rising from darkness to light."[95] Marx's katabatic encounter with "the truth of capitalism" in "*that* cave"—behind the factory door—emulated Engels' game-changing *Condition*.[96]

Dank, miserable, socially-murderous caves seem ubiquitous in proletarian life, and death, in Engels' book. He quoted from classical political economist Nassau Senior's 1837 account of working-class quarters in Manchester: "In one place we saw a whole street following the course of a ditch, in order to have deeper cellars (cellars for people, not for lumber) without the expense of excavations. *Not a house in this street escaped cholera.* … whole families occupy a corner of a cellar or of a garret."[97] Leaving aside Engels' discovery of industrial vivisepulture in the cavernous factory system—"condemnation to be buried alive in the mill … felt as the keenest torture by the operatives"—his methodical exploration of England's *bas-fonds* confirmed the prevalence of cave-like housing for working-class people.[98] In London, he saw "a great number of cellar dwellings out of which puny children and half-starved, ragged women emerge;" "more than 45,000 human beings [in Liverpool] live in narrow, dark, damp, badly-ventilated cellar dwellings;" "subterranean dens ... are general" in towns surrounding Manchester too; and so "the great multitude of the poor" throughout the land "are given damp dwellings, cellar dens that are not waterproof from below, or garrets that leak from above."[99] "For page after page," as Andy Merrifield put it, Engels ventured "deeper down the abyss, vividly evoking the horror" of his descent "into the ruined basements of the damned, 'natural' complements to the suburbs of the rich."[100] The horror of these sinister basements was enclosed in another horror: anthropogenic obnubilation. In Germany Engels had entered low, cave-like workrooms where people inhaled more coal fumes than oxygen, but in England he traversed entire industrial towns and cities that were like caves, since ceaseless smoke pollution blocked out the sun—factory towers, in Charles Dickens' Carlylean description, "never ceasing in their black vomit, blasting all things living or inanimate, shutting out the face of day, and closing in on all these horrors with a dense dark cloud."[101]

Marx's one-time mentor Moses Hess had a sanguine attitude to the coming of communism. Stathis Kouvelakis has paraphrased Hess: "nothing can prevent humanity from emerging from the cave."[102] Marx, however, wrote of workers being either returned to the cave or sent to an early grave, slain by social murder. In a draft article from 1845, he asserted that the only land that bourgeois domination allows workers to hold, whether in life or in death, is underground: "The nationality of the worker ... is *labour, free slavery, self-huckstering*. His government ... is *capital*. His native air ... is *factory air*. The land belonging to him ... lies a few feet *below the ground*."[103] Here Marx catechized the argument of his 1844 manuscripts that capital ceaselessly violates both the natural essence of humanity and the human essence of nature:

> Even the need for fresh air ceases to be a need for the worker. Man returns to a cave dwelling, which is now, however, contaminated with the pestilential breath of civilisation, and which he continues to occupy only *precariously*, it being for him an alien habitation which can be withdrawn from him any day — a place from which, if he does not pay, he can be thrown out any day. For this mortuary he has to *pay*. A dwelling in the *light*, which

Prometheus in Aeschylus designated as one of the greatest boons, by means of which he made the savage into a human being, ceases to exist for the worker. ...

We have said above that man is regressing to the *cave dwelling*, etc. — but he is regressing to it in an estranged, malignant form. The savage in his cave — a natural element which freely offers itself for his use and protection — feels himself no more a stranger, or rather feels as much at home as a *fish* in water. But the cellar dwelling of the poor man is a hostile element ... which he cannot regard as his own hearth — where he might at last exclaim: "Here I am at home" — but where instead he finds himself in *someone else*'s house, in the house of a *stranger* who always watches him and throws him out if he does not pay his rent. He is also aware of the contrast in quality between his dwelling and a human dwelling that stands in the *other* world, in the heaven of wealth.[104]

Factory air was naturalized, fresh air denaturalized. The acme of this pulmonary debasement of nature and the human was, in Engels' phrase, "the total pollution of the air."[105] In his and Marx's analysis of capitalist social reality's brutal depths and polluted atmosphere, alienation from the earth and ecological crisis comprise an everyday *mise en abîme*. Within the city-cave contaminated with the pestilential breath of civilization is the cave dwelling contaminated with the pestilential breath of civilization, and within the contaminated cave dwelling is the worker's concave chest contaminated with the pestilential breath of civilization. Capital is and means an unearthly pestilence.

Marx expanded the unearthly social-environmental concerns of his 1844 manuscripts in later works. In *Eighteenth Brumaire*, he observed that as capital's dominance of France became entrenched, cave dwelling was generalized: "Small-holding property, in this enslavement by capital to which its development inevitably pushes forward, has transformed the mass of the French nation into troglodytes. Sixteen million peasants (including women and children) dwell in hovels" — *caves* in some translations — "a large number of which have but one opening;" and so the *bourgeois régime* "has become a vampire that sucks out [the small-holders'] blood and brains and throws them into the alchemist's cauldron of capital."[106] In *Capital*, Volume 3, shades of Engels' 1843 denunciation of immoral huckstering of the land as well as Marx's

1844 lamentation for the worker barely occupying a rental mortuary appear in a profoundly moving passage about stricken workers forbidden to live on the earth without precarity, let alone to flourish with the earth untrammelled by the alien supremacy of property:

> the monstrous power wielded by landed property, when united hand in hand with industrial capital, enables it to be used against labourers engaged in their wage struggle as a means of practically expelling them from the earth as a dwelling place. One part of society thus exacts tribute from another for the permission to inhabit the earth, as landed property in general assigns the landlord the privilege of exploiting the terrestrial body, the bowels of the earth, the air, and thereby the maintenance and development of life.[107]

In *Capital*, Volume 1, workers living and dying in hand-dug caves in Derbyshire appear in a footnote where Marx has interpolated "(unter den Troglodyten)" into his quotation from *Public Health: Seventh Report* (1864):

> 'At Doveholes, a number of small excavations have been made into a large hillock of lime ashes (the refuse of lime-kilns), and which are used as dwellings [by railway labourers]. The excavations are small and damp, and have no drains or privies about them, and not the slightest means of ventilation except up a hole pulled through the top, and used for a chimney. In consequence of this defect, small-pox has been raging for some time, and some deaths' (amongst the troglodytes) 'have been caused by it.'[108]

This textual vivisepulture of a working-class community of cave-dwellers, buried in a note at the bottom of an arbitrarily-numbered page, like a collective grave for unnamed workers, symbolizes the position of proletarians in bourgeois society. Marx, of course, gave much more than this downward glance at *den Troglodyten* — a term that he used to denote, not deride, cave-dwellers.[109] He aggressively criticized "the life-situation in which capital places the working class," as he phrased it in *Economic Manuscript of 1861-63*: "the vacuity of their lives."[110] Cave-dwelling was, and is, not an abuse, aberration or exception to the laws of accumulation, but rather a truth of those laws, one expression among many of the general life-shortening, desolating sentence imposed on working people under capitalism.

Whenever and wherever capital sees plenitude arising from accumulation, the proletariat undergoes the hollowing out of life. So must the dwellers of capital's underground voids surface across the body of Marx and Engels' collected works. And as the simultaneous pileups of wealth and misery proceed apace today, "a new sort of cave dweller becomes rampant," as Kluge has observed: "Projects for the formation of new property — new media — reflect on this Robinsonian constitution of the modern house and cave dweller."[111] It is capitalism's "nature" to love a vacuum.

Earth be our Sepulchre

> Shrink to your cellars, holes, and cells –
> In hall ye deck another dwells.
> Why shake the chains ye wrought? Ye see
> The steel ye tempered glance on ye.
>
> With plough and spade and hoe and loom
> Trace your grave and build your tomb
> And weave your winding-sheet — till fair
> England be your Sepulchre.[112]

"The development of Modern Industry," Marx and Engels asserted in the *Communist Manifesto*, "cuts from under its feet the very foundation on which the bourgeoisie produces and appropriates products. What the bourgeoisie, therefore, produces, above all, is its own grave-diggers. Its fall and the victory of the proletariat are equally inevitable."[113] In other words, given the proletariat's chthonic existence and enchainment to capital, its self-emancipation will necessarily undermine, undo and overthrow the very ground of the bourgeoisie's mission to accumulate wealth by sucking out the guts of the earth and earthly life. Marx and Engel's epigrammatic formulation of "what has come to be known as the gravedigger thesis"[114] is the most prominent expression of their stressing, for propaganda purposes, "the victory of the revolutionary classes over the course of history — save in the exceptional case of [what they called] 'the common ruin of the contending classes.'"[115]

Their later works foresaw the universalization of local and regional ecological catastrophes, such as deforestation, desertification and toxic pollution of "our one and all," leading not to social revolution and sustainable, communist dwelling and flourishing with the earth, but rather to an uninhabitable planet and thence the death-throes of all humanity, not just the plutocrats of Plutus. In 1970, Henri Lefebvre found that Engels' findings about English pollution had been universalized: "Industrialization and urbanization, together or in competition, ravage nature. Water, earth, air, fire — the elements — are threatened with destruction. By the year 2000, whether or not there has been nuclear war, our water and air will be so polluted that life on earth will be difficult to maintain."[116] In 2019, Peter Osborne maintained that for the people reading his words, "capitalism is unlikely to die any kind of death during their lifetimes, unless it is a death of all."[117] Today, as the bourgeoisie robs, hucksters and squanders the earth unto its very end(s), "the common ruin of the contending classes" looms.[118] Under capital's abysmal accumulation of anthropogenic ecological catastrophe, social murder is universalized into social omnicide.

In formulating the "gravedigger thesis," Marx and Engels retooled Shelley's "Song to Men of England" as an incitement to insurrection. Whereas Shelley indirectly and negatively expressed the need for working-class people to revolt, instead of weaving their own winding-sheets and hoeing their own burial pits, Marx and Engels positively provoked their communist and working-class readers to dig the bourgeoisie's grave by struggling to transcend and end class-based society as such. Because capital's inherent tendency to ecological catastrophe is winning the world, turning it into a slaughterhouse of mass extinction, the classical-Marxist slogan "socialism or barbarism" has been revised to "ecosocialism or barbarism."[119] If the grave-digging of bourgeois society does not take a communist form — chthonic revolution to abolish capitalism and bring forth the earth as a home for all — the catastrophic default form will become inevitable: the earth as home to none, sepulchre for all. Out of the depths of the earth, the communist literature of Marx and Engels demonstrated that ruinous accumulation, cave-dwelling and bourgeois society's creation of its own gravediggers must necessarily remain core tendencies of capitalism until its blessed end.

Notes

1   Quotations of Marx and Engels are from their Collected Works, 50 vols. (London: Lawrence and Wishart, 1975-2004) and use the established acronym MECW, followed by the volume and page number(s), as per the form of this reference—MECW 35: 53.

2   *MECW* 35: 591.

3   Esther Leslie, *Synthetic Worlds: Nature, Art and the Chemical Industry* (London: Reaktion Books, 2005), 210.

4   Edward Aveling and Eleanor Marx Aveling, *Shelley's Socialism* (London: Journeyman, 1975), 4.

5   *MECW* 2: 101.

6   Percy Bysshe Shelley, *The Selected Poetry and Prose of Shelley*, ed. Bruce Woodcock (Ware, UK: Wordsworth Editions, 2002), 36.

7   John Bellamy Foster, "Engels's *Dialectics of Nature* in the Anthropocene," *Monthly Review* 72, no. 6 (2020): 15.

8   *MECW* 3: 429-30.

9   *MECW* 3: 172.

10 *MECW* 3: 170.

11 Shelley, *Selected Poetry and Prose*, 33.

12 *MECW* 35: 506-7.

13 See John Bellamy Foster and Brett Clark. "The Robbery of Nature: Capitalism and the Metabolic Rift," *Monthly Review* 70, no. 3 (2018): 1-20.

14 *MECW* 37: 799.

15 John Bellamy Foster, "Capitalism and the Accumulation of Catastrophe," *Monthly Review* 63, no. 7 (2011): 14.

16 Ned Lukacher, "Walter Benjamin's Chthonian Revolution," *boundary 2* 11, nos. 1-2 (1982-1983): 53, 55.

17 Pierre Macherey, *The Object of Literature*, trans. David Macey (Cambridge: Cambridge University Press, 1995), 87, 99, 104.

18 Alexander Kluge, *Difference and Orientation: An Alexander Kluge Reader*, ed. Richard Langston (Ithaca and London: Cornell University Press and Cornell University Library, 2019), 111.

19 *MECW* 35: 45.

20 Andreas Malm, *The Progress of this Storm: Nature and Society in a Warming* World (Verso: London and Brooklyn, 2018), 185.

21 *MECW* 35: 591.

22 *MECW* 35: 247.

23 See Foster and Clark, "The Robbery of Nature."

24 *MECW* 35: 54, 271.

25   Keston Sutherland, "The Poetics of *Capital*," in *Capitalism: Concept, Idea, Image –
      Aspects of Marx's* Capital *Today*, ed. Peter Osborne, Éric Alliez and Eric-John
      Russell (London: CRMEP Books, 2019), 205.
26   Shelley, *Selected Poetry and Prose*, 405. *MECW* 35: 241.
27   Foster and Clark, "The Robbery of Nature," 1-2.
28   Liebig quoted in Foster and Clark, "The Robbery of Nature," 5.
29   *MECW* 35: 384.
30   *MECW* 35: 143.
31   Hans Magnus Enzensberger, *Critical Essays*, ed. Reinhold Grimm and Bruce
      Armstrong (New York: Continuum, 1982), 212.
32   *MECW* 35: 750,
33   See Paul Burkett, "Marx's Vision of Sustainable Human Development,"
      Monthly Review 57, no. 5 (2005): 34-62; John Bellamy Foster, ""The Crisis of the
      Earth: Marx's Theory of Ecological Sustainability as a Nature-Imposed
      Necessity for Human Production," *Organization & Environment* 10, no. 3 (1997):
      278-95, and John Bellamy Foster, *The Return of Nature: Socialism and Ecology*
      (New York: Monthly Review Press, 2020).
34   *MECW* 37: 763.
35   *MECW* 5: 141.
36   John Bellamy Foster, *Marx's Ecology: Materialism and Nature* (New York:
      Monthly Review Press, 2000), 135. See Walt Sheasby, "Anti-Prometheus, Post-
      Marx: The Real and the Myth in Green Theory," *Organization & Environment*
      12, 1 (1999): 5-44.
37   Franklin Rosemont, "Karl Marx and the Iroquois," *Arsenal: Surrealist
      Subversion* 4 (1989): 203.
38   Keston Sutherland, "Marx's Defence of Poetry," *world picture* 19 (2015): 1.
39   Sutherland, "The Poetics of *Capital*," 207.
40   Foster, *The Return of Nature*, 179.
41   David McNally, *Monsters of the Market: Zombies, Vampires and Global Capitalism*
      (Leiden and Boston: Brill, 2011), 115.
42   Sutherland, "Marx's Defence of Poetry," 14 n. 40.
43   S. S. Prawer, *Karl Marx and World Literature* (Oxford: Clarendon, 1976). Paul
      Hamilton, *Historicism* (London and New York: Routledge, 1996), 109.
44   See William Clare Roberts, *Marx's Inferno: The Political Theory of Capital*
      (Princeton: Princeton University Press, 2018) and Jayson Althofer, "Friedrich
      Engels and Gothic Marxism: A Fairy-Tale Introduction," *Critical Imprints* VIII
      (2020): 77-94.
45   Lukacher, "Walter Benjamin's Chthonian Revolution," 52.
46   See G. M. Matthews, "A Volcano's Voice in Shelley," *ELH* 24, 3 (1957): 191-228.
47   Leslie, *Synthetic Worlds*, 74.
48   Georges Bataille, *Visions of Excess: Selected Writings, 1927-1939*, ed. Allan Stoekl
      (Minneapolis: University of Minnesota Press, 1985), 35.
49   *MECW* 1: 598, 619.
50   *MECW* 1: 577.
51   McKenzie Wark, *Capital is Dead* (London and New York: Verso, 2019), 168.
52   *MECW* 5: 6, 8.

53   Thomas Carlyle, *Past and Present* (Boston: Little and Brown, 1843), 227.
54   Leslie, *Synthetic Worlds*, 30.
55   *MECW* 35: 186, 261.
56   Peter Osborne, *How to Read Marx* (London: Granta, 2005), 94.
57   *MECW* 35: 251, 263 273, 283, 306.
58   *MECW* 28: 96.
59   *MECW* 1: 551.
60   *MECW* 1:11.
61   *MECW* 1: 18.
62   Sutherland, "Marx's Defence of Poetry," 1-2.
63   *MECW* 35: 19.
64   Sutherland, "Marx's Defence of Poetry," 2.
65   Sutherland, "Marx in Jargon," *world picture* 1 (2008): 6. See Osborne, *How to Read Marx*, 85-86.
66   *MECW* 1: 491.
67   *MECW* 2: 9.
68   Stanley Edgar Hyman, *The Tangled Bank: Darwin, Marx, Frazer and Freud as Imaginative Writers* (New York: Atheneum, 1962), 135.
69   *MECW* 2: 336.
70   Foster, *The Return of Nature*, 178.
71   *MECW* 3: 428, 432.
72   Foster, *The Return of Nature*, 178-79.
73   *MECW* 27: 387.
74   *MECW* 4: 528.
75   *MECW* 4: 411.
76   *MECW* 4: 128.
77   Leslie, *Synthetic Worlds*, 71.
78   Sutherland, "Marx's Defence of Poetry," 10.
79   Sutherland, "Marx's Defence of Poetry," 11, 10.
80   Sutherland, "Marx's Defence of Poetry," 11.
81   Sutherland, "Marx's Defence of Poetry," 12.
82   *MECW* 35: 639.
83   *MECW* 35: 639-40.
84   Joseph Fracchia, "Beyond the Human-Nature Debate: Human Corporeal Organisation as the 'First Fact' of Historical Materialism," *Historical Materialism* 13, no. 1 (2005): 57.
85   *MECW* 4: 394.
86   *MECW* 3: 314.
87   *MECW* 4: 80.
88   Bataille, *Visions of Excess*, 43.
89   Althofer, "Friedrich Engels and Gothic Marxism," 90-91.
90   *MECW* 6: 495.
91   Heinrich Heine, *The Works of Heinrich Heine*, Vol. VIII in 2 vols, Vol. II: Lutetia, trans. Charles Godfrey Leland (London: William Heinemann, 1893), 299, 301.
92   Heine, *Works*, 25-26.

93   Theodore Ziolkowski, *German Romanticism and its Institutions* (Princeton: Princeton University Press, 1990), 18.

94   Leslie, *Synthetic Worlds*, 71.

95   McNally, *Monsters of the Market*, 133-34.

96   Robert Paul Wolff, *Moneybags Must Be So Lucky: On the Literary Structure of Capital* (Amherst: University of Massachusetts Press, 1988), 53.

97   *MECW* 4: 364.

98   *MECW* 4: 466.

99   *MECW* 4: 333-45, 396.

100   Andy Merrifield, *Metromarxism: A Marxist Tale of the City* (New York and London: Routledge, 2002), 36-37.

101   Charles Dickens, *The Old Curiosity Shop* (Oxford: Oxford University Press, 1997), 348.

102   Stathis Kouvelakis, *Philosophy and Revolution: From Kant to Marx*, 2nd ed. (Verso: London and New York, 2018), 162.

103   *MECW* 4: 280.

104   *MECW* 3: 307-8, 314.

105   *MECW* 4: 346.

106   *MECW* 11: 190-91.

107   *MECW* 37: 760.

108   *MECW* 35: 658, no. 1.

109   Cf. Stephen Graham, *Vertical: The City from Satellites to Bunkers* (London and New York: Verso, 2016), 316.

110   *MECW* 30: 302.

111   Kluge, *Difference and Orientation*, 267. See Graham, *Vertical*, 313-21.

112   From Shelley's "Song to Men of England" in Shelley, *Selected Poetry and Prose*, 405.

113   *MECW* 6: 495-96.

114   Matt Vidal, "Was Marx Wrong about the Working Class? Reconsidering the Gravedigger Thesis," *International Socialism* 158 (2018): 65.

115   Michael Löwy, *Fire Alarm: Reading Walter Benjamin's 'On the Concept of History'*, trans. Chris Turner (London and New York: Verso, 2016), 39.

116   Henri Lefebvre, *The Urban Revolution*, trans. Robert Bononno (Minneapolis: University of Minnesota Press, 2003), 26

117   Peter Osborne, "Capitalism: Concept, Idea, Image," in *Capitalism: Concept, Idea, Image – Aspects of Marx's* Capital *Today*, ed. Peter Osborne, Éric Alliez and Eric-John Russell (London: CRMEP Books, 2019), 3.

118   *MECW* 6: 482.

119   Jane Kelly and Malone, Sheila, eds. *Ecosocialism or Barbarism* (London: Socialist Resistance, 2006).

Bibliography

Althofer, Jayson. "Friedrich Engels and Gothic Marxism: A Fairy-Tale Introduction." *Critical Imprints* VIII (2020): pp. 77-94.

Aveling, Edward, and Eleanor Marx Aveling. *Shelley's Socialism*. 1888. London: Journeyman, 1975.

Bataille, Georges. *Visions of Excess: Selected Writings, 1927-1939*. Edited by Allan Stoekl. Minneapolis: University of Minnesota Press, 1985.

Burkett, Paul. "Marx's Vision of Sustainable Human Development." *Monthly Review* 57, no. 5 (2005): pp. 34-62.

Carlyle, Thomas. *Past and Present*. Boston: Little and Brown, 1843.

Dickens, Charles. *The Old Curiosity Shop*. 1840-41. Oxford: Oxford University Press, 1997.

Enzensberger, Hans Magnus. *Critical Essays*. Edited by Reinhold Grimm and Bruce Armstrong. New York: Continuum, 1982.

Foster, John Bellamy. "Capitalism and the Accumulation of Catastrophe." *Monthly Review* 63, no. 7 (2011): pp. 1-17.

____. "The Crisis of the Earth: Marx's Theory of Ecological Sustainability as a Nature-Imposed Necessity for Human Production." *Organization & Environment* 10, no. 3 (1997): pp. 278-95.

____. "Engels's Dialectics of Nature in the Anthropocene." *Monthly Review* 72, no. 6 (2020): pp. 1-17.

____. *Marx's Ecology: Materialism and Nature*. New York: Monthly Review Press, 2000.

____. *The Return of Nature: Socialism and Ecology*. New York: Monthly Review Press, 2020.

Foster, John Bellamy, and Brett Clark. "The Robbery of Nature: Capitalism and the Metabolic Rift." *Monthly Review* 70, no. 3 (2018): pp. 1-20.

Fracchia, Joseph. "Beyond the Human-Nature Debate: Human Corporeal Organisation as the 'First Fact' of Historical Materialism." *Historical Materialism* 13, no. 1 (2005): pp. 33-62.

Graham, Stephen. *Vertical: The City from Satellites to Bunkers*. London and New York: Verso, 2016.

Hamilton, Paul. *Historicism*. London and New York: Routledge, 1996.

Heine, Heinrich. *The Works of Heinrich Heine*. Vol. VIII in 2 vols, Vol. II: Lutetia. Translated by Charles Godfrey Leland. London: William Heinemann, 1893.

Hyman, Stanley Edgar. *The Tangled Bank: Darwin, Marx, Frazer and Freud as Imaginative Writers*. New York: Atheneum, 1962.

Kelly, Jane and Malone Sheila, eds. *Ecosocialism or Barbarism*. London: Socialist Resistance, 2006.

Kluge, Alexander. *Difference and Orientation: An Alexander Kluge Reader*. Edited by Richard Langston. Ithaca and London: Cornell University Press and Cornell University Library, 2019.

Kouvelakis, Stathis. *Philosophy and Revolution: From Kant to Marx*, 2nd ed. London and New York: Verso, 2018.

Lefebvre, Henri. *The Urban Revolution*. 1970. Translated by Robert Bononno. Minneapolis: University of Minnesota Press, 2003.

Leslie, Esther. *Synthetic Worlds: Nature, Art and the Chemical Industry*. London: Reaktion Books, 2005.

Löwy, Michael. *Fire Alarm: Reading Walter Benjamin's 'On the Concept of History'*. Translated by Chris Turner. London and New York: Verso, 2016.

Lukacher, Ned. "Walter Benjamin's Chthonian Revolution." *boundary 2* 11, nos. 1-2 (1982-1983): pp. 41-57.

Macherey, Pierre. *The Object of Literature*. 1990. Translated by David Macey. Cambridge: Cambridge University Press, 1995.

Malm, Andreas. *The Progress of this Storm: Nature and Society in a Warming World*. Verso: London and Brooklyn, 2018.

Marx, Karl, and Frederick Engels. *Collected Works*. 50 vols. London: Lawrence and Wishart, 1975-2004.

Matthews G.M. "A Volcano's Voice in Shelley." *ELH* 24, no. 3 (1957): pp. 191-228.

McNally, David. *Monsters of the Market: Zombies, Vampires and Global Capitalism*. Leiden and Boston: Brill, 2011.

Merrifield, Andy. *Metromarxism: A Marxist Tale of the City*. New York and London: Routledge, 2002.

Osborne, Peter. "Capitalism: Concept, Idea, Image." In *Capitalism: Concept, Idea, Image – Aspects of Marx's Capital Today*, edited by Peter Osborne, Éric Alliez and Eric-John Russell, pp. 3-17. London: CRMEP Books, 2019.

____. *How to Read Marx*. London: Granta, 2005.

Prawer, S. S. *Karl Marx and World Literature*. Oxford: Clarendon, 1976.

Roberts, William Clare. *Marx's Inferno: The Political Theory of Capital*. Princeton: Princeton University Press, 2018.

Rosemont, Franklin. "Karl Marx and the Iroquois." *Arsenal: Surrealist Subversion* 4 (1989): pp. 201-213.

Sheasby, Walt. "Anti-Prometheus, Post-Marx: The Real and the Myth in Green Theory." *Organization & Environment* 12, no. 1 (1999): pp. 5-44.

Shelley, Percy Bysshe. *The Selected Poetry and Prose of Shelley*. Edited by Bruce Woodcock. Ware, UK: Wordsworth Editions, 2002.

Sutherland, Keston. "Marx in Jargon." *world picture* 1 (2008): pp. 1-25.

____. "Marx's Defence of Poetry." *world picture* 19 (2015): pp. 1-15.

____. "The Poetics of *Capital*." In *Capitalism: Concept, Idea, Image — Aspects of Marx's Capital Today*, edited by Peter Osborne, Éric Alliez and Eric-John Russell, pp. 203-218. London: CRMEP Books, 2019.

Vidal, Matt. "Was Marx Wrong about the Working Class? Reconsidering the Gravedigger Thesis." *International Socialism* 158 (2018): pp. 65-80.

Wark, McKenzie. *Capital is Dead*. London and New York: Verso, 2019.

Wolff, Robert Paul. *Moneybags Must Be So Lucky: On the Literary Structure of Capital*. Amherst: University of Massachusetts Press, 1988.

Ziolkowski, Theodore. *German Romanticism and its Institutions*. Princeton: Princeton University Press, 1990.

2

A Glance at the Whole:
Nature, Earth and Subjectivity in
Alexander von Humboldt's *Cosmos* and
Views of Nature

Mario Bosincu

At the beginning of his American scientific expedition, Alexander von Humboldt expressed his motto about life in a letter: "Man must have the will to accomplish great and good things. Everything else depends on destiny."[1] A sentence that foregrounds the theme of this chapter, in which I analyze Alexander von Humboldt's *Views of Nature* (1849) and *Cosmos* (1845-1862) in terms of the idea of the subject and, above all, of the *subject form* whose constitution these texts engage through a kind of nature writing based on ancient notions about self-formation. Specifically, my analysis begins with the Foucaultian conception of the subject as a socio-cultural construct informing Andreas Reckwitz's survey of the selfhood forms peculiar to various stages of the modern age. According to Reckwitz, modernity presents itself as a sequence of hegemonic subject cultures characterized by specific codes to which each subjectivity form must conform while constituting itself through standardized practices. In particular, Reckwitz sharply distinguishes outer and inner-oriented practices, the latter of which give rise to a complex inner sphere, as occurs through diaristic writing, a bourgeois technology of the self-enabling a richly hued autobiographical consciousness.[2] Christian Moser has also analyzed the relationship between the practices of reading and writing on the one hand and the process of self-constitution on the other hand. Regarding the history of premodern subjectivity, Moser has focused on the phenomenon of the book-based selfhood,[3] which emerged thanks to technologies of the self, that is, reading and writing. Moser has also argued that ancient philosophy was a form of *psychagogical* knowledge geared toward creating a specific mode of subjectivity.[4] In this light, Greco-Roman philosophical schools, for all their doctrinal differences, shared the goal of inducing their adherents to refashion themselves into radically different men. This means, in turn, that ancient philosophy as a whole was a part of what Foucault has defined as a *culture de soi*: a set of doctrines and social practices for working on oneself in order to achieve self-transfiguration by means of spiritual exercises, strategies intended "to effect a modification [...] in the subject who practiced them."[5] Specifically, the exercitant could achieve *wisdom*, a mode of being characterized by autarchy, ataraxy, and cosmic consciousness, the "dilation of the self into the totality of the real."[6]

It is worth outlining the moral topography that underlies this concept of wisdom. As Charles Taylor has pointed out, the "inside-outside" opposition plays an important role in the language of modern self-understanding, which describes feelings and ideas as being inside us.[7] This semantics of inner and outer was also central to ancient thought, as indicated by the Stoic distinction between the "goods of the mind" — such as the "virtuous acts" depending on man — and the "external goods"[8] that were not in man's power, as Humboldt acknowledged in the above-quoted letter. This "inside-outside" opposition lay at the heart of Stoic ethics. In stressing the fickleness of chance,[9] Seneca distinguished the ephemeral "delight in adventitious things," which is at the mercy of chance, and lasting joy, which "springs wholly from oneself,"[10] i.e., from one's inner depths. In this way, he employed the language of inwardness, which was his major contribution to Western thought.[11] Hence, he exhorted Lucilius to rejoice only in his "very self,"[12] which could not "be given or snatched away"[13]: his reason. Reason enabled man to formulate correct judgments on the events happening to him and to attain "the Good which is [...] beyond the reach of threats,"[14] namely, wisdom, "the only immortal thing that falls to mortal lot,"[15] which makes man happy and "free from both fear and desire."[16]

In their pursuit of happiness, the Greco-Roman philosophical schools often resorted to physics, a view of nature specific to each doctrine that functioned as a spiritual exercise. For instance,

Epicurus expressed his psychagogical conception of cosmology by writing that natural philosophy did not create "boastful men [...] who show off the 'culture' which the many quarrel over, but rather strong and self-sufficient men."[17] More important, this lived physics was often bound up with the spiritual practice of the view of the cosmos or Earth from above, which originates in a well-known passage of Plato's *Republic* and which Hadot has classed among the topoi of meditation running through Western thought. Attempting to define the distinguishing mark of a philosophical nature, Socrates observes,

> Small-mindedness, I would imagine, is the last thing you want in a soul which is going to spend all its time reaching out for the wholeness and totality of things — divine and human.'
> 'That's very true,' he said.
> 'Do you think, then, that the mind which is not afraid of great things, and can contemplate the whole of time and the whole of reality, is likely to regard human life as of any great importance?'
> 'No, that's impossible.[18]

Moreover, what is at stake here is the ancient conception of the *theoria* as the practice of "gazing" upon nature as a whole and upon what was divine[19] in accordance with the original meaning of θεωρία: the journey undertaken to consult oracles or witness festivals in honor of the gods. In Marcus Aurelius' *Meditations*, the *theoria* of the cosmos often takes the form of a spiritual exercise of "imaginative 'overflight'"[20]: "You can strip away many unnecessary troubles which lie wholly in your own judgement. And you will immediately make large and wide room for yourself by grasping the whole universe in your thought."[21]

The Roman emperor calls for a shift from the dominant vision of reality to a view that resituates each event within the perspective of universal nature to understand an event as the necessary outcome of the overall cosmic process made up of interrelated elements: "All things are meshed together, and a sacred bond unites them. Hardly a single thing is alien to the rest: ordered together in their places they together make up the one order of the universe."[22] Hence, the conception of every fact as something that "has been fated by the Whole from the beginning and spun for your own destiny"[23] and that is to be joyfully accepted because "what comes to each individual is a determining part of the welfare [...] of that which governs the Whole."[24] Thus, Marcus Aurelius' meditations shed light on the constitutive elements of the ancient *askēsis* elucidated by Foucault: the "ethical substance"—i.e., the prime material of the work on oneself (in the emperor's case his desires and emotions in relation to the events occurring in man's life)—and its *"telos,"*[25] such as the nature-attuned form of subjectivity and the cosmic consciousness he strives for.

A further key aspect of the imaginative exercise of the cosmic flight was the *topos* of the view of the Earth from above: "Well then, will a little fame distract you? Look at the speed of universal oblivion, [...] the tiny room in which all this is confined. The whole earth is a mere point in space: what a minute cranny within this is your own habitation, and how many and what sort will sing your praises here!"[26]

This topical meditation on the tininess of the Earth found its most influential expression in Cicero's treatise *On the Republic*, specifically in the chapter in which Scipio Africanus Minor relates the dream in which his grandfather, Scipio Africanus Major, after carrying him up to the Milky Way, lets him behold the Earth: "Earth itself now seemed so small to me that I was discontented with our empire."[27] Hence, his grandfather recommends that he look always heavenward and scorn human things. In this way, Cicero's text makes it possible for the reader to cast an imaginary glance at the Earth as a whole and thereby offers a veritable spiritual exercise in conformity with a central feature of ancient philosophical works. In fact, these works were structured as a set of exercises intended to allow readers to experience a "spiritual metamorphosis,"[28] such as the inner renewal that Seneca wished Lucilius to undergo. Seneca himself further developed the *topos* of the view of the Earth from above in his *Natural Questions*. In the preface to the first book, the knowledge of the universe culminates in a scornful glance at the Earth and worldly things:

> The full consummation of human felicity is attained when [...] the soul seeks the heights and reaches the inner recesses of nature. What joy then to roam

> through the very stars, to look down with derision on the gilded saloons of the rich and the whole earth with its store of gold! [...] Only when one has surveyed the whole universe can one truly despise grand colonnades, ceilings glittering with ivory, trim groves and cooling streams transported into wealthy mansions. From above, one can now look down upon this narrow world [...]. That is a mere point in which you sail, and war, and dispose your kingdoms.[29]

The contemplation of the Earth from the heights of the cosmos, therefore, serves to attain the high-mindedness—the disdain for human things—extolled by Plato in the *Republic*. Foucault has interpreted the above-cited passage as key to understanding what he termed "spiritual knowledge" in his characterization of spirituality as the "experience through which the subject carries out the necessary transformations on himself in order to have access to the truth."[30] According to the French philosopher, during the modern age, the subject-shaping knowledge of spirituality was gradually supplanted by a different mode of knowledge, "le *savoir de connaissance*"—modern science—which triumphed over the former by adopting "a number of its elements."[31]

Another ancient writer relevant to understanding the conceptual framework of the *Views of Nature* and of *Cosmos* is Pliny the Elder. In his *Natural History*, he eloquently elaborated the *topos* of the view of the Earth from above:

> subtract all these portions from the earth or rather from this pin-prick, as the majority of thinkers have taught, in the world—for in the whole universe the earth is nothing else: and this is the substance of our glory, this is its habitation, here it is that we fill positions of power and covet wealth, and throw mankind into an uproar, and launch even civil wars and slaughter one another to make the land more spacious![32]

At the same time, he further underscored the psychagogical function ascribed to knowledge by portraying, with Lucretian pathos, the astronomers, "who have discovered the law of those great divinities"—the stars—and "released the miserable mind of man from fear," as "mighty heroes."[33] Pliny also expressed his pantheistic view of the world as a "deity."[34] Indeed, Pliny's work is suffused with a sense of religious awe in the face of "the grandeur of nature,"[35] whose "power and majesty [...] lacks credence if one's mind embraces parts of it only and not the whole."[36] In this respect, *mirabilia* are reported to illustrate nature's different facets, such as the wildness and cruelty of the *bellum omnium contra omnes* spectacularly raging among animals.[37]

In *Cosmos*, Alexander von Humboldt chose the passage from Pliny on the power and majesty of nature as the epigraph to the book and explicitly designated him as a model because of his awareness of the need to present the universe "as a great and concurrent whole."[38] No wonder, then, that he adopted the totalizing perspective at the center of the ancient *theoria*, maintaining that the fundamental principle of his work consisted in "the constant [...] endeavor to embrace the phænomena of the universe as a natural Whole"[39] and that the goal of "physical geography" was "the investigation of the Common and Intimately-connected in all terrestrial phænomena."[40] Hence, he searched for the stylistic devices needed to depict nature as a whole and took an interest in the "vivid and graphical descriptions of the vegetable and animal world."[41] In other words, he drew on the rhetorical tradition of the *ekphrasis* in the conviction that, as an Arabic saying goes, "the best description is that in which the ear is transformed into an eye."[42] Aristotle stressed the capacity of metaphors to place something before listeners' eyes.[43] This was the point of an *ekphrasis*, a speech characterized by *enargeia*, the power to set matters before the eyes of the audience,[44] which an orator could acquire thanks to visualization exercises that made him *euphantasiōtos* ("good at imagining"), as Quintilian put it.[45] Conjuring their own vision of a scene to be evoked, orators managed to bring it vividly before the eyes of their audience, who they called upon to "re-enact internally the act of seeing such a sight."[46] This also explains why the description of the speaker as a guide and the "analogy between a speech and a journey in which the speaker leads the audience"[47] were frequent in the ancient rhetorical tradition. This tradition emphasized the "time-warping action of *enargeia*,"[48] ascribing to a skilled orator the power to make the audience feel present, as it were, at past and future events by means of a *metastasis*.[49]

There is evidence that the ekphrastic tradition during modernity intersected with the practice of imaginative spiritual exercises, bound up with the technology of the self of meditative reading. As Karl Enenkel and Walter Melion demonstrated, in the late medieval and early modern period, the reception of texts always included a form of *meditatio*, the "self-imposed disciplinary regime" consisting of mental exercises such as "techniques of visualization,"[50] so that books themselves functioned as a spiritual guide. A paramount example is Louis Richeome's text entitled *La peinture Spirituelle* (1611), in which the French Jesuit offered to the reader verbal descriptions of religious scenes aimed at evoking in his mind vivid images destined to aid him "in his admiration of all God's works, so as to thereby come into the presence of God himself, as the prerequisite for loving him."[51] Behind Richeome's book lies the tradition of the spiritual exercises of Ignatius of Loyola, who recommended the *composition of place (compositio loci)*, which includes visualizing scenes from the life of Christ in order to bring one to intimacy with him.[52] He also improved the technique of the application of the senses, allowing exercitants to activate their senses and witness, as it were, the scenes they imagined. Even the prefaces to early modern texts implied visualization strategies and offered instructions on how to employ them to work on oneself. The dedicatory preface to Petrarch's *On the Solitary Life* exemplifies this kind of paratext that created "meditative frames,"[53] thereby guiding textual readings, since Petrarch asked the dedicatee to imagine the poet's humanistic life style in order to imitate it.

Humboldt's 1808 preface to the *Views of Nature* may be read as a kind of meditative frame:

> I humbly extend to the public a series of works that came into being within the contemplation of great objects in Nature [...]. Individual fragments were recorded at the place and time and only later forged together as a whole. A far-reaching overview of Nature, proof of the cooperation of forces, and a renewal of the delight that direct experience of the tropics gives to a person of feeling are the goals to which I strive. [...] This aesthetic treatment of matters of natural history [...] carries with it tremendous difficulties of composition. The richness of Nature encourages an agglomeration of individual images that disturbs the calmness and the overall impression of the portrait. In appealing to feeling and fancy, style easily degenerates into poetic prose.[54]

The German writer presents himself as a sort of "painter", working *en plein air* to depict *ekphraseis* so that the reader, following him as a guide "into the thickets of the forest, into the immeasurable steppes, and out upon the spine of the Andes range,"[55] may imaginatively reconstruct the places portrayed and thereby work on himself. Descriptions therefore function as ekphrastic exercises for the visualization of nature. Humboldt demonstrates his knowledge of the tradition of spiritual exercises by referring not only to the *Natural Questions*[56] and to the *Somnium Scipionis* in Cicero's dialogue *On the Republic*,[57] but, above all, through a footnote in *Cosmos*[58] that indicates the following passage from the *Academica*: "For the study and observation of nature affords a sort of natural pasturage for the spirit and intellect; we are uplifted, we seem to become more exalted, we look down on what is human, and while reflecting upon things above and in the heavens we despise this world of our own as small and even tiny."[59]

Moreover, Humboldt, transforms the spiritual motif of the glance cast at the Earth into the structural principle underlying his exposition of a modern *savoir de connaissance*:

> When we strive, in thoughtful contemplation of existing things, to penetrate the life of Nature in its ample fullness, and to unveil the empire of her various forces, we feel ourselves raised to an eminence, whence, in the wide-spread horizon around, individualities present themselves gathered into groups, and surrounded with a kind of vaporous haze. [...] We begin with the depths of space, and the region of the farthest nebulæ; we descend, step by step, through the stratum of stars to which our solar system belongs, and at length set foot on the air- and sea-surrounding spheroid we inhabit, discussing its form, its temperature, and its magnetical tension, till we reach the LIFE, that, under the stimulus of light, is evolved upon its surface.[60]

Even more significant is that he clearly refers to this exercise of the view from above at the beginning of the *Ideas for a Physiognomy of Plants*: "When a person possessed of an active mind explores Nature, or ponders in imagination the broad range of organic creation, no single one among the manifold impressions that occur to him has so deep and powerful an effect as that of the ubiquitous abundance of life."[61] Thus, he reestablishes the link between the theoric aspiration to grasp nature as a whole and the spiritual *topos* of the imaginary overflight, but he modernizes it by focusing not on the tininess of the Earth but on nature's plenitude of being.

Interestingly, Humboldt professed in *Cosmos* his faith in the "safe path"[62] of modern inductive science and sharply criticized the "intoxicating delirium"[63] of the Romantic *Naturphilosophie*. Yet, he approvingly referred also to the Romantic conception of nature as "the Ever-becoming, the Ever-engaged in fashioning and evolving"[64] and wrote that, far from being a "dead aggregate," it was, "as Schelling grandly expressed himself, in his admirable *Discourse on the Fine Arts*," "'the holy, the eternally creative prime mover of the universe, engendering and evolving all things out of her pregnant self'.'"[65] Humboldt therefore turns out to be a deeply ambivalent figure at the intersection of empirical science, spiritual knowledge, and Romantic resacralization of Nature. In this respect, the following passage is emblematic of this cross-fertilization: "Thus do the races of men die away. The admirable lore of the different peoples fades away. But with the wilting of each blossom of the spirit, whenever, in the storm of the times, the works of creative art are scattered, so forever will new life sprout forth from the womb of the Earth. Restlessly, procreative Nature opens her buds."[66]

Humboldt resorts to the *topos* of the transience of everything, which ancient writers often employed in the genre of the *consolatio*. For instance, Seneca, in his *Consolation to Polybius*, availed himself of this motif, evoking a cosmic dimension to offer solace to his addressee: "What folly, then, for anyone to weep for the lives of individuals, to mourn over the ashes of Carthage and Numantia and Corinth and the fall of any other city, mayhap loftier than these, when even this universe will perish though it has no place into which it can fall."[67] Strikingly enough, both Humboldt and Seneca go beyond the boundaries of the human sphere to focus on nature, except that for Humboldt nature is not transient but eternal and ever-productive, thus presenting itself as a source of consolation. Indeed, following Pliny, the German writer sees nature as endowed with godlike qualities, so that wonder at the "plenitude of life that flows throughout creation"[68] replaces the high-mindedness that ancient philosophers thought of as the goal of the contemplation of nature.

The will to depict wonder-inspiring natural scenes lies at the core of the *Views of Nature*; they are therefore to be placed not only within an ancient rhetorical tradition but also within the anti-hegemonic subject culture of Romantic selfhood. In opposition to the hegemonic bourgeois culture, Romanticism worked out an antithetical subject code, which made a strong case for deepening one's inner world through imagination and lived experiences.[69] In other words, Romanticism opposed to the bourgeois inwardly rationalized subject a self-sensitized selfhood form to be fashioned through a search for emotionally intense moments,[70] inner-oriented practices such as the experience of nature — sensing the presence of an entity that transcended the human ego[71] — and the solitary reading of texts that stimulated the imagination, thereby offering a refuge from everyday life.[72] The Romantic instant-focused consciousness structure clearly emerges in this passage from the *Views of Nature*:

> Through Ehrenberg's excellent work *Über das Verhalten des kleinsten Lebens*, in the tropical ocean and within the floating and stationary ice of the South Pole, the sphere of organic life, indeed the horizon of life itself, has broadened before our eyes. Siliceous-shelled polygastria, the coscinodiscuses with their green ovaries, have been found 12° from the pole, alive and encased in ice; in the same way, the Podurellae and the little black glacier flea, *Desoria glacialis*, inhabit narrow tubes in the ice of the Swiss glacier investigated by Agassiz. [...] In the ocean, gelatinlike sea microbes, now alive, now dying out, appear as glimmering stars. Their phosphorescence transforms the greenish surface of the immense ocean to a sea of fire. I will never forget those tropical nights in the South Sea, when the constellations of the high-flying ship Argo and the setting Southern Cross poured out their mild planetary light from the blue gossamer of the heavens while the dolphins drew their glowing wakes in the foaming flood of the sea.[73]

This excerpt displays the key aspects of Humboldt's essay collection, in which the will to offer scientific information[74] merges with a recollection-based and wonder-suffused *ekphrasis*. This, in turn, allows the reader to re-enact the narrator's imaginative act of seeing, thereby undertaking an exercise of *compositio loci naturae*, so to speak, that enables him to have contact not with the Christian

God but with all-living nature. In *Ideas for a Physiognomy of Plants*, the author therefore takes up the ancient thought scheme of the imaginary overflight to focus first on the "empire of nature"[75] and then on scenes that provide thrilling in*sight* into nature's creative power. This represents a shift from a spiritual exercise, typical of the ancient *culture de soi* and aimed at modifying one's mode of being, to a Romantic inner-oriented practice granting access to lived experiences. In this sense, the conclusion of the essay deserves particular attention:

> The sickly plants within our greenhouses provide but a weak image of the majesty of tropical vegetation. But in the refinement of our language, in the incandescent imagination of the poet, in the depictive art of the painter there open rich wellsprings of compensation. From this, the power of our imagination creates a living picture of exotic Nature. In the cold of the North, in the starkness of the heath, the lone individual can acquire for himself that which is being explored in the most distant latitudes, and thus create within himself a world that is the work of, and is as free and immortal as, his own spirit.[76]

These remarks find a parallel in the *Essay on the Geography of Plants* (1807), in which Humboldt praises the works of art thanks to which man, "in the solitude of a barren heath creates for himself, as it were, an inner world" and thereby enjoys "an intellectual pleasure and an inner freedom that, beneath the blows of fate, cannot be destroyed by any external power."[77] These observations show the extent to which the German naturalist writer reconceptualized the Stoic distinction between the internal and the external goods he referred to in the letter quoted at this chapter's outset. In terms of a new language of inwardness, the goods represented by the reason and by the "immortal" wisdom that Seneca described as beyond the reach of chance give way to the pleasure and the freedom that a lonely reader (a modern form of the book-based selfhood) derives from his capacity to conjure up an "immortal" and exciting fictional world. Thus, the ancient man in search of inner peace transforms into the modern daydreamer, as the *telos* of a new practice whose ethical substance manifests itself in the emotions in which the "person of feeling" (*der fühlende Mensch*[78]) is expected to revel.

Humboldt places high value on the 'cosmogonic' power of creative imagination in a passage of his *magnum opus*, too: "He who is awakened to a spiritual self-activity, and who delights to build up a world within himself, fills the amphitheatre of the boundless ocean with the lofty image of the INFINITE and the ENDLESS."[79] The essay *Concerning the Structure and Action of Volcanoes in Various Regions of the Earth* best illustrates the new *telos* of the *emotion-arousing* work on oneself advocated by the Romantic subject culture. In this text, the comparative study of telluric phenomena results in a narration that, by means of a *metastasis*, allows both the reader and his 'guide' to imagine "the youthful days of our planet," when "the materials of the interior that had remained fluid forced their way through the cracks that were everywhere in the Earth's crust," "spreading in layers atop one another."[80] In this way, the reader gains insight into the world as a wild and protean whole totally independent of man. This imaginative exercise of *compositio loci naturae* climaxes in the following passage: "The depth at which the planetary body may be considered a molten mass has been calculated. The primitive cause of this subterranean heat is, as with all planets, the process of formation itself, the coalescence of a sphere-forming mass from a vaporous cosmic fluid, the cooling of the layers of the Earth at different depths through radiation."[81]

Humboldt, marching "far beyond the blazing battlements of the world,"[82] in the words of Lucretius, who evidently influenced him,[83] opens his and the reader's mind to a cosmic perspective. He then concludes his overflight by refocusing on the primeval Earth:

> Tropical animal forms, arborescent ferns, palms, and bamboo plants lie buried in the frigid North. [...] In the places where the deeply fissured crust of the prehistoric world radiated heat from its clefts, there, for perhaps centuries and over vast stretches of land, palms, arborescent ferns, and all the animals of the torrid zone could thrive. By this view of things, [...], the temperature of volcanoes would be that of the interior of the terrestrial body itself; and the same cause that now brings about such frightful devastation may once, upon the newly oxidized crust of the Earth and on the deeply riven layers of rock, have been able to bring forth in any zone the most luxuriant of vegetation. [...] It is the privilege of the curious and active mind of humanity to occasionally drift out of the present and into the darkness of prehistory, to gain a sense of what cannot yet be clearly discerned, and thus

to take delight in the ancient myths of geognosy in their many recurring forms.[84]

His scientific essay therefore, culminates in the staging of an inspiring cosmic spectacle. At the same time, Humboldt seems to draw on the ancient tradition of the physics as spiritual exercise, reframing it in terms of the scientific and Romantic subject culture, as this passage from *Cosmos* demonstrates:

> General views accustom us to regard each organic form as a portion of a whole; to see in the plant and in the animal less the individual or dissevered kind, than the natural form, inseparably linked with the aggregate of organic forms. General views give an irresistible charm to the assurance we have from the late voyages of discovery [...]; general views enlarge our spiritual existence, and bring us, even if we live in solitude and seclusion, into communion with the whole circle of life and activity — with the earth, with the universe.[85]

Humboldt thus, perceives natural science as a mental strategy giving rise to a form of Whole-consciousness, whose *telos* is nevertheless no more than the production of an *ēthos*, namely of a new mode of being, as was the case with Marcus Aurelius' decision to conform his desires to the overall cosmic process. Along the same lines, Seneca drew the following picture of the Stoic sage: "The soul that gazes upon truth, [...] the soul that penetrates the whole world and directs its contemplating gaze upon all its phenomena, one which no violence can shatter, one which acts of chance can neither exalt nor depress."[86]

The expansion of the self into the infinite is not related to the constitution of a subject impervious *to the blows of fortune; it* leads only to a cognitive and emotional enrichment of the mind devoted to science. As a consequence, the new holistic consciousness of the connecting mind, which sees nature in every region of the Earth as "a reflex of the whole,"[87] replaces the ancient sapiential cosmic awareness. The high value ascribed to cognitive activity also emerges from Humboldt's praise of Philolaus, Aristarchus and Hipparcus as "the heroes of the early and limited knowledge of that age."[88] We should read this against the background of the above-cited passage from *Natural History*, to which the German writer implicitly refers and that stressed, on the contrary, the psychagogical importance of the ancient astronomers' discoveries. In a similar vein, Humboldt outlined a thought experiment endowed with a scientific function:

> If we imagine, as in a vision of the fancy, the acuteness of our senses preternaturally sharpened, even to the extreme limit of telescopic vision, and incidents compressed into a day or an hour, which are separated by vast intervals of time, everything like rest in spacial existence will forthwith disappear. We shall find the innumerable host of the fixed stars commoved in groups in different directions; nebulæ drawing hither and thither, like cosmic clouds; the milky way breaking up in particular parts, and its veil rent; motion in every point of the vault of the heaven, as on the surface of the earth.[89]

Small wonder, therefore, that his reference to Anaxagora's axiom that "the destruction of matter" is "a mere separation of parts,"[90] has nothing to do with Marcus Aurelius' attempt *to banish* the *fear of death*.[91] Instead, this reference relates to the will to understand that the world "is apparently a laboratory of [...] decay."[92] This also explains why he, presenting "the history of the gradually developed knowledge [...] of the Universe as a whole,"[93] defines it as "the loftiest pinnacle which the intelligence of man can attain."[94] In short, Humboldt's text reflects the transition from the domain of spiritual knowledge to the sphere of the *savoir de connaissance*, from the ancient *culture de soi* striving for a new *ēthos* to the modern scientific culture idealizing the mere knowledge subject.

In the context of modern science practices, Humboldt's critique of the Linnean "linear enchainment"[95] of organic forms and his plea for "a general concatenation [...] in reticulate or more intricate modes"[96] acquire a specific meaning. In fact, he aims to provide a glimpse of man's dependence on nature, emphasized in his remarks on the Guarani people:

> Even now, the Guarani owe the preservation of their physical and perhaps even their moral independence to the loose, semifluid bog soil [...]. The Mauritia, however, provides not only safe living quarters but abundant food as well. Before the tender blossom spathe bursts forth on the male palm, and only in this phase of the plant's metamorphosis, the pulp of the trunk contains a meal similar to sago, which, like the meal of the Jatropha root, is dried into thin, breadlike wafers. [...]. Thus do we find, at this most basic level of human intellectual development, the existence of an entire people

bound (like the insect that is restricted to certain parts of a blossom) almost solely to a single tree.[97]

In his effort to describe "the regularly woven [...] network of animated natural creation,"[98] Humboldt rejects the millennia-long model of the "chain of beings,"[99] which placed man at the summit of nature, and he opens the reader's eyes to his real position in the cosmos: far from being the culmination of creation, man is only a marginal part of it, wholly dependent on nature and thus assimilable to an *insect*. By means of ethnographic observations, Humboldt therefore seeks to free readers from their anthropocentric delusions and to induce them to *recosmicize* themselves by acknowledging themselves as a thread in the interconnected web of life.

Furthermore, following Pliny's and using the narrative strategy of the *mirabilia*-account and its theatrical imagery, Humboldt portrays nature as a violence-ridden dimension:

> The capturing of the gymnotids affords a picturesque spectacle. Mules and horses, encircled by Indians, are driven into a swamp, until the bold fish are excited by the unaccustomed noise into attacking. One sees them swimming like snakes in the water and slyly crowding under the bellies of the horses. Of these, many succumb to the power of invisible strikes. [...] This is the wondrous struggle of the horses and fish. That which, invisible, is the living weapon of this denizen of the water; which, awakened by the contact of moist and dissimilar parts, races through all organs of animals and plants; which thunderingly inflames the broad roof of the heavens, binds iron to iron, and steers the silent, returning motion of the guiding needle — all, like the colors of the refracted beam of light, flow forth from One Source; all melt together in an eternal, all-encompassing power.[100]

The passage culminates in a hieratic meditation on nature, transfigured into a metaphysical power through a resacralizing rhetoric and in terms reminiscent of the Neoplatonic light-metaphor. The essay *The Nocturnal Wildlife of the Primeval Forest*, too, hymns nature's all-embracing presence:

> The sun stood at zenith [...]. All the blocks of stone and naked boulders were covered with innumerable large, thick-scaled iguanas, geckos, and colorfully speckled salamanders. Immobile, their heads lifted and mouths opened wide, they seem to inhale the hot air with delight. The larger animals are hiding now in the thickets of the forest, the birds under the foliage of the

trees or within the clefts of the cliffs; if one were to listen now, however, for the quietest tones that come to us in this apparent stillness of Nature, then one perceives close to the ground and in the lower layers of the atmosphere a muffled sound, a whirring and buzzing of insects. Everything announces a world of active, organic powers. In every shrub, in the cracked bark of the trees, in the loose earth where live the hymenoptera, Life audibly stirs. It is one of the many voices of Nature, discernible to the pious, receptive mind of humanity.[101]

This *ekphrasis* functions as an exercise of *compositio loci naturae* through which the German naturalist strives to activate readers' senses of sight and hearing in order that they may *perceive* the presence of a force underlying the forest's teeming life and thereby experience a feeling of *Naturfrömmigkeit*.[102] For all his insistence on scientific data, Humboldt's essay collection culminates *in an art-mediated experience* of the *sacrality* of *nature*.

Notes

1   Alexander von Humboldt, *Die Jugendbriefe Alexander von Humboldts 1787-1799* (Berlin: Akademie Verlag, 1973), 664.

2   Andreas Reckwitz, *Das hybride Subjekt. Eine Theorie der Subjektkulturen von der bürgerlichen Moderne zur Postmoderne* (Weilerswist: Velbrück Wissenschaft, 2006), 40.

3   Christian Moser, *Buchgestützte Subjektivität. Literarische Formen der Selbstsorge und der Selbsthermeneutik von Platon bis Montaigne* (Tübingen: Max Niemeyer Verlag, 2006).

4   As Foucault remarked with a view to Greco-Roman philosophy: "we can [...] call 'psychagogical' the transmission of a truth whose function is not to endow any subject whomsoever with a series of abilities [...], but whose function is to modify the mode of being of the subject to whom we address ourselves." Cf. Michel Foucault, *The Hermeneutics of the Subject. Lectures at the Collège de France* (New York: Palgrave Macmillan, 2005), 407.

5   Pierre Hadot, *What Is Ancient Philosophy?* (Cambridge, MA: Harvard University Press, 2002), 6.

6   Hadot, *What Is Ancient Philosophy?*, 202.

7   Charles Taylor, *Sources of the Self. The Making of the Modern Identity* (Cambridge, MA: Harvard University Press, 1989), 111.

8   Diogenes Laertius, *Lives of Eminent Philosophers*, vol. II (London: William Heinemann LTD, 1925), 203.

9   Cf. Lucius Annaeus Seneca, *Ad Lucilium Epistulae Morales*, vol. II (London: William Heinemann LTD, 1920), 433.

10   Lucius Annaeus Seneca, *Ad Lucilium Epistulae Morales*, vol. III (London: William Heinemann LTD, 1925), 119.

11   On this concept, see Alfonso Traina, *Lo stile 'drammatico' del filosofo Seneca* (Bologna: *Pàtron* Editore: 2011), 22.

12   Lucius Annaeus Seneca, *Ad Lucilium Epistulae Morales*, vol. I (London: William Heinemann LTD, 1917), 163.

13   Seneca, *Ad Lucilium Epistulae Morales*, vol. I, 277.

14   Seneca, *Ad Lucilium Epistulae Morales*, vol. III, 121.

15   Seneca, *Ad Lucilium Epistulae Morales*, vol. III, 125.

16   Lucius Annaeus Seneca, *Moral Essays*, vol. II (London: William Heinemann LTD, 1958), 111.

17   Brad Inwood and L. P. Gerson (eds.), *The Epicurus Reader* (Indianapolis: Hackett Publishing Company, 1994), 38.

18   Plato, *The Republic* (Cambridge: Cambridge University Press, 2000), 188-189.

19   Joachim Ritter, *Subjektivität. Sechs Aufsätze* (Frankfurt am Main: Suhrkamp Verlag, 1974), 144.

20   Pierre Hadot, *Philosophy as a Way of Life. Spiritual Exercises from Socrates to Foucault* (Oxford: Blackwell, 1995), 98

21   Marcus Aurelius, *Meditations* (London: Penguin Books LTD, 2006), 90.

22   Marcus Aurelius, *Meditations*, 59.

23   Marcus Aurelius, *Meditations*, 28.

24   Marcus Aurelius, *Meditations*, 38.

25   Michel Foucault, *The History of Sexuality, Vol. II: The Use of Pleasure* (New York: Vintage Books, 1990), 26-28.

26   Marcus Aurelius, *Meditations*, 24.

27   Marcus Tullius Cicero, *On the Republic* (Ithaca: Cornell University Press, 2014), 120.

28   Hadot, *Philosophy as a Way of Life. Spiritual Exercises from Socrates to Foucault*, 23.

29   Lucius Annaeus Seneca, *Physical Science in the Time of Nero, Being a Translation of the Quaestiones Naturales of Seneca* (London: Macmillan and Co., 1910), 5.

30   Foucault, *The Hermeneutics of the Subject. Lectures at the Collège de France*, 15.

31   Foucault, *The Hermeneutics of the Subject*, 309.

32   Pliny, *Natural History*, Vol. I (London: William Heinemann LTD, 1938), 309.

33   Pliny, *Natural History*, Vol. I, 203.

34   Pliny, *Natural History*, Vol. I, 171.

35   Pliny, *Natural History*, Vol. I, 245.

36   Pliny, *Natural History*, Vol. II (London: William Heinemann LTD, 1942), 511.

37   For the theatrical imagery employed by Pliny to describe the violence endemic to the animal world, cf. Pliny, *Natural History*, Vol. III (London: William Heinemann LTD, 1940), 298-299.

38   Alexander von Humboldt, Cosmos: A Sketch of a Physical Description of the Universe, Vol. II (London: Brown, Green, and Longmans, 1849), 197.

39   Alexander von Humboldt, Cosmos: A Sketch of a Physical Description of the Universe, Vol. III, Part I (London: Brown, Green, and Longmans, 1851), 9.

40   Alexander von Humboldt, *Cosmos: A Survey of the General Physical History of the Universe* (New York: Harper & Brothers, 1845), 17.

41   Von Humboldt, *Cosmos: A Sketch of a Physical Description of the Universe*, Vol. II, 4.

42   Von Humboldt, *Cosmos: A Sketch of a Physical Description of the Universe*, Vol. II, 71.

43   Cf. Aristotle, *On Rhetoric* (Oxford: Oxford University Press, 2007), 220.

[44]   R. Dean Anderson Jr., *Glossary of Greek Rhetorical Terms* (Leuven: Peeters Publishers, 2000), 43.

[45]   Ruth Webb, *Ekphrasis, Imagination and Persuasion in Ancient Rhetorical Theory and Practice* (Farnham: Ashgate Publishing Company, 2009), 95.

[46]   Webb, *Ekphrasis, Imagination and Persuasion in Ancient Rhetorical Theory and Practice*, 128.

[47]   Webb, *Ekphrasis, Imagination and Persuasion in Ancient Rhetorical Theory and Practice*, 54.

[48]   Webb, *Ekphrasis, Imagination and Persuasion in Ancient Rhetorical Theory and Practice*, 100.

[49]   The term metastasis refers "to the vivid presentation of some real or fictive action from the past or future to the audience as if it were happening before their eyes" (R. Dean Anderson Jr., *Glossary of Greek Rhetorical Terms*, 73).

[50]   Karl Enenkel and Walter Melion (eds.), *Meditatio – Refashioning the Self. Theory and Practice in Late Medieval and Early Modern Intellectual Culture* (Leiden-Boston: Brill, 2011), 1.

[51]   Judi Loach, "Jesuit Ekphrastic Meditation: Louis Richeome's Painting in the Mind," in *Meditation in Judaism, Christianity and Islam*, ed. Halvor Eifring (London: Bloomsbury, 2013), 166.

[52]   Cf. Philip Shano, "Mysticism and Ecology. Ignatian Contemplation and Participation," *The Way*, 102 (2001): 108.

[53]   Karl Enenkel, "Meditative Frames as Reader's Guidance in Neo-Latin Texts," in Karl Enenkel and Walter Melion (eds.), *Meditatio – Refashioning the Self. Theory and Practice in Late Medieval and Early Modern Intellectual Culture* (Leiden-Boston: Brill, 2011), 32-33.

[54]   Alexander von Humboldt, *Views of Nature* (Chicago-London: The University of Chicago Press, 2014), 25.

[55]   Von Humboldt, *Views of Nature*, 25.

[56]   Cf. Von Humboldt, *Cosmos: A Survey of the General Physical History of the Universe*, 112.

[57]   Cf. Alexander von Humboldt, *Cosmos: A Sketch of a Physical Description of the Universe*, Vol. IV (London: Henry G. Bohn, 1852), 432.

[58]   Cf. Von Humboldt, *Cosmos: A Sketch of a Physical Description of the Universe*, Vol. II, 198.

[59]   Marcus Tullius Cicero, *De Natura Deorum. Academica* (London: William Heinemann LTD, 1987), 633.

[60]   Von Humboldt, *Cosmos: A Survey of the General Physical History of the Universe*, 27.

[61]   Von Humboldt, *Views of Nature*, 155.

[62]   Von Humboldt, *Cosmos: A Sketch of a Physical Description of the Universe*, Vol. III, 49.

[63]   Von Humboldt, *Cosmos: A Survey of the General Physical History of the Universe*, 22.

[64]   Von Humboldt, *Cosmos: A Survey of the General Physical History of the Universe*, 8.

[65]   Von Humboldt, *Cosmos: A Survey of the General Physical History of the Universe*, 12.

[66]   Von Humboldt, *Views of Nature*, 129-130.

[67]   *Seneca, Moral Essays*, vol. II, 357-359.

[68]   Von Humboldt, *Cosmos: A Survey of the General Physical History of the Universe*, 6.

69 Reckwitz, *Das hybride Subjekt. Eine Theorie der Subjektkulturen von der bürgerlichen Moderne zur Postmoderne*, 232.

70 Reckwitz, *Das hybride Subjekt. Eine Theorie der Subjektkulturen von der bürgerlichen Moderne zur Postmoderne*, 209.

71 Reckwitz, *Das hybride Subjekt. Eine Theorie der Subjektkulturen von der bürgerlichen Moderne zur Postmoderne*, 224.

72 Reckwitz, *Das hybride Subjekt. Eine Theorie der Subjektkulturen von der bürgerlichen Moderne zur Postmoderne*, 261.

73 Von Humboldt, *Views of Nature*, 156-157.

74 Annette Graczyk, *Das literarische Tableau zwischen Kunst und Wissenschaft* (München: Wilhelm Fink Verlag, 2004), 257.

75 Alexander von Humboldt, *Briefe aus Amerika 1799-1804* (Berlin: Akademie Verlag, 1993), 85.

76 Von Humboldt, *Views of Nature*, 169.

77 Alexander von Humboldt, *Schriften zur Geographie der Pflanzen*, in *Studienausgabe*, Bd. I (Darmstadt: Wissenschaftliche Buchgesellschaft, 1989), 66 (my translation).

78 Alexander von Humboldt, *Ansichten der Natur*, in *Studienausgabe*, Bd. V (Darmstadt: Wissenschaftliche Buchgesellschaft, 1987), IX.

79 Von Humboldt, *Cosmos: A Survey of the General Physical History of the Universe*, 94.

80 Von Humboldt, *Views of Nature*, 254-255.

81 Von Humboldt, *Views of Nature*, 255.

82 Titus Lucretius, *On the Nature of Things* (Indianapolis: Hackett Publishing Company, 2001), 5.

83 "The great poem [...] of Lucretius", Humboldt remarked, "embraces the whole Cosmos." Cf. *Von Humboldt, Cosmos: A Sketch of a Physical Description of the Universe, Vol. II*, 16.

84 Von Humboldt, *Views of Nature*, 256-257.

85 Von Humboldt, *Cosmos: A Survey of the General Physical History of the Universe*, 8.

86 Seneca, *Ad Lucilium Epistulae Morales*, vol. II, 7.

87 Von Humboldt, *Cosmos: A Sketch of a Physical Description of the Universe, Vol. II*, 86. On "Humboldt's concern with holistic structures," cf. Malcolm Nicolson, "Alexander von Humboldt and the Geography of Vegetation," in Romanticism and the Sciences, eds. Andrew Cunningham and Nicholas Jardine (Cambridge: Cambridge University Press, 1990), 173.

88 Von Humboldt, *Cosmos: A Sketch of a Physical Description of the Universe, Vol. IV*, 356.

89 Von Humboldt, *Cosmos: A Survey of the General Physical History of the Universe*, 47.

90 Alexander von Humboldt, *Cosmos: A Sketch of a Physical Description of the Universe*, Vol. V (London: George Bell and Sons, 1883), 7.

91 Cf. Marcus Aurelius, *Meditations*, 15.

92 Von Humboldt, *Cosmos: A Sketch of a Physical Description of the Universe*, Vol. V, 7.

93 Von Humboldt, Cosmos: A Sketch of a Physical Description of the Universe, Vol. II, 353.

94 Von Humboldt, *Cosmos: A Sketch of a Physical Description of the Universe*, Vol. II, 103.

95 Von Humboldt, *Cosmos: A Survey of the General Physical History of the Universe*, 21.

96 Von Humboldt, *Cosmos: A Survey of the General Physical History of the Universe*, 11.

97   Von Humboldt, *Views of Nature*, 36-37.

98   Von Humboldt, *Views of Nature*, 243.

99   Von Humboldt, *Cosmos: A Sketch of a Physical Description of the Universe*, Vol. III, Part I, 14.

100   Von Humboldt, *Views of Nature*, 40.

101   Von Humboldt, *Views of Nature*, 146. I have modified the translation by substituting the term "pious" for "solemn" to translate the German adjective "fromm."

102   On Humboldt's *Naturfrömmigkeit*, cf. Bettina Hey'l, *Das Ganze der Natur und die Differenzierung des Wissens. Alexander von Humboldt als Schriftsteller* (Berlin: De Gruyter, 2007), 295. On Humboldt's remythologizing rhetorics, see Heinrich Detering, *Menschen im Weltgarten. Die Entdeckung der Ökologie in der Literatur von Haller bis Humboldt* (Göttingen: Wallstein Verlag, 2020), 332-333.

Bibliography

Anderson, R. Dean Jr. *Glossary of Greek Rhetorical Terms*. Leuven: Peeters Publishers, 2000.

Aurelius, Marcus. *Meditations*. London: Penguin Books LTD, 2006.

Aristotle. *On Rhetoric*. Oxford: Oxford University Press, 2007.

Cicero, Marcus Tullius. *De Natura Deorum. Academica*. London: William Heinemann LTD, 1987.

Cicero, Marcus Tullius. *On the Republic*. Ithaca: Cornell University Press, 2014.

Detering, Heinrich. *Menschen im Weltgarten. Die Entdeckung der Ökologie in der Literatur von Haller bis Humboldt*. Göttingen: Wallstein Verlag, 2020.

Enenkel, Karl. "Meditative Frames as Reader's Guidance in Neo-Latin Texts." In *Meditatio — Refashioning the Self. Theory and Practice in Late Medieval and Early Modern Intellectual Culture*, edited by Karl Enenkel and Walter Melion. Leiden-Boston: Brill, 2011.

Foucault, Michel. *The History of Sexuality, Vol. II: The Use of Pleasure*. New York: Vintage Books, 1990.

Foucault, Michel. *The Hermeneutics of the Subject. Lectures at the Collège de France*. New York: Palgrave Macmillan, 2005.

Graczyk, Annette. *Das literarische Tableau zwischen Kunst und Wissenschaft*. München: Wilhelm Fink Verlag, 2004.

Hadot, Pierre. *Philosophy as a Way of Life. Spiritual Exercises from Socrates to Foucault*. Oxford: Blackwell, 1995.

____. *What Is Ancient Philosophy?*. Cambridge, MA: Harvard University Press, 2002.

Hey'l, Bettina. *Das Ganze der Natur und die Differenzierung des Wissens. Alexander von Humboldt als Schriftsteller*. Berlin: De Gruyter, 2007.

Inwood, Brad and Lloyd P. Gerson, eds. *The Epicurus Reader: Selected Writings and Testimonia*. Indianapolis: Hackett Publishing Company, 1994.

Laertius, Diogenes. *Lives of Eminent Philosophers*, vol. II. London: William Heinemann LTD, 1925.

Loach, Judi. "Jesuit Ekphrastic Meditation: Louis Richeome's Painting in the Mind." In *Meditation in Judaism, Christianity and Islam*, edited by Halvor Eifring. London: Bloosmsbury, 2013.

Lucretius, Titus. *On the Nature of Things*. Indianapolis: Hackett Publishing Company, 2001.

Moser, Christian. *Buchgestützte Subjektivität. Literarische Formen der Selbstsorge und der Selbsthermeneutik von Platon bis Montaigne*. Tübingen: Max Niemeyer Verlag, 2006.

Nicolson, Malcolm. "Alexander von Humboldt and the Geography of Vegetation." In *Romanticism and the Sciences*, edited by Andrew Cunningham and Nicholas Jardine. Cambridge: Cambridge University Press, 1990.

Plato, *The Republic*. Cambridge: Cambridge University Press, 2000.

Pliny. *Natural History*, Vol. I. London: William Heinemann LTD, 1938.

____. *Natural History*, Vol. III. *London: William Heinemann LTD, 1940.*

____. *Natural History*, Vol. II. *London: William Heinemann LTD, 1942.*

Reckwitz, Andreas. *Das hybride Subjekt. Eine Theorie der Subjektkulturen von der bürgerlichen Moderne zur Postmoderne*. Weilerswist: Velbrück Wissenschaft, 2006.

Ritter, Joachim. *Subjektivität. Sechs Aufsätze*. Frankfurt am Main: Suhrkamp Verlag, 1974.

Seneca, Lucius Annaeus. *Physical Science in the Time of Nero, Being a Translation of the Quaestiones Naturales of Seneca*. London: Macmillan and Co., 1910.

____. *Ad Lucilium Epistulae Morales*, vol. I. London: William Heinemann LTD, 1917.

____. *Ad Lucilium Epistulae Morales*, vol. II. London: William Heinemann LTD, 1920.

____. *Ad Lucilium Epistulae Morales*, vol. III. London: William Heinemann LTD, 1925.

____. *Moral Essays*, vol. II. London: William Heinemann LTD, 1958.

Shano, Philip. "Mysticism and Ecology. Ignatian Contemplation and Participation." *The Way*, 102 (2001): pp. 107-123.

Taylor, Charles. *Sources of the Self. The Making of the Modern Identity*. Cambridge, MA: Harvard University Press, 1989.

Traina, Alfonso. *Lo stile 'drammatico' del filosofo Seneca*. Bologna: Pàtron Editore: 2011.

Von Humboldt, Alexander. *Cosmos: A Survey of the General Physical History of the Universe*. New York: Harper & Brothers, 1845.

____. *Cosmos: A Sketch of a Physical Description of the Universe*, Vol. II. London: Brown, Green, and Longmans, 1849.

____. *Cosmos: A Sketch of a Physical Description of the Universe*, Vol. III, Part I. London: Brown, Green, and Longmans, 1851.

____. *Cosmos: A Sketch of a Physical Description of the Universe*, Vol. IV. London: Henry G. Bohn, 1852.

____. *Cosmos: A Sketch of a Physical Description of the Universe*, Vol. V. London: George Bell and Sons, 1883.

_____. *Die Jugendbriefe Alexander von Humboldts 1787-1799*. Berlin: Akademie Verlag, 1973.

_____. "Ansichten der Natur." In *Studienausgabe, Bd. V*. Darmstadt: Wissenschaftliche Buchgesellschaft, 1987.

_____. "Schriften zur Geographie der Pflanzen." In *Studienausgabe, Bd. I*. Darmstadt: Wissenschaftliche Buchgesellschaft, 1989.

_____. *Briefe aus Amerika 1799-1804*. Berlin: Akademie Verlag, 1993.

_____. *Views of Nature*. Chicago-London: The University of Chicago Press, 2014.

Webb, Ruth. *Ekphrasis, Imagination and Persuasion in Ancient Rhetorical Theory and Practice*. Farnham: Ashgate Publishing Company, 2009.

3

Romantic Earth/Art? "Impossible": Re-Locating Romantic Inheritance in the Contemporary Critical Thought

Ratul Nandi

In an answer to the question of how far the aesthetic space of literature can afford a dwelling place for our beloved earth, the English literary critic Jonathan Bate in his book *The Song of the Earth* exultantly claims that the literary or the poetic indeed houses a place "...where we save the earth."[1] Even though Bate's proposition is predicated upon his conviction in the power of poetics, in general, to restore to humanity the enchantment and mystery of the earth from which it stands increasingly alienated, one does not fail to notice how his project aligns itself to a particular tradition of thought in the nineteenth century widely noted for an intense desire to treat the aesthetic as a fecund turf for cultivating a green sensibility, a tradition which Bate calls "Romantic Ecology." Standing at the dawn of what later emerges as a modern-day scientific ecology, this tradition of poetic idolization of earth, according to Bate, functions as a moral corrective to a society fallen out of harmony with the earth for its relentless pursuit of material acceleration. Offering an authentic dwelling, the general economy of Romantic poetry as such strives to overcome the earth/art rift in its experiment "to see what happens when we regard poems as imaginary parks in which we may breathe an air that is not toxic and accommodate ourselves to a mode of dwelling that is not alienated" (Bate 2001, 322). Indeed, very few literary epochs have been as sensitive to and self-reflectively aware of the question of man's poetic dwelling on earth as the poetry of English Romantics. In a sense, we have never quite been able to outgrow the influence of this romantic ecology since it continues to act as the foundational hinge of our most basic sense of earth-consciousness, even when we are thinking about the most pressing environmental issues like global warming, climate change or the extinction of human race in future: the human rhetoric of care and sustainability, though faced with the most challenging issues of survival like never before, have remained invariably romantic.

Romantic Ecology and the Interior Self

Perhaps the greatest achievement of Bate's model of "romantic ecology", illustrated principally with the poetry of William Wordsworth, is its power to convince its readers that poetry is, in fact, an extension of our earth; reading Wordsworth's poetry is the same as taking an evening stroll through a green landscape filled with the throb of its natural life. In bringing us close to the earth, the role of a poet, in Wordsworthian sense, is that of a therapist who relieves the wounds inflicted upon the psyche brought about by the ills of a human-centric world which is "too much with us."[2] Thus, opening oneself up to the earth requires one gives up on one's impulse of wealth accumulation and recalibrate and strengthen one's *Natural Contract*[3] with the external world. Being a "romantic" in this sense, therefore, means conceiving of the earth fundamentally as a space of unspoiled greenery untarnished by the industrial encroachment. Poetry to this end has a decisive role to play. It is the germinal site which triggers our earth-consciousness, an eco-*poiesis* (in the sense of "making") which guides individuals to forge an integrated perception of themselves in harmony with the earth and, thus, emerge as a "complete" man: "not the Power Man, not the Profit Man, not the Mechanical man, but the Whole Man."[4] It is in this earnest poetic claim, however, to embrace the earth, or in the moral drive to build the "whole man" after the earth that Wordsworth 's poetic persona, almost on each occasion, finds itself paradoxically removed from what it so lovingly describes. The earth as a *tópos* or a place is valued in so far as it serves as a means to a covert poetic ambition: to help the poet achieve the "growth of mind", to build a subjective consciousness so powerful that can reflect on the world and on itself by holding the earth at arm's length. Thus, if one takes together the familiar "nature poems" by William Wordsworth (whether the lengthy poems like "The Prelude", "Tintern Abbey", "Ode: Intimations of Immortality" or the short ones like "Daffodils", "The Solitary Reaper", "The World Is Too Much with Us") one can trace a conscious poetic design played out over and again, where every encounter with the earth—whether natural objects or people, animate or inanimate—is ultimately seized as take-off points that would help Wordsworth to turn from the landscape to mindscape, to build the privileged interiority of the mind that would, in the end, *consume* the earth. Time and again, we encounter/return to the poetic persona in Wordsworth's poems which dwells on its earthly experiences of green countryside strewn with lakes, valleys and the humble folks of rural town who people the idyllic greenscape with their quiet, proto-ecological lives, only to arrive at conscious mind-palace where the sense-certainty of raw and natural objects are processed into "a mansion for all lovely forms."[5] Poems of William Wordsworth almost transform ordinary persons, objects and sites of his Lake District almost into a picturesque spectacle of an eco-tourist advert, a romantic fallacy that Timothy Morton identifies with what he qualifies as a kind of "aesthetic consumerism."[6] Such romantic idealization of the earth often turns out to be counterintuitive: produced through the use of the studied and deft textuality, in which the earth is called to emulate the "picturesque" art, the earth in such picture-postcard representations appears to transform the real landscape into a reified "consumer object" that systematically places itself beyond the reach of its readers/viewers. Alien and alienated, the readers of his poems are invited to act like self-contented voyeurs relishing immersions in the aestheticized landscape while being kept safely quarantined from encountering a world of real objects all the same. The aura of the earth is sustained by its "thereness", by the inevitable rupture it occasions between itself and the romantic subject. The "distance" as such works wonders for the subject as well: The depth of poetic subjectivity with its intuitive grasp of the physical world so often leads to moments of intense perceptual wisdom (for example, "Nature never did betray the heart that loved her") is ironically forged and fostered through the process of the subject's distance from the earth. Thus, tempting his readers with a glimpse of sublime earth, the great "Nature" poems of William Wordsworthian at best leaves his readers with his "egotistical sublime" wherein the poet is more intent on observing his self than the physical landscape.

The Romantic tradition spearheaded by Wordsworth, though fundamentally a poetic one, has a decisive and lasting impact on the way its ramification could be traced on the successive generation of poets and thinkers of environment. Any discerning reader of Henry David Thoreau's *Walden* (1854) would hardly miss seeing his desire to live in isolation from urban life in the woods beside the Walden pond *à la* Wordsworthian insistence on embracing the earth to recover one's true identity; as if we visit external landscape only to have our authentic selves recuperated. John Ruskin, William Morris, Aldo Leopold among others in the nineteenth century continue this tradition through their unflagging repudiation of anti-industrial arguments. It is in the twentieth century, however, that this particular stance signals its strongest exposition through writings from a diversity of sources: from critical thinkers of Frankfurt School like Theodore Adorno and Max Horkheimer to literary critic-sociologist Lewis Mumford, from political philosopher Murray Bookchin and anthropologist Gregory Bateson to poets such as Gary Snyder, Mary Oliver, W. S. Merwin, and Wendell Berry. One can see how the Wordsworthian shadow expands to encapsulate many of contemporary critical thoughts and tendencies cutting across a range of disciplinary enclosures. For instance, Deep Ecology, one of the most celebrated branches of Environmental philosophy, in its conviction on the significance of one's place-based identity seem to find an obvious parallel with Wordsworthian romantic ecology as much as in its celebration of the doctrine of pantheism that does not endorse a belief in a separate anthropomorphic god. Furthermore, in proposing a perception of the earth as a living organism with a manifestation of "one life" expressing through connections between its different organic and non-organic parts, scientist James Lovelock's immensely popular Gaia hypothesis strikes a profound Wordsworthian ring. Wordsworth has always been the most trusted ground for thinkers of the environment and this holds true even at a time today when the questions concerning the protection and preservation of the earth have reached a stage where it can no longer be discounted.

The Earth Becomes a Romance at One's Own Peril

The image of immaculate earth adorned with rounded pictorial metaphors and facilitating a subjective consciousness often works to disguise the violence that may otherwise accompany such thought. The poetic use of metaphors takes away the mystery of the earth and transforms it into an object of human knowledge while denying complicity in any form of violence it may unintendedly have engendered. Our human gaze which finds romance in an idea of a beautiful place or a utopian community often proceeds through habitual blindness to the underlying truths which can reveal the unremarkable dull cake of reality underneath the aesthetically colourful candy sprinkles of romance. A perfect illustration of this can be found in Anthropologist Shepard Kreech's insightful book *The Ecological Indian: Myth and History* (2000) which bursts the most cherished contemporary romantic myth about the ancient native American Indians. Through painstaking details, Kreech demonstrates that far from being some exemplary community known for its ecologically balanced livelihood, the lives lived by the Indians leave behind signs of exploitation and violence as any human community anywhere. Held accountable for the extinction of many large-scale mammals and for causing massive geological shifts due to over-irrigation of crops and over-salination of the water bodies, Kreech believes, the community as such can qualify as organic and ecological only at the price of overlooking such disturbing facets of their lives. When not seen through the rose-tinted romantic glasses, Wordsworth's euphoric celebration of Lakeland cottage firms of his native place — as offering some kind of a spiritual answer to the rapacious tendencies of industrial city life — also appears to reveal its own internal anomalies. Wordsworth rhapsodic idealization of a rural landscape with its local flora and fauna works only through a systematic erasure of the fact such regions have their "origins in the prehistoric destruction of forests to make space for domesticated livestock, its bears and wolves long killed off."[7] However much he despised industrial economy, there is hardly any doubt that Wordsworth's rural economy of cottage holders, even in his own time, was already a thriving economy (although a pre-capitalist one) "with its own laws of ownership and inheritance and a strong division of labour between the sexes" (Clark 2011, 19).

It is clear from the references given above that the attempts to capture the earth poetically in a way that poetry orchestrates the song of the earth, that poetry has an unmediated access to earth's being in a non-ideological way is itself an ideology of the most deceitful kind. It does raise an uneasy question about the unholy nexus between poetry and the idea of place as when poetry helps appropriate only a specific type of image of the earth which, then, subsequently leads to the politics of (literary) canon formation. Finally, it implicates the earth in the formation of one's socio-political identity in the sense how one's notion of political identity gets determined by the way one's relationship to the particular locale or place is appropriated. Wordsworth's ecopoetics (in the sense Jonathan Bate uses the term) remains an exercise in affecting a symbolic reunion between the Earth and Art by calling readers attention to the "inherent greenness" of the poetic language. This "greenness" is, in effect, the power of figurative or metaphorical language to conjure up the semblance of the real earth, to simulate or represent something that exists perennially outside the ambit of the art. Poetics, for Wordsworth and his followers, is, a kind of a "possibility" space which ultimately secures an authentic dwelling place for the earth by attempting to overcome the earth/art split through enacting a mode of heightened self-consciousness that eventually ends up absorbing/subsuming the earth into its symbolic economy.

The Keatsian Impossibility

The poetic oeuvre of John Keats stands at the farthest extreme from almost everything we come to associate with Wordsworth. If poetry for Wordsworth is all about foregrounding the poetic self in dialogue with earth, for Keats, the experience of poetry is consistent with the experience of obliteration of self. While Wordsworth is a believer in the "use" of poetic metaphors to reproduce the earth, like some "reality Tv shows", as a strategy to dissolve the boundary between the earth and the human, Keats inspires a fundamental re-thinking of earth-art dialogue based on the "impossibility" of knowing earthly beings or objects in their entirety. The force of such impossibility is to raise doubts about the *usefulness* of the aesthetic form and the metaphorical language to truthfully re-present or "copy" the world external to itself. Unlike Wordsworth's self-obsessed egotism that seeks to transcend the earth through refined language, Keats celebrates the "negative capability" in the poet which is never a matter of knowing, seizing, explaining the earth under the aegis of human reason but the capacity to be precisely incapacitated and *useless* or as he says "when a man is capable of being in uncertainties, Mysteries, doubts, without any irritable reaching after fact & reason."[8] The result of such ontological doubt is to question the very efficacy of earth-consciousness forged through the power of metaphors in language and thus ironically open the language to its own finitude; that is, our reliance upon language that we can never master. Thus, thinking Green studies with Keats could indicate a fresh terrain of romantic inquiry far remote from the established green cannon framed regularly after the eco-romantic paradigm left by Wordsworth. The "impossibility" of Keats poetic art is the moment of its breach from the world-of-objects-that-exist-outside-it and questions the justification of the role of poetry or art to faithfully capture the earth. Exposed to the radical finitude of its own limit, the metaphorical language reflects an inescapable irony wherein the literary art simultaneously aspires to capture the earth, yet realizes painfully how such endeavour is doomed to remain incomplete. The impossibility in Keats is not to be taken simply as the antithesis of possibility but as a Derridean "im-possibility" signifying an intractable in-betweenness or undecidability poised between both.

Moving from Wordsworth to Keats is the same as transitioning from being an ardent apostle of poetry capable of "representing" the earth to being a sceptic who nonetheless resorts to poetic art knowing for certain that the earth as a *thing-in-itself* is impossible to be captured completely by the poet. Wordsworth's poems are *logical* structures which solicit the image of a "real" earthy landscape through a series of closely-knit (linguistic) propositions that resolutely seek to obliterate the process of these prepositions with the effect that readers invariably accept the given textual image of earth as a closed or "finished" product from the beginning. In contrast, Keats' characteristic move is always to expose art's im-possibility through an ironic response in which he both desires to capture the true essence of the world of objects and things through poetry but ends up acknowledging the fundamental impossibility of such ambition by drawing attention to the necessary incompleteness of the poetic form. One finds this structure repeated in Keats many times, especially in his great odes where he is found to engage with (due to default structure of Ode form) objects of diverse nature—nightingale, urn, autumn etc. only to arrive at the ungraspability of these objects: (i) the nightingale leaves the poetic self in the state of uncertainty, (ii) the urn resists the poetic comprehension by speaking back and (iii) the autumnal season of "mellow fruitfulness" is not restricted to its anthropocentric "use" but opens up "to a nonhuman phenomenology of wonder beyond fact, reason, and mimetic description."[9] Whereas Wordsworth, to quote Timothy Morton, uses art as "candy coating on top of facts",[10] Keats relentlessly seeks to align himself with what Morton identifies as OOO approach as opposed to Wordsworthian approach to the earth. Indeed, Keats's poetic meditation is focused more on the "attuning" power of the non-human objects of his intentional consciousness rather than on the consciousness itself in transcendent or pure form (as in Wordsworth). Meditative thinking, as Morton correctly reminds us, is already "in itself, a relation to the non-human, insofar as the logical content of one's thought is independent of the mind thinking about itself" (Morton 2013, 198). Thinking, in this sense, is intrinsically contemplative and like Wordsworth one does not have to obtrusively reflect "on" some object or thing (like the earth) as subject of poetic consciousness. Like a poet in the vein of OOO

(Object Oriented Ontology), Keats seeks to think about the objects, whereby thinking is not about overcoming or "annihilating" them into some conceptual fixity but allowing their essential uncanny opacity to retain in a way that destabilizes poetic identity. Thus, if one discovers in Wordsworth advocacy of certain Hegelian *Aufhebung,* (annihilation), Keats's poetic method undoubtedly echoes what Heidegger calls the "Stepping backwards"(*Schritt zurück)* which does not view the earth as an object to be *consumed* but promotes an ontological interruption between the earth's objects and the poet by opening him up to the abysmal and unfathomable dimension of objects. Romantic poetry, for Keats, is invariably the "fragmented absolute"[11] since poetic representation of earth is always *other* than the earth itself: the things and objects of the earth are never exhausted by their poetic *use*. It is in this sense poetry is close to its original Greek sense of *poiesis* which implies primordial creativity or *making* of some external form to capture the earth. As "poiesis," then, poems are constantly attempting ironically to remind how poetic art forever fails to make poetry a proper dwelling place for the earth. For Keats, the art in its split from the earth is itself "impossible."

Negative Capability and the 'Earth'

If Keats' romantic paradigm is one where art and language fail to embed the earth, then how does the earth thrust itself up in the work of poetry at all? The answer lies, again, in what Keats called the "negative capability," a faculty which helps poets face up to the fundamental impossibility or the uncertainty inherent in the human attempt to make sense of life. Keats, in this sense, is close to German Romantics of Jena circle who posited a fundamental distinction between Greek words *theoria* (knowledge) and *poiesis* (making). In contrast to the inflexible foundation of knowledge of the earth desired by *theoria*, *poiesis* holds that the world/earth is, in essence, finite, incomplete and fragmented, and thus cannot ever be known in its entirety. Recognizing the essential negativity in the art, where art is forced to appear in its own "uselessness" (*désœuvrement*)[12] where it eschews its responsibility to *represent* and begins to reflect its own materiality or status as a thing or an object: it is a moment when art singularizes existence, making it "singular" from general where it foregrounds its original negativity. To read Keats, then, is to be moved by the overwhelming presence of his poetic subjects — be it the nightingale, the urn or the autumn — which tend to grow on the readers and start to look unfamiliar as reading moves on. It is less a Wordsworthian exercise of imposing poet's "subjective impression" on the earth, but more of pursuing the impossible, that which refuses to be fully conceptually domesticated.

Keatsian poetic impossibility finds striking resemblances to Heidegger's concept of the "earth." Even though Jonathan Bate's *The Song of the Earth* situated Heidegger's thinking in respect to Wordsworth's romantic ecology, one finds the negatively enabled Keatsian poetic space more suited to the general tenor of Heideggerian thought on the environment, especially to what he implies by "earth" which is replete with a negative undertone in the sense of being ungraspable or impenetrable. As Timothy Clark explains, "Earth means not just the physical environment without which no human world would exist, but also the very resistance to understanding and knowledge inherent to the non-human."[13] Crucially then, attending to the negative capability makes the poet also respond to everything non-anthropocentric in the world, including the poetics or the literary itself; drawing the attention back to the very material grounding of the poetry, to the internal "environment" of the poetic text in a way that makes the readers acknowledge how the concept of earth or nature is itself produced through textuality. As Claire Colebrook explains the very notion of poetry or literary art presupposes an "arche-environmentality" of its own:

> There is something essentially counter-ecological in the very notion of the literary: a text needs to be read on its own terms, as though the text itself were a bounded whole, akin to a living being or organism with no reference to anything other than itself .... one might argue that there is an ecological tension or problem both in the concept of text and in the concept of Oikos from which both "ecology" and "economy" derive. First, a text is (especially in its literary mode) akin to a living being or organism; insofar as it is woven

from interrelated aspects that make sense in their relation to a whole, a text seems to possess a certain autonomy or apartness.[14]

Emerging through poetic making, the "earth" appears both as a *topos* (place) and *atopos* (non-place): it both appears but remains hidden. According to Keats, Poetic or literary art can only save or reflect the earth by disclosing its negative capability, that is, by showing its very "un-sayability." The earth speaks through its "unspeakability."

Environmental Thought & Keats's Contemporaneity

Paul de Man in his own readings identifies Keats a "prospective" writer, as someone whose work is always oriented towards the future as opposed to someone like Wordsworth whom de Man calls a "retrospective" writer. For de Man, Keats was much preoccupied with the excitement of opening oneself to the not-yet rather than being contented with "meditative reflections on past moments of insight and harmony."[15] This question of openness to radical futurity aligns Keats with the thinking of some noted critical minds working in the contemporary academia today, thinkers who primarily turn their back on mainstream liberal environmentalism of Wordsworthian tradition and proceed to uphold a form environmental thinking inspired broadly by the Derridean deconstruction. In contrast to the romantic eulogy of earth seen as a principle of harmony, these thinkers consider the effect of current global ecological catastrophe as destructive of all our inherited concepts of romantic earth and, thus, set out to embrace moments of "crisis" itself as the only ethical response to the situation. Thinkers like Timothy Morton, Tom Cohen, Claire Colebrook, Timothy Clark, David Wood, etc. view how the environmental crisis like the Anthropocene challenges our anthropocentric illusion of mastery (either literal or conceptual) of earth and provoke us to reject or at least be critical of all pursuit of "representable" knowledge. Keatsian poetic perception, with its emphasis on negative capability, seems to fit squarely with the scope and goal of such a deconstructive environmental paradigm. Even though a fuller exposition of Keatsian environmental thinking requires a space beyond what I can offer here, it is nonetheless useful to cite at least one instance which may give us an indication as to how Keats' poetic insight can be brought into a productive dialogue with the current global environmental emergency. David Wood, in his book *The Step Back: Ethics and Politics After Deconstruction* (2005) admirably works with the Keats' poetic insight of negative capability as a way to deal with the critical challenges to human faculty of creativity and thinking an event like Anthropocene summons today. Since global climate change warrants a general uncertainty regarding our system of knowledge, Wood considers Keats's negative capability to be the redemptive principle of humanity in such fallen times: instead of trying to overcome the onto-epistemic problem of uncertainty, it would be best to embrace the uncertainty itself as the only certainty. The underlying idea is that environmental problems such as climate change are so pressing and so recalcitrant in the same breath that our realization of it demands we give up our obsessively logical pursuit of it as a "problem" requiring human determination. Following Keats in this way, Wood believes, could help us learn how to be open to our own finitude in the sense of being capable of being acted upon by the outside. In the context of climate change, this Keatsian approach of poetic negativity could lead us to reconcile with such inherent negativity within ourselves and help us acknowledge the very limit of "thinking" as well as the thinking of "limit". Thus, thinking with Keats can open up new vistas of critical thinking that can recalibrate a new shift in our very doing of environmental humanities. Working with a "negative" Keatsian approach can provide a fundamentally ironical response to the question of saving the earth through art. it is not a question of success or failure of art: poetic works can save the earth in its utter "impossibility".

Thus, as one can see, the two modes of romantic thought eventually culminate into two distinct strands of green literary criticism and although both schools attend to the question of finding in poetry a proper dwelling place for the earth, their respective approaches to the issue are radically opposed to one another: one asserts the poetics of possibility, the other upholds impossibility. While the influence of Wordsworthian romantic ecology is widely recognized as a theoretical paradigm today, Keats's thought, for the most part, remained obscured from green literary criticism. But with the kind of critical engagement with his work has just started, as indicated above, one feels that his time has just arrive.

Notes

1   Jonathan Bate, *The Song of the Earth* (Pan Macmillan, 2001), 12.

2   William Wordsworth, "The World Is Too Much With Us". *Poetry Foundation*. https://www.poetryfoundation.org/poems/45564/the-world-is-too-much-with-us.

3   Michel Serres, *The Natural Contract* (The University of Michigan Press,1995). Serres' book is a must read for anyone interested in the question of how earth or nature is not just a simple antithesis of humanity, but a force that disrupts and precedes all our dualistic and inherently violent sense of human instrumentalization.

4   Lewis Mumford, *Let Man Take Command* (Saturday Review of Literature, 20th October, 1948), 35.

5   William Wordsworth, *Tintern Abbey, Lyrical Ballads* (Project GutenbergeBook #9622, January, 2006), 44. http://www.gutenberg.org/files/9622/9622-h/96 22-h.htm#poem23.

6   Timothy Morton, *Ecology Without Nature: Rethinking Environmental Aesthetics* (Harvard University Press, 2007). Morton's contribution to literary ecological field has assumed canonical status with his particular focus on modes of ecological consumerism in the poetry of English Romantic poets at large.

7   Timothy Clark, *The Cambridge Introduction to Literature and the Environment* (Cambridge University Press, 2011), 19.

8   John Keats, *The Complete Poetical Works and Letters of John Keats* (Cambridge Edition. Houghton, Mifflin and Company, 1899), 277. The poetics of "nihilism" one encounters in Keats has relevance beyond his immediate poetic context. The ambiguity and destruction of self coming though the experience of language which never really allows for complete "self-presence" is something that always binds this outlook with a certain Deconstructionist premise.

9   Ron Broglio, *Romantic Self and Posthumanism* in *Critical Posthumanism,* July 2, 2019. https://criticalposthumanism.net/the-romantic-self-and-posthumanism/.

10   Timothy Morton, *Hyperobjects: Philosophy and Ecology After the End of the World* (University of Minnesota Press, 2013), 182.

11   *Romanticism 20: Keats and Shelley and OOO* (WEDNESDAY, MAY 30, 2012, http://ecologywithoutnature.blogspot.com)http://ecologywithoutnature.bl ogspot.com/2012/05/romanticism-20-keats-and-shelley-and.html

12   See Maurice Blanchot, *The Space of Literature* (University of Nebraska Press, January1,1989). *Désoeuvrement,* translated mostly as "worklessness" in English, which Blanchot uses to question hermeneutical drive for "meaning" and

thereby, expose the work to its inherent "negativity". The strategic similarity of the term to Keats' "Negative Capability" is undeniable.

13   Clark, *The Cambridge Introduction*, 57.

14   Claire Colebrook, "Ecocriticism" in *The Bloomsbury Handbook of Literary and Cultural Theory*, ed. Jeffrey R. Di Leo (Bloomsbury Academic, 2019),173.

15   Paul de Man, "Introduction to the Poetry of John Keats," in *Critical Writings 1953–1978*, ed. Lindsay Waters (Minneapolis: University of Minnesota Press, 1989), 181.

Bibliography

Bate, Jonathan. *The Song of the Earth*. London: Pan Macmillan, 2001.

Broglio, Ron. "Romantic Self and Posthumanism." *Critical Posthumanism*. July 2, 2019. https://criticalposthumanism.net/the-romantic-self-an dposthumanism/.

Blanchot, Maurice. *The Space of Literature*. Nebraska: University of Nebraska Press. 1889.

Clark, Timothy. *The Cambridge Introduction to Literature and the Environment*. Cambridge: Cambridge University Press, 2011.

Colebrook, Claire. "Ecocriticism." In *The Bloomsbury Handbook of Literary and Cultural Theory*, edited by Jeffrey R. Di Leo. New York: Bloomsbury Academic, 2019.

Man, Paul de. "Introduction to the Poetry of John Keats." In *Critical Writings 1953–1978*, edited by Lindsay Waters. Minneapolis: University of Minnesota Press, 1989.

Ghosh, Ranjan. "Globing the Earth: The New Eco-logics of Nature." *SubStance* 41, no. 127 (2012): pp. 3-14. DOI: 10.1353/sub.2012.0008.

Hutchings, Kevin. "Ecocriticism in British Romantic Studies." *Literature Compass* 4, no. 1 (2007): pp. 172–202.

Keats, Jhon. *The Complete Poetical Works and Letters of John Keats*. Houghton: Mifflin and Company, 1899.

McKusick, James C. *Green Writing: Romanticism and Ecology*. New York: St Martin's Press, 2000.

Morton, Timothy. *Ecology Without Nature: Rethinking Environmental Aesthetics*. Cambridge, MA, and London: Harvard University Press, 2007.

_____. *Hyperobjects: Philosophy and Ecology After the End of the World*. Minnesota: University of Minnesota Press, 2013.

_____. "Romanticism 20: Keats and Shelley and OOO." Ecology Without Nature. Accessed on 10 October 2020. http://ecologywithoutnature. blogspot.com)http://ecologywithoutnature.blogspot.com/2012/05 /romanticism-20-keats-and-shelley-and.html

Mumford, Lewis. "Let Man Take Command." Saturday Review of Literature. 20 October, 1948. Accessed on 15 November 2020.

Serres, Michel. *The Natural Contract*. Michigan: The University of Michigan Press, 1995.

Wordsworth, William. "The World Is Too Much With Us." *Poetry Foundation*. https://www.poetryfoundation.org/poems/45564/the-world-is-too-much-with-us.

_____. "Tintern Abbey." *Lyrical Ballads*. Project Gutenberg Book. http://www.gutenberg.org/files/9622/9622-h/9622-h.htm#poem23.

4

Green Thumbs:
Floral Geopoetics in the Poetry of
Sarah Maguire

Pavlína Flajšarová

Geopoetry is no newcomer in the history of Anglophone literature; however, the term itself seems to be rather a novelty. Previously, in the context of writing in English, the label of "topographical literature" was preferred. It was defined by Dr. Johnson as "local poetry, of which the fundamental object is some particular landscape [...] with the addition of [...] historical retrospection or incidental meditation."[1] John Denham with his poem "Cooper's Hill" is considered as the founding father of this genre. The term "topographical" is a clear reference to a specific place to which the literary text directly or indirectly relates. For example, Wordsworth's poem "Lines Composed a Few Miles above Tintern Abbey, On Revisiting the Banks of the Wye during a Tour. July 13, 1798" has a clear reference to the geographical frame in Wales. Moreover, the first generation of the English Romantics made the Lake District famous and derived their inspiration from this picturesque landscape. A similar sensibility to specific locations can be witnessed in other national literatures and art. In Germany, for instance, the foundations were laid by the "Sturm and Drang" ("Storm and Drive") movement and Romantic painters such as Caspar David Friedrich or Philipp Otto Runge and writers such as Novalis, Johann Wolfgang Goethe, Heinrich Heine, Johann Gottfried Herder, E.T.A. Hoffmann, and Heinrich von Kleist and supported by the philosophy proposed by Wilhelm Heinrich Wackenroder, Friedrich Wilhelm Joseph Schelling, and Friedrich Schleiermacher. The theoretical treatise of German Romanticism and the nature of poetry by the Schlegel brothers found a fruitful response in England. For example, Friedrich Schlegel claimed in 1798 in *Athenaeumsfragment* that

> Romantic poetry is said there to be a "progressive, universal poetry, ... the only kind of poetry that is more than a kind, that is, as it were, poetry itself: for in a certain sense all poetry is or should be romantic." The task of such poetry, he claims in this fragment, should be to "fuse poetry and prose, inspiration and criticism, the poetry of art and the poetry of nature; and make poetry lively and sociable, and life and society poetical; poeticize wit and fill and saturate the forms of art with every kind of good, solid matter for instruction, and animate them with the pulsations of humor.[2]

His theory was mirrored by Wordsworth in his *Preface* which also deals with the purpose and character of poetry and its language. Access to the ideas and works of the German writers and philosophers in England was mediated by Samuel Taylor Coleridge, who translated the seminal works by the Germans. The English Romantics were to profit from the path beaten by the Germans; in particular, their sensitivity to a specific space in the world of nature was admired. In addition, the English were at first also excited about the ideas of the French Revolution of 1789. The inspiration from the French, however, soon evaporated with the emergence of Terror. Nevertheless, this outcome of the Revolution caused a return to Inspiration and a closer attachment to the British landscape.

In the twentieth century, the landscape remained a prolific source of Inspiration for British writers. However, a new element was added, namely the dimension of ecology, which became prominent after the Second World War. The term "landscape", although still in use, was slowly replaced by "geopoetry", which seemed a more fashionable term. Its dominance was proved when Kenneth White, a poet who was Scottish by birth and settled in France, officially coined the term "geopoetics" in 1979, although it then existed only in a sketchy form in his diary notes. However, approximately a decade later, he was the founding father of the *Institut international de Géopoétique*. He explained the motivation for its establishment thus:

> If, around 1978, I began to talk of "geopoetics", it was for two reasons. On the one hand, it was becoming more and more obvious that the earth (the

biosphere) was in danger and that ways, both deep and efficient, would have to be worked out in order to protect it. On the other hand, I had always been of the persuasion that the richest poetics come from contact with the earth, from a plunge into biospheric space, from an attempt to read the lines of the world. Since then, the word has been picked up and used, in various contexts. The moment has come to concentrate those currents of energy into a unitary field. That is why we have founded the *Institute of Geopoetics*. The geopoetic project is not one more contribution to the cultural variety show, nor it is a literary school, nor it is concerned with poetry considered as an art of intimacy. It is a major movement involving the very foundations of human life on earth.[3]

As is obvious from White's words, he enriches the genre of "landscape" poetry with an ecological aspect because environmental protection became a pressing international issue. In addition, in his view, poetry deriving its inspiration from a specific place had to transcend the *genius loci* to a multicultural and multidisciplinary dimension. As vague as the terms "geopoetics" or "geopoetry" might be, they seem to have acquired the critical attention of, for example, Erika Schellenberger-Diederich or Fernando Aínsa.[4] Neither of these, however, provided a universally suitable and accepted definition. The vagueness or even lack of precise definition gives the discipline of geopoetics a flexible frame of reference that might include both ontological and epistemological dimensions.

If we focus on the specific situation of geopoetry in the United Kingdom, especially in modern Anglophone literature, it is represented by several writers who build upon the English Romantic tradition. Kathleen Jamie, Ian Duhig and Kenneth White can be named as the most prominent contemporary writers working within this genre. Special attention should also be devoted to Sarah Maguire (1957-2017), whose work will be the focus of this chapter, in which it is compared to that of her predecessors and contemporaries. She left school at the age of seventeen to become an apprentice gardener for three years. This experience brought the poet closer to the soil. She is someone who truly represents the symbiosis between nature and ecology on the one hand and the world of poetry on the other hand. It was only after she had spent several years earning her living as a gardener that she returned to education to gain a degree in English literature and even to proceed to doctoral studies in English at Cambridge University. She therefore, profited from double expertise: a horticulturalist and an English scholar. The hard work of raking leaves and lifting the heavy poisoned turf in London parks contrasts with the tenderness with which she describes the activity of planting trees, which resembles giving birth to an organism, and the delicate treatment of individual plant species. She exchanged physical drudgery for pen and ink, which she describes thus: "since leaving the Parks Department I've hardly ever picked up a hoe. But I picked up the language."[5] The language she uses fits the definition of William Wordsworth which he introduced in his 1802 *Preface to Lyrical Ballads*. He gives preference to simple language used by people of rural origin over the elevated artificial language that had been used by writers in the past. Wordsworth postulates:

> Low and rustic life was generally chosen, because in that condition, the essential passions of the heart find a better soil in which they can attain their maturity, are less under restraint, and speak a plainer and more emphatic language; because in that condition of life our elementary feelings co-exist in a state of greater simplicity, and, consequently, may be more accurately contemplated, and more forcibly communicated; because the manners of rural life germinate from those elementary feelings; and, from the necessary character of rural occupations, are more easily comprehended, and are more durable; and lastly, because in that condition the passions of men are incorporated with the beautiful and permanent forms of nature. The language, too, of these men is adopted (purified indeed from what appear to be its real defects, from all lasting and rational causes of dislike or disgust) because such men hourly communicate with the best objects from which the best part of language is originally derived; and because, from their rank in society and the sameness and narrow circle of their intercourse, being less under the influence of social vanity they convey their feelings and notions in simple and unelaborated expressions. Accordingly, such a language, arising out of repeated experience and regular feelings, is a more permanent, and a far more philosophical language, than that which is frequently substituted for it by Poets, who think that they are conferring honour upon themselves and their art, in proportion as they separate themselves from the sympathies of men, and indulge in arbitrary and capricious habits of expression, in order to furnish food for fickle tastes, and fickle appetites, of their own creation.[6]

Nature and poetry came close to one another in the hands of Sarah Maguire. She epitomises the Ideal proposed by Wordsworth.

Moreover, she also fulfils the Wordsworthian ideal of deriving the sources of inspiration directly from nature and from the simple life in the country. Wordsworth formulated it in the following way:

> the principal object, then, which I proposed to myself in these Poems was to chuse incidents and situations from common life, and to relate or describe them, throughout, as far as was possible, in a selection of language really used by men; and, at the same time, to throw over them a certain colouring of imagination, whereby ordinary things should be presented to the mind in an unusual way; and, further, and above all, to make these incidents and situations interesting by tracing in them, truly though not ostentatiously, the primary laws of our nature: chiefly, as far as regards the manner in which we associate ideas in a state of excitement.[7]

The coming together of nature and language in the work of Sarah Maguire was also possible because she learnt the names of the plants both in English and in Latin and thus, the plants became "living objects" for her. Maguire comments on this transformation: "it wasn't just necessity that made me learn the names of plants. It was pleasure. I loved the sound of these strange words, their Latinate abstractions, the sense of order they implied. And I'm still delighted and astonished when, even now, the botanical identity of some nondescript shrub swims into view."[8] Although she started writing poetry in her early twenties, it was only with the publication of her two first volumes, *Spilt Milk* and *The Invisible Meander*, that she concentrated on the world of plants: "I've found myself writing poems about individual plants as a starting point for poems that take off in many different directions, such as the night time bike-ride through the suburbs of Marrakesh in my poem Hibiscus."[9]

Another formative element in the life of Sarah Maguire was her residency at the Chelsea Physic Garden in 1998, which aimed at bringing poetry and gardening close to one another. Interestingly, the Chelsea Physic Garden was founded in 1673 by the Worshipful Society of the Apothecaries of London. Back then, the garden served primarily for scientific purposes as at Chelsea the students of medicine studied the healing effects of individual plants. Returning to what Wordsworth postulated, he distinguishes the description and use of nature by a poet and by a scientist:

> ... the Poet, prompted by this feeling of pleasure which accompanies him through the whole course of his studies, converses with general nature with affections akin to those, which, through labour and length of time, the Man of Science has raised up in himself, by conversing with those particular parts of nature which are the objects of his studies. The knowledge both of the Poet and the Man of Science is pleasure; but the knowledge of the one cleaves to us as a necessary part of our existence, our natural and unalienable inheritance; the other is a personal and individual acquisition, slow to come to us, and by no habitual and direct sympathy connecting us with our fellow-beings. The Man of Science seeks truth as a remote and unknown benefactor; he cherishes and loves it in his solitude: the Poet, singing a song in which all human beings join with him, rejoices in the presence of truth as our visible friend and hourly companion. Poetry is the breath and finer spirit of all knowledge; it is the impassioned expression which is in the countenance of all Science.[10]

Therefore, whereas the former principal use of the Chelsea Physic Garden was purely scientific, during Maguire's residency, she attempted to draw the attention of the visitors to the poetic uses of this specific place. In her essay "Cross-Fertilisation: Poet in Residence at the Chelsea Physic Gardens", she comments on the purpose of her residency: "The aim of this small project was to stimulate the connections between poetry and gardens; to interest horticulturists in poems about plants, and to inspire poets and poetry-readers to look at plants afresh" (Maguire). She refused to organise only workshops on botanical poetry because such an activity seemed to be a road that was too well-travelled. Instead, she initiated a project which brought poems to plant labels in the flowerbeds. The labels contained not only the names of the individual plants but also a poem about the species. In order to be innovative she researched the history of botanical verse and discovered that the tradition of using specific flowers "as subjects of a poem ... [was] relatively rare until the Romantic period, and it's not until the twentieth century that poets really begin to write about a large variety of plant species."[11] This tendency went hand in hand with a great interest in the exotic. Simultaneously with spatial exploration and British colonialism, interest in the beauty of plants and flowers in particular was cultivated in eighteenth and nineteenth-century Britain by art movements such as the Pre-Raphaelites and the Aesthetic movement, which brought a third element into play, namely, the visual arts. The triangle of botany, the visual arts and poetry, became a springboard for the exploration of hitherto unnoticed relations. For example, Christina Rossetti throughout her poetry uses botanical verses to encode femininity and feminine sensibility. Emily Dickinson employs complex botanical metaphors to disguise hints about female sexuality in "There Is A Flower That Bees Prefer".

As a result of the expeditions to distant regions and continents, British gardens were enriched with many new plant species. In addition, British colonialism stimulated interest in new plants as these were imported from far corners of the world. An example illustrating this phenomenon is Kathleen Jamie's poem "Rhododendrons" where she describes the effects of colonialism in a positive sense because new plants found their way to British gardens. In her case, she turns the attention to rhododendrons and describes how they travelled from the Himalayas to Scotland. She opens with a dedication to British naval exploration:

> They were brought under sail
> from a red-tinged east,
> carried down gangplanks
> in dockers' arms. Innocent
> and rare. Their thick leaves
> bore a salt-damp gleam,
> their blooms a hidden gargle
> in their green throats.[12]

After a difficult and turbulent journey, the plants are incorporated into Scottish gardens as if they have always belonged there:

> So we step out from their shade
> to overlook Loch Melfort
> and the bare glens, ready now
> to claim this flowering, purple
> flame-bright exotica as our own;
> a commonplace, native
> as language or living memory,
> to our slightly acid soil.[13]

The Scottish landscape has appropriated a formerly exotic plant into British scenery. The rhododendrons became a "commonplace, native" and acquired the ability to represent the language or a living memory. A similar process was described by Wordsworth in "Tintern Abbey" to whose location he in his memory returns as it brings him pleasure. He believes that it is possible because of

> the breath of this corporeal frame
> And even the motion of our human blood
> Almost suspended, we are laid asleep
> In body, and become a living soul.[14]

The very place initiates a memory of something dear, something that inherently belongs to the specific locality. The objects that trigger this might vary; and in the hand of Wordsworth, the recollections are brought about by the ruin of an abbey while in Jamie's case by the formerly exotic rhododendrons.

To import various plants to Britain was feasible because of the prosperity that was made possible, thanks to British plantations and trade overseas. It is interesting to note that the new plant species primarily intended for the embellishment of ornamental gardens could have been imported to Britain due to the wealth gained through the business involving plant commodities such as sugar cane, tea, tobacco, opium, coffee, cocoa, cotton, rubber, and various spices such as cinnamon, curry, and vanilla. Therefore, on the one hand, there were plants in Victorian England and even earlier that served commercial purposes and were true signs of family wealth, and, on the other hand, there were plants that were solely intended to embellish the gardens of the upper class. These, however, were also implicit signifiers of prosperity, as only wealthy people could afford to acquire exotics. Such social development is well reflected in the poems written prior to the Romantic period. If any flower was mentioned predominantly, it was rose, which is, after all, the national flower of England. However, poems hardly ever had flowers which acted as the sole lyrical object, as is the case with William Shakespeare, Andrew Marvell, George Herbert, and many others. On the contrary, the English Romantics would carefully look at natural objects, flowers being among them. An interesting case is William Blake's "Ah Sunflower", which nominates the sunflower as a silent historian of time:

Ah Sun-flower! weary of time,
Who countest the steps of the Sun:
Seeking after that sweet golden clime
Where the traveller's journey is done.[15]

This particular poem was later mentioned by the American poet Allen Ginsberg in his "Sunflower Sutra", thus creating a "botanical" dialogue across centuries and continents. Similarly, to Blake, Ginsberg assigns a historical memory of the sunflower:

> I walked on the banks of the tincan banana dock and sat down under the huge shade of a Southern Pacific locomotive to look at the sunset over the box house hills and cry.
> ....
> Look at the Sunflower, he said, there was a dead gray shadow against the
>   sky, big as a man, sitting dry on top of a pile of ancient sawdust—
> —I rushed up enchanted—it was my first sunflower, memories of Blake—
>   my visions—Harlem
> and Hells of the Eastern rivers, bridges clanking Joes Greasy Sandwiches,
>   dead baby carriages, black treadless tires forgotten and unretreaded, the
>   poem of the riverbank, condoms & pots, steel knives, nothing stainless,
>   only the dank muck and the razor-sharp artifacts passing into the past—
> and the gray Sunflower poised against the sunset, crackly bleak and dusty
>   with the smut and smog and smoke of olden locomotives in its eye.[16]

Whereas Blake's treatise is a lyrical one, Ginsberg makes direct reference to the products of his time, by which he provides, similarly to Blake, a criticism of the consumerist way of life. In the same vein, in "Spilt Milk" Maguire talks about civilisation that has become tainted. The pessimism that permeates her poem is supported by the atmosphere created by substantial rain.

> The whole world seems to slide into the drain by my window.
> It has rained and rained since you left, the streets
> black and muscled with water. Out of pain and exhaustion you came
> into my mouth, covering my tongue with your good and bitter milk.
> ... I sit here in a circle
> of lamplight, studying women of nine hundred years past.
> ... I drain the glass.
> I still want to return to that hotel room by the station
> to hear all night the goods trains coming and leaving.[17]

Civilisation seems to be interested only in commercial profit and feelings do not count any more. Modern society has succumbed to isolation and only the background noise of the railway station seems to be the possible or desired company for the poet. The theme of isolation is often the topic of Maguire's poetry. Her seminal poem "Florist's at Midnight" shows the contemporary superfluous obsession for cut flowers embellishing public and private places. In the poem, the stems bleed, there are zinc buckets, dark water, the flowers in the shop are solitary and alert, they have been uprooted in both the physical and metaphorical sense as they were transported across the continents, fading far from their place of origin, and now they are cloistered in cellophane. The total isolation, decay, and death signified by the ambiguous reference to zinc (which acts as a bucket for the flowers as well as for zinc coffins for the intercontinental transport of corpses), the cloister, and the process of fading juxtapose the vitality of the flowers and their being abandoned at the florist at night, obviously acting as a symbol of darkness and approaching death. A similar approach can be detected in the poetry of Anglophone postcolonial poets such as Grace Nichols, Derek Walcott, Lorna Goodison, Jean Binta Breeze or Olive Senior, who derive their visual and textual imagination from their native Caribbean culture. Interestingly, however, they also combine the colonial heritage, which is the sensibility they share with the English Romantics that they were taught at school, with the local botanical species. It seems to be a colonisation in reverse that plants such as daffodils, representing the colonisers, are exotic in the colonies, whereas local plants such as hibiscus are tokens of domesticity, and vice versa. Therefore, it is possible to claim that botanical verses well reflect the political and social developments in the United Kingdom and in the British Empire in general. In addition, the flowers the postcolonial writers employ in their poetry indirectly signify the diaspora. The recollections of flowers that are domestic in their home (is-lands) are the dear memories they immaterially take with them to their hostile new lands of residence. This is in line with Sarah Maguire's belief that "poetry is the best way of finding out about another culture."[18] She manifests this idea very carefully in her collection *The Pomegranates of Kandahar* (2007), which is inspired by her residence in Palestine under the auspices of the British Council. In that volume, as Robert Potts argues, she presents

> a willingness to nurture her material until it can find its appropriate form. Her poetry clearly emerges from patient, attentive contemplation; her descriptions are visually accurate, sensuous, palpable. Many of the poems employ poems short line, spare, unwasteful, with a delicate music. They proceed gradually, gently, affording the readier a comparable intensity of attention.[19]

In that respect, she utilises the method so frequently employed by the English Romantics, that is, a careful scrutinising of nature and seeing individual natural objects as integral parts of the larger whole. By doing so, she becomes a modern representative of Romantic pantheism, holding a lamp to nature and mirroring it in her work. Robert Potts holds a similar view when he postulates that Maguire

> captures a significant aspect of her work: when she evokes an environment, she does not efface herself from it, nor (despite the clarity of her eye) stand apart from it. Instead, through unrushed, unegotistical contemplation, she integrates herself. Some of the most affecting poems in the book are those in which Maguire mediates desire and grief through atmosphere alone, by faithful and particular detail.[20]

A different approach to isolation, and yet with a sensibility similar to Maguire's, is shown by Samuel Taylor Coleridge in his "This Limetree Bower My Prison". He does not lament it. Instead, he lets his imagination flourish and works with "feelings recollected in tranquillity,"[21] as his friend Wordsworth would urge him. Although the poem was occasioned by an incident in which hot milk was spilt on his foot, which prevented him from walking for a number of days, he turns his disadvantage of having to stay at home to his own benefit. He turns his attention to all the possible plants and trees that surround him and imbues them with meanings beyond their physical connotation.

> Now, my friends emerge
> Beneath the wide wide Heaven — and view again
> The many-steepled tract magnificent
> Of hilly fields and meadows, and the sea,
> With some fair bark, perhaps, whose sails light up

The slip of smooth clear blue betwixt two Isles
Of purple shadow!
....

A delight
Comes sudden on my heart, and I am glad
As I myself were there! Nor in this bower,
This little lime-tree bower, have I not mark'd
Much that has sooth'd me. Pale beneath the blaze
Hung the transparent foliage; and I watch'd
Some broad and sunny leaf, and lov'd to see
The shadow of the leaf and stem above
Dappling its sunshine! And that walnut-tree
Was richly ting'd, and a deep radiance lay
Full on the ancient ivy, which usurps
Those fronting elms, and now, with blackest mass
Makes their dark branches gleam a lighter hue
Through the late twilight: and though now the bat
Wheels silent by, and not a swallow twitters,
Yet still the solitary humble-bee
Sings in the bean-flower! Henceforth I shall know
That Nature ne'er deserts the wise and pure;
No plot so narrow, be but Nature there,
No waste so vacant, but may well employ
Each faculty of sense, and keep the heart
Awake to Love and Beauty![22]

For Coleridge, nature remains the most inspirational and pleasurable nurturer of the heart's feelings.

Via her botanical verse, Maguire combines Romantic sensibility and modern poetics. As the introduction to the poet by the Poetry Archive indicates, "few other contemporary British poets combine the intensity of Sarah Maguire's lyrical imagination with the breadth of her geopolitical reach."[23] A very fine example of this strategy materialises in the poem "The Grass Church at Dilston Grove". This opening of the poem was inspired by a rare artistic enterprise in which, in a disused church in London, in the docklands area, grass seeds were sown, creating a unique scene of grass covering the old church. Potts points out that "the diligent description of the scent and appearance of the living grass and the abandoned building gives way to self-contemplation, then to beautifully deployed rhythms of ritual incantation, and finally to a moment poised perfectly between self and oblivion: laden with the inevitability of death, yet balanced perfectly by quiet, determined, resourceful life."[24] In addition, the poem evokes, and alludes directly, to the atmosphere created by Philip Larkin in his "Church Going". Maguire closes the poem by claiming that it is necessary to have one's roots firmly planted into the soil. This is perhaps an ambiguous metaphor referring both to her being adopted from an orphanage and, second, the multinational and multiethnic society in contemporary London. As Maguire explained in an interview, "I still love London enormously. I love the mess of it. Also the multicultural aspect of London. I couldn't live in another part of England. I love the fact there are 300 languages spoken in this city. I love the mongrel nature of London. There are more mixed race babies born in London than in any other city on the planet, which is great. I love the buildings (even the bad ones)."[25] Dilston Church is a very fine example of a building that has no appealing exterior but an interior with excellent artistic quality. It is in line with the Romantic theory of the inward-looking eye which takes its perception primarily from the exterior but progresses towards the interior. In the poem, Maguire attempts to find the extraordinary in the everyday. She is in line with Wordsworth's claim in his Preface that "by fitting to metrical arrangement a selection of the real language of men in a state of vivid sensation, that sort of pleasure and that quantity of pleasure may be imparted, which a Poet may rationally endeavour to impart."[26] She takes the reader to a disused and deconsecrated building which was the first concrete church in England. The building is not an immediately appealing one; rather the contrary effect is often produced. The interior has been vacated and no furniture was left there when services ceased to be actively conducted in the church. Nevertheless, new life was fed into the building in 2003 when clay and grass seeds were applied there by Heather Ackroyd and Dan Harvey. Interestingly, the artists did not do the obvious, that is, to lay the lawn on the ground; rather, they covered the walls with a green grass carpet. Another important element is the light coming through the large stained-glass windows. As the artists say:

through the application of clay, germinating grass seed, water and natural light the boundary between growth and decay, reverie and renewal was exposed within this repository of spiritual memory. The artists regarded the architectural structure as in some sense being inert, brooding and boarded up, no longer functioning in the community. Bringing memory to the surface, the living skin of grass literally drew life back within the fabric of the church. A momentary resurrection."[27]

The project was developed further so that the visitors could listen to the music composed by Graeme Miller, who created tunes specifically for this project. Maguire picks up the motif of a disused church and transforms it into a concerto of sensory perceptions. She compares the church to a toolshed as they share the same smell: "The church is damp, it smells of a toolshed."[28] She pays attention to the minute details driving the thoughts behind the scene because, as a trained horticulturalist, she imagines what nutrition, such as soil and minerals, is necessary in order for the grass to grow. Looking at the grass-covered walls, "a box of green metaphors opens as I watch," initiates meditation, such as "memories of redemption." By the end of the poem, Maguire comes to a Hardy-like conclusion that "everything the grass has asked of me I have done. / I have taken the grass for my path, for my playground, and for my bed."[29] Therefore, she paints a life circle, similarly to other Romantics, such as Shelley in his "Ode to the West Wind", from the playground to the bed, which is the grave. However, she does not want to succumb to death yet; she repeats her devotedness to grass as a double-edged sword signifying both life and death and concludes the poem with a few exceptions she names: "everything the grass has asked of me on this earth I have done / except give myself up, except lie under its sky of moving roots."[30] She does not want to give up vitality for passivity; rather, she celebrates the ability of the grass to put down roots and to live on. She appreciates the stability of the grass and employs the metaphor of roots as she herself was adopted and does not want to feel uprooted again. Both the church, with its walls and ceiling that are covered with grass, and the poem create a very delicate contrast and counterbalance between growth and decay. A similar setting is employed by Philip Larkin in his "Church Going". He stops at a still active church, but it is empty when he enters. He observes silence and reverence with much distance and the flowers in the interior catch his attention. The flowers, although they are mentioned only generally, symbolise the decay of the institution of the church as they are fading, "sprawlings of flowers cut / For Sunday brownish now."[31] In the course of the poem, the speaker arrives at a partial conclusion that the church was not worth stopping at, "Yet stop I did."[32] However, in the lines that immediately follow, he re-evaluates his view by saying,

> in fact I often do
> And always end much at a loss like this
> Wondering what to look for; wondering too
> When churches fall completely out of use
> What we shall turn them into if we shall keep
> A few cathedrals chronically on show
> Their parchment plate and pyx in locked cases
> And let the rest rent-free to rain and sheep.
> Shall we avoid them as unlucky places?[33]

This indicates that there must be some element that made him not only to stop but stay in the church and his meditation about the sense of life continues. After making a small donation, the speaker "Reflect[s] the place was not worth stopping for. / But superstition like belief must die / And what remains when disbelief has gone? / Grass weedy pavement brambles buttress sky."[34] Both Larkin and Maguire contemplate the future use of the church, Larkin, however, thinks about death more explicitly:

> I wonder who
> Will be the last the very last to seek
> This place for what it was
>
> Through suburb scrub because it held unspilt
> So long and equably what since is found
> Only in separation--marriage and birth
> And death and thoughts of these--for which was built
> This special shell? For though I've no idea
> What this accoutred frowsty barn is worth
> It pleases me to stand in silence here.[35]

Sarah Maguire did not only write botanical poems but she also carefully researched the tradition of botanical verse. She claims that "of all flowers, the rose is unsurpassed in its rich symbolic associations."[36] In her anthology *Flora Poetica*, Maguire not only presents her deep knowledge about the individual plants, but also demonstrates a profound insight into the history of English and world poetry. There she has accumulated a collection of poems about plants from all over the world and by juxtaposing them with the English examples, she indirectly compares and contrasts them. The order of the poems is interesting, as she did not choose geographical or chronological order, but, behaving like a true horticulturalist, the poems are grouped according to their species. In accordance with the Latin taxonomy created by Carl Linneaus, Maguire explains her strategy: "I've ordered the book by plant families, which was really enjoyable to do, and one of the great things about doing this is you get poets who wouldn't usually be alongside each other. Strangely, Aphra Behn shares with Tom Paulin and Sylvia Plath and Ted Hughes still share the same bed!"[37]

Both in her poetry and her community work, Maguire therefore stimulates great interest in botanical poetry, which represents a subgenre of geopoetics. She plants poetry among the plants and makes geopoetry part of our everyday lives. Like the Romantics, Maguire not only shares an interest in the intersection of poetry and science but also the language these fields naturally employ and the way they employ it.

Notes

1   Samuel Johnson, *Lives of the English Poets*, ed. G. B. Hill, vol. 1 (Oxford: Oxford University Press, 1905), 22.

2   Friedrich Schlegel, *Kritische Schriften*, ed. Wolfdietrich Rasch (Munich: Carl Hanser Verlag, 1958), 37-38.

3   Kenneth White, "For the Institute of Geopoetics." 28 April 1989. https://www.institut-geopoetique.org/en/presentation-of-the-institute.

4   See Erika Schellenberger-Diederich, *Geopoetik. Studien zur Metaphorik des Gestein in der Lyrik von Hölderlin bis Celan*, Bielefeld, 2006; Joan Brandt, *Geopoetics. The Politics of Mimesis in Poststructuralist French Poetry and Theory*, Stanford CA, 1997; Fernando Aínsa, *Del Topos al logos: propuestas de geopoética*, Madrid, 2006.

5	Sarah Maguire, ed. "Introduction," *Flora Poetica* (London: Chatto and Windus, 2003), xvii.
6	William Wordsworth, *Preface to Lyrical Ballads*, http://www.gutenberg.org/cache/epub/8905/pg8905.html.
7	William Wordsworth, *Preface to Lyrical Ballads*.
8	Sarah Maguire, ed., "Introduction," xvii.
9	Sarah Maguire, ed., "Introduction," xviii.
10	William Wordsworth, *Preface to Lyrical Ballads*.
11	Sarah Maguire, ed., "Introduction," xviii.
12	Kathleen Jamie, "Rhododendrons," *Flora Poetica* (London: Chatto and Windus, 2003), 102.
13	Kathleen Jamie, "Rhododendrons," 102.
14	William Wordsworth, "Lines Composed A Few Miles Above Tintern Abbey, on Revising the Banks of the Wye during a Tour, July 13, 1798," *The Poetical Works of William Wordsworth*, ed. William Knight, vol. 2 (1896), https://www.gutenberg.org/files/12145/12145-h/12145-h.htm.
15	William Blake, "Ah, Sun-flower," *Flora Poetica* (London: Chatto and Windus, 2003), 72.
16	Allen Ginsberg, "Sunflower Sutra," *Flora Poetica* (London: Chatto and Windus, 2003), 73-74.
17	Sarah Maguire, "Spilt Milk," in *Spilt Milk* (London: Secker and Warburg, 1991), 10.
18	James Byrne, "Interview with Sarah Maguire," *The Wolf*, vol 6. http://www.wolfmagazine.co.uk/6_interview_sm.php
19	Robert Potts, "All this time on my knees—The Pomegranates of Kandahar by Sarah Maguire review." *The Guardian*. London. https://www.theguardian.com/books/2007/jul/21/poetry.featuresreviews1
20	Robert Potts. "All this time on my knees."
21	William Wordsworth, *Preface to Lyrical Ballads*.
22	Coleridge, "This Lime-Tree Bower My Prison," *The Complete Poetical Works of Samuel Taylor Coleridge*, ed. Ernest Hartley Coleridge (Oxford: Clarendon, 1912), https://www.gutenberg.org/files/29091/29091-h/29091-h.htm.
23	"Sarah Maguire," https://poetryarchive.org/poet/sarah-maguire/.
24	Robert Potts. "All this time on my knees."
25	James Byrne, "Interview with Sarah Maguire."
26	William Wordsworth, *Preface to Lyrical Ballads*.
27	"Dilston Grove." https://www.ackroydandharvey.com/dilston-grove/.
28	Sarah Maguire, "The Grass Church at Dilston Grove," "Sarah Maguire," https://poetryarchive.org/poet/sarah-maguire/.
29	Maguire, "The Grass Church at Dilston Grove."
30	Maguire, "The Grass Church at Dilston Grove."
31	Philip Larkin, "Church Going," *Less Deceived* (Hessle: Marvell Press, 1955), 29.
32	Philip Larkin, "Church Going."
33	Philip Larkin, "Church Going."
34	Philip Larkin, "Church Going."
35	Philip Larkin, "Church Going."
36	Sarah Maguire, ed., "Introduction," xxii.
37	James Byrne, "Interview with Sarah Maguire."

Bibliography

Blake, William. "Ah, Sun-flower." In *Flora Poetica*. London: Chatto and Windus, 2003.

Byrne, James. "Interview with Sarah Maguire." *The Wolf*. 6. http://www.wolfmagazine.co.uk/6_interview_sm.php.

Coleridge, Samuel Taylor. "This Lime-Tree Bower My Prison." In *The Complete Poetical Works of Samuel Taylor Coleridge*, edited by Ernest Hartley Coleridge. Oxford: Clarendon, 1912. https://www.gutenbe rg.org/files/29091/29091-h/29091-h.htm.

____. "Dilston Grove." https://www.ackroydandharvey.com/dilston-gr ove/.

Jamie, Kathleen. "Rhododendrons." In *Flora Poetica*. London: Chatto and Windus, 2003.

Johnson, Samuel. *Lives of the English Poets: Volume 1*. Edited by G. B. Hill. 22. Oxford: Oxford University Press, 1905.

Larkin, Philip. "Church Going." In *Less Deceived*. Hessle: Marvell Press, 1955.

Maguire, Sarah. "The Grass Church at Dilston Grove." https://poetryarch ive.org/poet/sarah-maguire/.

____. "Spilt Milk." In *Spilt Milk*. London: Secker and Warburg, 1991.

____. "Cross-Fertilisation: Poet in Residence at the Chelsea Physic Gardens." *The Poetry Society*. http://archive.poetrysociety.org.uk/content/archives/places/maguire/.

Maguire, Sarah, ed. *Flora Poetica*. London: Chatto and Windus, 2003.

Potts, Robert. "All this time on my knees — The Pomegranates of Kandahar by Sarah Maguire review." *The Guardian*. https://www.theguardian.com/books/2007/jul/21/poetry.featuresreviews1.

Schlegel, Friedrich. *Kritische Schriften*. Edited by Wolfdietrich Rasch. Munich: Carl Hanser Verlag, 1958.

White, Kenneth. "For the Institute of Geopoetics." 28 April 1989. https://www.institut-geopoetique.org/en/presentation-of-the-institute.

Wordsworth, William. *Preface to Lyrical Ballads*. http://www.gutenberg.org/cache/epub/8905/pg8905.html.

5

The Memory of Here and Elsewhere: Geopoetics and Literary Fiction

Ankita Sharma

> We were the people who were not in the papers. We lived in the blank white spaces at the edges of print. It gave us more freedom. We lived in the gaps between the stories.
> —Margaret Atwood, *The Handmaid's Tale*

The Spaces of Human-ness

While recent geographic scholarship has time and again reiterated the spatial production of social and collective identity through maps, monuments, memorials and museums; the conscious efforts of memory scholars to elicit the humanist and emotional values of geographical knowledge through its interactions and negotiations with the non-tangible spaces of memory seem completely warranted. Such emplacement of geography within the memory discourse points to the emotional, sensorial and physical responses offered by the linkage between memory and building a sense of place in the world.

In the COVID-19 pandemic predicament, when the spaces are confined more than ever, the prescience of understanding our embodied existence through spatial experiences can help organise the inside-outside and then-now coordinates of shared time and space. As the entire species has been pushed into the "corners" of immobility, the process of this "inward-looking" approach to "geopoetics" is timely. It becomes a necessary condition to stabilise anxieties about human existence when the outside world is full of uncertainties and danger, unable to promise a secure future. The reflection on the interpenetration of space, memory and emotion in being "locked into a place of loneliness, vulnerability, and desperation, rocked by desires to be 'normal' and understood"

(Davidson 2000, 4), seems urgent and necessary in the time of the pandemic.

The shifts in the relation between the physical environment and human perception are recorded and transmitted through memory. Places are conceived and mobilised through real and fictive narratives that act as the model for understanding the spaces around us and our own place and that of others within those spaces. Space here is made intelligible in both realistic and representational manner, imbued with the layers of history, memory, imagination, spatiality and futurity.

Andersons's noteworthy editorial "Emotional Geographies" confronts the challenges posed to the approach of cultural geography that validates the engagement of emotion and affect in the domain of research and policy-making in geographical knowledge. The political operations and gendered biases towards an emotional understanding in social scholarship are clearly pointed out in his research: "marginalisation of emotion has been part of a gender politics of research in which detachment, objectivity and rationality have been valued, and implicitly masculinised, while engagement, subjectivity, passion and desire have been devalued, and frequently feminised" (Anderson 2001, 2). He posits that discounting the emotional way of being, knowing and doing any space delays the activation of one's "geographical imagination" and "geographical sensibility" that helps designate personal and collective meanings to spaces in society (5).

Narratives of space function as signposts in tracing the human dimensions of spatial relationships in society. Through them, we know about the earth we inhabit and share with others. Literary landscapes serve as "provisional landmarks" in our mental mapping and align our thoughts and experiences of physical space through its representation in literary imagination, history and memory.

The experience of spatiality requires the interpretive memory tool to recognise the places and objects that constitute the landscape's history and location within the contemporary world. In turn, "placing" the memory facilitates the subjectivity to the participants within a shared space. Memory carries the imprints of familiar spaces like home and remembrances of places visited and inhabited. Through this process of signification, we tend to conceive a sense of place in the world.

The body provides the primary localisation to the human perception of space. It allows us to retain the impressions of our experiences on the "bodies, which do not forget" and map them through memories later (Bachelard 1994, 15). "Foremost, most immediate and intimately felt geography is the body," says Davidson, "the site of emotional experience and expression par excellence. Emotions, to be sure, take place within and around this closest of spatial scales" (Davidson 2004, 523). Concurrently, the physical environment's bodily interpretation is extended onto the home, community, city and the world. The movement between these overlapping territories engages the subject's memory in the process of mapping these places with the self.

According to the Field Theory developed by Kurt Lewin, the social behaviour of a subject is determined by the totality of the experiences stamped into the "life space"[1] region. It can be understood as a self-referential map that uses topological systems to ascertain the psychological-being for a subject.

Place is more than a setting or a backdrop. Various thinkers and scholars have conceptualised the social nature of spaces through the architecture and culture of "home". Bachelard's romanticised childhood home is a "group of organic habits", Morrison's Bluestone 124 reveals the horrors of unresolved trauma against the backdrop of slavery and racism; and Woolf's room (of one's own) is the private space that nurtures creativity and fosters spaces of economic self-reliance for female artists.

Alderman brings together the discussions around the social and spatial nature of memory to highlight how Robben Island gathered global signification over time, from being a physical site of exile for crushing political dissent to a social space promoting peace-building strategies against apartheid in South Africa. The experience of memory practices that sanction human values of affect is also evident in the exploration of performative rituals and celebrations as sites to examine the "geographies of memory" by Connerton. In addition to the material landscapes and commemorative architecture, the embodied acts of social memory "read" the spaces through the framework of bodily experiences, without much reliance upon the actuality of those geographic places.

Said's "invention" of memory and tradition ties his "geographical designations" to power and dominance that underpin his concept of "imaginative geography." For him "memory is not necessarily authentic, but rather useful" (Said 2000, 179). In his analysis, he observes that the geographical knowledge of a place reveals a physical locus embedded within its imperial reality. The conflicts arising from shuffling power dynamics continuously re-write the places so that the invented memory narratives can act as "instrument[s] of rule."

This explication shows that trauma can be conceptualised through spaces and in historical events like Holocaust, "[t]he 'unrepresentable' character of trauma is thus due not to its being 'originary' and hence, beyond history and representation. Rather, it has to do with the enforced rupture with precolonial pasts and the prohibitions against remembrance enforced by particular regimes of power" (Forter 2014, 77). This understanding also raises foundational questions like: How does memory control space? How does space control memory?

To navigate this thought structure, this chapter uses two compelling accounts of memory or "memory-scapes"[2] that evoke the memory of spatiality as a dimension of being. The first account presents Yoko Ogawa's *Memory Police*, a narrative of systemic disappearances of everyday objects and human notions, that dictate the lives of inhabitants on an unnamed island. The second account is represented through *Clone* by Priya Sarukkai Chabria where the norms of life are governed by the Global Community in a world inhabited by twenty-fourth century clones who were once humans. Both fictional accounts present the psycho-geographical mapping of the landscapes. The dystopian worlds of Ogawa and Chabria are sites of examination to analyse the control over the process of remembering and forgetting and possibly "carry memory traces beyond" their immediate locality in the psycho-geographical mapping of the world.

The 'Hidden Room,' 'Secret Drawers' and 'Trapped Voices' in *Memory Police*

> I'm here, you're there, and the question is floating between us.
> — Yoko Ogawa, "Cafeteria"

> No one knows what the future holds. Someday, even the Memory Police are bound to disappear. That's what happens to everything on this island. I don't know. Maybe there's a place out there where people whose hearts aren't empty [of memories] can go on living.
> — Yoko Ogawa, *Memory Police*

The element of uncertainty floats through almost every narrative of Yoko Ogawa. Her writing probes into the gaps of human presence through the trope of place. *Memory Police* offers a poetic meditation on "life spaces" and their entanglement with memory. Set in an unnamed Japanese island where "disappearances" dictate the course of life, the dystopian narrative reveals the horrors of control and manipulation of memory-processes and perception under totalitarianism. The motives for this surveillance are never communicated in the narrative, but the totalitarian system maintains its operations of fear, discipline, erasure and retribution through a surveillance-reinforcing body called the Memory Police, acting on behalf of the authoritarian masters. Their sole purpose is to ensure that people forget particular objects and ideas when it is determined that they should disappear from the world. The protagonist, a young female writer, attempts to intervene in the process and reconfigure her fading memories by creating a new space for their preservation and continuation. The act of revolt provides a new interpretation of social existence through spatial re-imagination.

Robert Tally argues that "we navigate our world by mapping it" and "in mapping a place, one also tells a story" (Tally 2014, 2). The places and objects design the symbolic sense-making system of our territorial consciousness. A rose garden is identifiable by its roses, the red of their colour and the smell. It ceases to exist without the roses. Similarly, the job of a hat maker is dependent on the hats he creates. What happens when the roses and the hats disappear, and their memories vanish from the world? How do the meanings and spaces alter with this changing physical reality? These are some of the initial questions that Ogawa's novel raises.

Ogawa's narrative shapes itself as a moving metaphor of memory. Deriving and expanding on the traditional tropes of trauma and memory propounded by Orwell, Morrison, Atwood and Anne Frank among others, her allusive narrative traces a historiography of loss and awakens the totality of human existence by raising consciousness of the emotional gaps in the official history of the island. The deprivation of emotional consciousness of the present reality delays the cognitive process of trauma. It is well informed at the beginning of the novel that "there were many more things here...transparent things, fragrant things...fluttery ones, bright ones...wonderful things you can't possibly imagine" and that these are only a few "among all the things that have vanished from the island" (Ogawa 2020, 3). The readers and the narrator are warned of their losing grip on memory "to hold such marvellous things in their hearts and minds" (3).

The first elaborate description of disappearance in the novel is unsettling for readers as it is not a material object but the disappearance of a bird that is being dispensed with. The inhabitants on the island do not immediately react to the loss but respond to the changed environ nonetheless. They notice the "sign of a disappearance" but create no "fuss" and "soon enough, things are back to normal, as though nothing had happened, and no one can even recall what it was that disappeared" (4). The memories, feelings and the meaning of the word 'bird' are erased from the consciousness of the people on the island in a mechanical manner, posing questions on the representation of human-ness in Ogawa's speculative writing.

This emotional inertia and the unspeakability of trauma has been the subject of inspection for Caruth and her contemporary trauma theorists exploring the pathological features of trauma in Freudian understanding, such as PTSD. Further developments in contemporary trauma theory assimilate reflections on traumas that are not "punctual" and have bearings on the ongoing practices of everyday life. These less "socially specific" forms of trauma define themselves against the "historical events of such singularity, magnitude and horror that they can be read as shocks that disable the psychic system," such as the Holocaust (Forter 2007, 259). Forter asserts that:

> Such traumas are also so chronic and cumulative, so woven into the fabric of our societies, that they cannot count as "shocks" in the way that Nazi persecution and genocide do in the accounts of Caruth and others. They are emphatically social disturbances, but have been thoroughly naturalised in ways that make it necessary to excavate and "estrange" them in order to see them as social trauma." (260)

Accordingly, Ogawa shuffles her speculative narrative to move beyond the mimetic representation of the psychic anxieties of "punctual" traumas and effortlessly blends elements of routinised "systemic traumatisations", to expose the socio-political mechanisms of the culture of vigilance/surveillance in the contemporary world.

In the novel, the enforcement of surveillance over the private and social life on the island is regulated by the men of Memory Police. The guardians equipped with the power of erasure wore "dark green uniforms...nearly identical, with only three badges on their collars to tell them apart" (Ogawa 2020, 12). These uniforms resonate with the deep red dresses worn by Atwood's handmaids that "defined" them. The "overalls" worn by Chabria's clones are symbolically charged in the same vein. The material clothing acts as visual codes of reinforcing pre-determined singular identities for their subjects. Any transgression outside the codified behaviour is marked as severe offence, so the Memory Police performed its operations "efficiently, thoroughly, systematically, and without any trace of emotion" (150).

This emotionless conduct not only distances them from other inhabitants, but also depletes the emotional spaces within them as they remain unaffected by the disappearances. They lose their individual identity and distinct voices like the character of the typist that the narrator sketches for her novel, with the help of her editor, R. As the Old Man says, "it didn't really matter" (53). Even after the disappearance of the "left leg", they walked, "perfectly in balance, as though the disappearance had caused them no difficulty—as though they had been training for just this eventuality" (249). Imposed amnesia or forgetfulness is the referred eventuality here. Ogawa's island is full of people but devoid of unique subjectivities. The inhabitants live in a shared space but share only a little. Bound by a collective history of loss and the awful disappearances, they remain divided by their ability to either remember or forget. The people who are immune to this forced amnesia, lack any "distinguishable features" but still find it impossible to "blend in" with the rest. One such force of defiance is R, whose heart is "full of so many forgotten things" (81). Another central character, the Old Man also becomes a passive agent in this resistance, but unlike R, does not question the "holes," "absences" and "gaps on the island" (54). Once reminiscing about old times on the island he tells the narrator that before he was born the place was "a lot fuller, a lot more real...as things got thinner, our hearts got thinner, too, diluted somehow" (54). The Old Man lost his occupation after the ferry's disappearance and had gotten "quite accustomed to these losses" (65). Consoling the narrator after the roses disappear from the island, he urges her to accept the disappearances as "there's no way of knowing...no one knows and no one needs to know [the truth behind them]" (51).

The brutal "methods" of Memory Police signify the efforts of totalitarianism to assert power over 'truth' and manufacture a monolithic version of history that requires submission and compliance of the participants to further its political agendas. Their men invaded "any space where someone could be hidden" (64). The desire to achieve the knowledge of truth behind the systemic violence and erasure enforced by the Memory Police disturbs the fragmented consciousness of the narrator. R constantly persuades her to realise this knowledge through remembering (and writing), he urges the narrator: "you may think that the memories themselves vanish every time there's a disappearance, but that's not true. They're just floating in a pool where the sunlight never reaches. All you have to do is plunge your hand in and you're bound to find something. Something to bring back into the light.

You have to try. I can't just stand by watching as your soul withers" (177).

The "deserted factories", "abandoned elementary school" and "old renovated theatre" that served as the headquarters for Memory Police indicate the dysfunctional physical geographies of an organic life on the island that permeate through the personal geographies of self. R has a nearly intact memory and "a heart that has no shape, no limits" (81). In contrast, the narrator had a "hollow heart full of holes" and felt jealous of R whose "transparent" heart offered resistance (82).

The narrator is motivated to imbibe this resistance and forge spaces (of memory) that would contain the memory of the things that had disappeared through R. Her father was an ornithologist and the Memory Police had ruthlessly paraded and violated their house looking for any remnants of the disappearance but couldn't notice the storage room that later becomes the hiding place for R. Like the basement studio of her mother, this was "a place far removed from the outside world" (67).

Hiding R from the outside world becomes the first act of resistance by the narrator and the "hidden room" becomes the locus of storage, retrieval, transmission and continuation of the memories. Much later in the novel the narrator discovers the truth of the "secret drawers" and the possible reasons for the disappearance of her mother who was a sculptor. A few of her sculptures are returned to the narrator by the Inui family who go into hiding to avoid the Memory Police. These sculptures remain hidden for years and become the (safe)house for some of the disappeared objects. Through them the narrator becomes aware of the personal and collective forms of resistance that her precursors had exhibited. This is possibly how Ogawa dispels the narrator's anxieties of disappearing "without a trace" and grasps the transient nature of life (53).

The ordinary objects that retain the memory of human presence in the novel are codes of retrieving those lost histories. Ogawa doesn't stop there and urges the creation of another space through the parallel story of the typist who had lost her voice, thus forging the space of language that gives voice to "the self" that the narrator puts into her novels. The narrator's slippery conviction in her own writing after the disappearance of novels invites contemplation on the relationship between memory and language that attributes and locates the semiotic spaces of meaning-making and belonging. "With the calendars gone, no matter how long we wait, we'll never get to a new month...so spring will never come" (135). The despondent note in Ogawa's novel about the disappearance of the calendars reminds of Shelley's "can Spring be far behind?" from the "West Wind." And like Shelley's desire for a fresh perspective and novel thoughts hints at the possibility of hope. On being asked, "what can the people on the island create" the Old Man replies "grand stories" (52, 53). Fostering personal spaces through powerful stories emerging from the memories of the past that extend as metaphors of the imagination of plausible futures thus seems to be Ogawa's message for knowing and being.

Writings and documentation in print and web are material commodities, the product of economic and cultural forces in society. Autobiographical writing functions as personal archives but their social register expands much larger than their territorial locations, integrating elements of oral tradition and historicity. Ogawa and Chabria create fluid temporal spaces through multiple acts of archiving: Ogawa's narrator's novel about a voiceless typist, the hidden diary of Clone 14/54/G[3] in the form of a chipset and the Original Aa-Aa's[4] pillow book. These texts transmit more than the concretised history of personal experiences.

"Morphing the Consciousness" through Memory in *Clone*

> *Are empty chrysalises homes of memories that have fled? Do you*
> *collect these? Whose memories*
> *are you retaining? Yours or*
> *someone else's? Will anyone*
> *retain memory of you?*
> — Priya Sarukkai Chabria, "Memory"

Chabria's *Clone* serves as a parallel effort to Ogawa's *Memory Police* — to map the structural trauma that affects the being of all humans. The tentacles of her narrative are spread all over the transhumanist conditioning of the lives of her twenty-fourth century clones. Contemporary philosopher Nick Bostrom defines transhumanism as "the intellectual and cultural movement that affirms the possibility and desirability of fundamentally improving the human condition through applied reason, especially by using technology to eliminate ageing and greatly enhance human intellectual, physical, and psychological capacities" (Bostrum 2014, 1).

Chabria's clones are augmented by advanced scientific systems of the Global Community that endow them with enhanced functional capacities. The clones possess adjustable bio clocks and can quickly shuffle between multiple modes of existence such as "sloth mode", lite-doze mode" and "slow mode." Their functionality is suited to only serve the Global Community's purposes and the vision of a transformed future for their capacities relies on forgotten information and replaced ideals in genetic inheritance. The more forgetful these clones are about their human ancestors called Originals, the more critical they become for the Global Community. Continuing with the legacy of *Generation 14*, Chabria envisions the world of *Clone* in a future that is looking backwards.

In the population of the Global Community, the Originals alone have "life," among other categories such as Firehearts, Superior Zombies, Clones and the hidden mutants. Similar to the people on Ogawa's island, the life-forms are controlled here by naturalised hierarchical divisions. The protagonist, Clone 14/54/G does not identify herself as a mutant but recognises that her consciousness had been changing nonetheless as "she remembers" (Chabria 2018, 1).

The Global Community issues threats at the sniff of a revolt: "there is only one space: the imperium of our Global Community, and time is what we have ordained it" (102). In such a controlled environment, the clones are made to believe that they are "fit and perfectly normal" all the time and that they would "long live [in] the Global Community." They are "strapped" for routine scans to ensure there are no "aberrations" or "malfunctions" and the norm to pass these tests is their supposed ability to "lack imagination" and being in a state of absolute forgetfulness about the past (8).

Frederick Nietzsche writes in *Thus Spoke Zarathustra* that "man is something that shall be overcome" (Nietzsche 1978, 12). Postcolonial science fiction has embraced this desire to "overcome" human limitations through the healing, correcting and enhancing intervention by cognitive technologies, projecting a transformed future. In the novel, these scientific advances of the Global Community are not able to eradicate complete traces of human history. On being prompted to find the records of the "saddest dirge" at the Museum of Civilization, Clone 14/54/G returns with an "endless" list and gets shocked to learn that the "human history seems full of sorrow" (Chabria 2018, 20). The Fireheart, Blank Verse affirms by adding, "but the Global Community has forgotten so" (24). Towards the end of the novel when another Fireheart, Couplet, inquires if Clone 14/54/G was in pain after being tortured during the investigation, she answers with a rhetorical question, "who isn't?" thereby commenting on the morbid condition of existence caused as a result of the cloning of humans (278).

Clone 14/54/G proclaims that Firehearts are the poets of the Global Community and "being poets, they cannot lie" (4). They possess "limitless consciousness" and "extraordinary memory" (27). These features make them the closest to bespoke human ecology. Clones do not require a "freed consciousness" like their Originals as their pre-determined levels of consciousness function well in maintaining the order in the Global Community – "they order, we do" (27). It is ironic that the monthly meetings of clones are intended to instil "camaraderie" amongst them, and yet each movement is closely monitored there. During one of the dances at the meets, Clone 14/54/G makes acquaintance of another clone sharing her Original's DNA, Clone 14/53/G, and learns about the mutants called the Others. These are the clones whose malfunctions or abnormality helped them remember.

I term these organisers of protest for democratic aspirations as the "mutants of memory", who create spaces of individuality in poetry, storytelling, remembrance and narratives. In a way, R and the narrator in *Memory Police* can also be seen as mutants as they realise the potential of memory through disobedience and protest for the island's surveillance culture.

The protests through remembrance are nipped in the bud in the Global Community. Slightest aberrations can cause the "withdrawal" of a clone and long durations of isolation in a "Recovery Pad", which is the rehabilitation centre for quashing the protest through seduction and torture. Watchdog clones are assigned to monitor the deflections of the body and the mind, while the Firehearts are made to scrape the bottoms of their soul, to look for those meanings hidden in language. Blank Verse, a Fireheart who is designated to investigate the malfunctioning in Clone 14/54/G learns that the stories that she experiences as "visitations" are rich with the historical and mythological tales of ancient and medieval India. The visitations do not emerge from the creative imagination of Clone 14/54/G, nor fantasies or dreams. They appear to be what Morrison calls the "re-memories."[5] These overpowering visitations occupy a significant portion in the textual space of the novel and become the window for "looking inwards" and "looking backwards" for Clone 14/54/G.

Visitations of Clone 14/54/G invite inquiry into their historical embedment and raises philosophical questions from the readers. Clone 14/54/G finds the visitations confusing as she is surrounded by questions outside the purview of her "nominal notions", and her primary response to them is bewilderment and dismissal: "why was I there? Rather, what was my Original's interest in that far time? For I am but her pale copy, and my duties are different" (13). Later again, in an attempt to establish connections between Global Communities' forgetting and her own remembering process of her Original's traces, she instantly retracts from her meditation: "I am a Clone and will ignore it" (24).

Powerless in their position, the "gaze" of surveillance induces the fear of "disappearance" or "withdrawal" in its receivers. The authority's most powerful tool to ensure the death of the protest is silence and disillusion of freedom. It is proclaimed that "nobody gets killed" in the Global Community. Originals "pass away", Firehearts are "interned", Superior Zombies are "returned", and Clones are "withdrawn" (15). Clone 14/54/G inherits her DNA from her Original, Aa-Aa, a writer who meets an untimely death. She was unable to finish her last composition, "The Great Inescapable Great Fading" about pain and death, "the same for all and for all species, without distinction" (112). Her expression corresponds with John Donne's reflection on, "death [that] comes equally to us all, and makes us all equal when it comes" (1640). Aa-aa died working on her last poem to be recited at the Celebrations. A revolutionary poet, she writes in her pillow book, "maybe a later generation of Clones will trip into consciousness and another understanding of Freedom" (Chabria 2018, 140).

The route to liberty is paved by remembrance but the clones "don't remember ever being free" (141). Clone 14/54/G experiences loneliness and incompleteness in her identity after the self-destruction of the watchdog clone, Bullet, who unrestrained by bloodlust destroys itself watching the gladiators at the Celebrations. The Philimix river that sprung at her feet at the time; and the robot eye of Bullet that she hides in her cell constitute Clone 14/54/G's mnemonics of loss and the foundation stones of the revolt.

The simmering revolt in the changing consciousness of Clone 14/54/G manifests itself on her body too in the shape of a mole: "beneath my overalls I grew hair. At work, I made no error. I was allowed full rations. I was living in two worlds. Is this what is meant by loneliness? That you don't belong to any world. Not the old one. Not the new. You don't even seem to belong to yourself" (48).

Ogawa and Chabria have a cognate vision for the characterisation of their "mutants of memory." Even in absence, the dead Leader empowers Clone 14/54/G the same way the narrator's mother does. Clone 14/53/G's efforts and eventual death resonate with the support of the Old Man, who embarks on the same journey with the narrator, but meets an early death than the protagonists. Lastly, Couplet's constant reminders to Clone 14/54/G to retrieve Aa-aa's story are similar to R's assertion on the need (and the duty) to remember.

Aa-aa stories are repeated several times in the novel. Each time they reveal new information and invigorate new emotions and sensibilities. R explains to the Old Man and the narrator that "memories don't just pile up-they also change over time. And sometimes they fade of their own accord...even if they fade. Something remains" (Ogawa 2020, 81). *Clone* takes a full circle of memory with the visitations being repeated and getting more detailed towards the end. Vrikama's story features as the first visitation in the novel and is retold again in the end. The difference in the voice is striking as the language becomes more emphatic in the retelling by Clone Aa-aa 14/54/G and bears a tone of compassion for human suffering. It appears as if the language of the novel has become more human, adding elements of a human voice with each recollected memory and in the end there remains just a voice—of protest, liberation and human-ness.

In an insightful study on the culture of surveillance in the twenty-first century, David Lyon exposes the limitations of the Orwellian tradition of vigilance. He suggests that these former spaces of control were centred on being watched by others; and supplements new ways of "watching" that actively involves the one who is under observation, through his research on digital life and popular culture.

Using the example of two episodes of the popular television series, *Black Mirror*, he highlights how the spaces of digital consumerism are made up with the building blocks of the desire for "visibility." He warns against feeding the memory system with a "remember it all" approach without assimilation of information and realising how your own participation in the system defines it and can probably change it in some way. In his study, Lyon examines the failure of a "transparent" society as the reason for Foucault's disdain in utopia and suggests that dystopian literature serves as the "black" mirror to reflect the new surveillance condition. His study offers an opportunity to turn the tool of oppression against the oppressors.

Ogawa and Chabria have skilfully employed this strategy in their respective narratives, by regaining control over one's memory and creating spaces of resistance. Ogawa's narrator initiates the disappearance of R for the outside world monitored by the Memory Police. She accomplishes the final story about the mute typist after the disappearance of novels and words from the island. Her participation in the shared pool of collective memories opened up by the melodic remembrance of the music box with R and the Old Man brings even her forgotten memories to the surface. She is also able to know and get inspired by her mother's resistance against the oppressive regime through the hidden objects inside her sculptures.

Similarly, Clone 14/54/G finally speaks her own story through Aa-Aa. She tells the Leader, "yesterday it was me who spoke, not Aa-aa. Those were my words" (Chabria 2018, 105). This records her returning confidence like her human vocabulary that keeps growing until it became her own voice proving that these spaces of literature and memory make one "remember one's self" and create a subjectivity of something more and multiple (85, 80).

Spaces of Literature, Mutants of Memory

Postcolonial science fiction today is deeply engaged in learning the truths beyond terrestrial existence and underlining the multiverse phenomenon. The changing relation between man and earth has been captured and problematised by authors such as Orwell, Bradbury and Atwood exhibiting their specific interest in the politics of control and its reflection in society. Popular culture has advanced the projection of the culture of vigilance through televised anthology series like *Black Mirror*, using techniques such as logical extrapolation and cognitive estrangement. The latter concept, developed by Darko Suvin, borrows from the Brechtian concept of alienation. These strange worlds provide "an imaginative framework alternative to the author's empirical environment" (Suvin 1979, 8).

The worlds of the two novels reflect the rhythms of life and death. Ogawa's language is subtle and poetic while Chabria's prose initially seems cluttered with alien and mechanical lexicon seemingly out of the world. The former induces a numbing pain of nothingness while the latter demands attentiveness to piece together the disjointed "actuality" of being. Both of them are keen on grasping the world far removed from the human language of connectedness and an organic way of living. Both narratives resist an easy interpretation and dissolve into open endings, thus extending the navigation of the narrative to the readers. The agency is liberating but not without risks. The complex meanings entailed in the narratives demand reading between the sentences without being allured by the language of estrangement.

The authority of the respective regimes over the population is suffocating to the point that the characters in both the narratives experience loneliness and the society remains divisive. Yet it is difficult to tap into the specific historical amnesias that have inspired the authors' meditations on losses — of objects, people, places and meanings. Again in the episode of burning books in *Memory Police* and the incidents at the Museum of Civilization in *Clone*, expressing discouragement for ~~of~~ the poets of society and research on the "unspeakable grief" in the Global Community, concerns such as intellectual censorship are clearly highlighted.

Ogawa and Chabria present a critique of the control over expressions of plurality — of histories, geographies, narratives and memory. The authors collectively expose the "danger[s] of a single story" (Adichie 2009). Ordained by the ruling authority, the regulated narratives of totalitarianism remain incomplete without any contestation from the marginalised participants of the society. Chabria's "visitations" in *Clone* respond to this practice of prescribing homogenous narratives of history by bringing the stories of the bereaved and the ostracised to the fore. Ogawa foregrounds her analysis of the social domination and spatial praxis in *Memory Police* by resisting a fossilised understanding of spatial reality. Creating plural spaces of expression, her novel encourages dialogism between the collective and individual. The depictions of "monstrous forgeries in historiography" (Finigan 2011, 332) by the two authors complicate the relationship of time and space for "retrieving" multiple truths and varieties of consciousness and "creating" alternate spaces for their continuation.

The impressions of life experiences and stories are transmitted through memory-narratives. "The extent to which the art of memory for the modern world is both for historians as well as ordinary citizens and institutions," has, according to Said, "… something to be used, misused, and exploited, rather than something that sits inertly there for each person to possess and contain" (Said 2000, 179). The novelists' foray in the memory discourse is futuristic yet embracing the past. Their literary landscapes approach time and space from opposing directions of presence and absence to articulate loss. The two narratives converge in their common objective of redefining shared humanity through "memory-scapes."

This unique and comprehensive understanding of spaces allows the optimisation of "emotions as ways of knowing, being and doing in the broadest sense; and using this to take geographical knowledges– and the relevance that goes with them– beyond their more usual visual, textual and linguistic domains" (Anderson 2001, 3). In doing so, this paper utilises Forter's emphasis on Freud's original theories of trauma over his later model. He posits that:

> "Rather than seeing events that cause trauma as potentially pathogenic in the future, this theory sees them as effractions that evict us from the movement of historical time from the start. Rather than emphasising the significatory content of trauma-meanings internalised too early yet too late, a subject who comes to be "always already" shaped by meanings with which he must contend this view emphasises the purely non-significatory effect of shock, the brute intrusion of unmasterable stimuli upon an unprepared psyche. And rather than viewing even this shock as producing a range of differential effects in the subject's subsequent life (symptoms, character traits, etc.), this view posits the initial event as one that the subject literally repeats in a kind of transfixed and atemporal nightmare." (269)

This implies the creation of new psycho-geographical spaces that are not limited to their socio-historical relevance but expand beyond it to represent or rather "transmit" miseries of human existence ontologically, outside of their temporal specificity as well. In creating such spaces the subject is liberated from the patterns of systemic domination.

Storytelling and poetry constitute the effect of voice in the two novels. The narrator in Ogawa's narrative finds the words that have disappeared from the island and gives a dreadful ending to the story of the typist mirroring her own loss. Clone 14/54/G completes Aa-aa's stories and gains a new reality for herself as

Clone Aa-aa 14/54/G. She manifests the hope to be able to tell those stories her own way someday with the sensibility to "love tremendously beyond [her]self" (Chabria 2018, 281). Reading, writing, and above all remembering thus become acts of resistance that constitute the language of human-ness and open up the "sanctifying" spaces of being (280). Ultimately, putting it in Chabria words "what are we made of? Are we only what is seen, and known? What of the spaces of thought and emotion, and that something else that makes us human, that something else that makes us grieve with others? What makes us feel thankful precisely because we are, in the end, not different, but governed by the same vast laws of life?" (278).

Notes

1   "Life space" can be identified as the map of a person's experiences. American social psychologist Kurt Lewin developed the concept of "life space" using topological systems, which states that the behaviour of an individual at a given time is based on the aggregate of the facts in the psychological field, including one's internal thoughts and the external environment. He explains the cognitive process of determining reality by an individual through these parameters.

2   The notion expresses that geographical landscapes accrue layered meanings through understanding their relevance vis-a-vis memory processes.

3   Clone 14/54/G is the narrator of Chabria's novel set in the twenty-fourth century. The fourteenth-generation clone is an engineered manifestation of her Original (a category of life-form in the novel) called Aa-aa, a human. The various life-forms and life-processes in the novel provide philosophical experience of human life and memory.

4   Aa-aa, the Original to the narrator, Clone 14/54/G, was a twenty-first century writer who died during a controversial public address without being able to reveal her final message.

5   In a narrow sense, "re-memories" can be understood as recurring figurations of traumatic memories in a way that they aren't frequent but distant. Set deep inside the psychological realms, these disturbing episodes become repressed and seem to be forgotten and un-familiarised.

Bibliography

Adichie, Chimamanda Ngozi. "The Danger of a Single Story." Speech, TED Talk, July 2009.

Anderson, Kay, and Susan J. Smith. "Editorial: Emotional Geographies." *Transactions of the Institute of British Geographers* 26, no. 1 (2001): 7-10.

Atwood, Margaret. *The Handmaid's Tale*. Canada: McClelland and Stewart, 1985.

Bachelard, Gaston. *The Poetics of Space*. Boston: Beacon Press, 1994.

Bergson, Henri. *Matter and Memory*. (Reprint of MacMillan Co., New York, 1912 edition). Translated by N. Margaret Paul and W. Scott Palmer. New York: Dover Publications, 2014.

Black Mirror series. Created by Charlie Brooker. Zeppotron (2011-13) and House of Tomorrow, (2014-19). 22 episodes & 1 film, Netflix.

Bostrom, Nick. "Introduction—The Transhumanist FAQ: A General Introduction." In *Transhumanism and the Body*. New York: Palgrave Macmillan, 2014, pp. 1-17.

Caruth, Cathy. *Unclaimed experience: Trauma, Narrative, and History*. Baltimore: Johns Hopkins University Press, 2016.

Chabria, Priya Sarukkai. *Clone*. New Delhi: Zubaan, 2018.

Colombo, Pamela, and Estela Schindel. "Introduction: The Multi-Layered Memories of Space." In *Space and the Memories of Violence*. London: Palgrave Macmillan, 2014, pp. 1-17.

Connerton, Paul. *How Societies Remember*. Cambridge: Cambridge University Press, 1989.

Davidson, Joyce, and Christine Milligan. "Embodying emotion sensing space: introducing emotional geographies." *Social and Cultural Geography* 5, no. 4 (2004): 523-532.

Davidson, Joyce, Mick Smith, and Liz Bondi, eds. *Emotional Geographies*. Farnham: Ashgate Publishing, 2007.

Donne, John. *LXXX Sermons*. 1640.

Finigan, Theo. "'Into the Memory Hole': Totalitarianism and Mal d'Archive in Nineteen Eighty-Four and The Handmaid's Tale." *Science Fiction Studies* 38, no. 3 (2011): 435-459.

Forter, Greg. "Freud, Faulkner, Caruth: Trauma and the Politics of Literary Form." *Narrative* 15, no. 3 (2007): 259-85.

Hoelscher, Steven, and Derek H. Alderman. "Memory and Place: Geographies of a Critical Relationship." *Social & Cultural Geography* 5, no. 3 (2004): 347-355.

Lyon, David. "Introduction: Surveillance Culture Takes Shape." *The Culture of Surveillance: Watching as a Way of Life*. New Jersey: John Wiley & Sons, 2018.

Morrison, Toni. *Beloved*. New York: Knopf, 1987.

Nietzsche, Friedrich. *Thus Spoke Zarathustra: A Book for None and All*. Translated by Walter Kaufmann. New York: Penguin, 1978.

Ogawa, Yoko. *The Memory Police*. Translated by Stephen Synder. London: Vintage, 2020.

Said, Edward W. "Invention, Memory, and Place." *Critical Inquiry* 26, no. 2 (2000): 175-192.

Suvin, Darko. "Cognition and Estrangement." *Metamorphoses of Science Fiction*. New Haven: Yale University Press, 1979, pp. 3-15.

Tally, Robert T. "Introduction: Mapping Narratives." In *Literary Cartographies*. New York: Palgrave Macmillan, 2014, pp. 1-12.

6

Reef Thinking:
Coral Reefs, Materialism and Ecology
at the End of Nature

Oriol Batalla

Melting Theories

To recognize nature's own agency means to recognize that the anthropocentric perception and understanding of time needs to be switched away from conventional, rather Cartesian/Spinozian, timespace models. Humans have not been able to come to terms with the issues the Anthropocene entails due to such perspective. Ecology needs to veer from such rationality and turn towards an ecological rationality in which "the match or fit between an agent's choices, actions and effects and that agent's overall desires, interests and objectives as they require certain ecological conditions for their fulfilment" (Plumwood 2002, 68), understanding ecology as an epistemological system grounded on understanding of such nonlinear timespaces governed by nonlinear causality (Guattari, 2000). Such approach, in turn, could help us rethink time, agency and ecosystems as a whole.

Anthropocentric practices where brought to an expansive, accumulative, vampire-like motion with the establishment of capitalism as a world-system and meta-narrative, perpetuating accumulation and the Money-Commodities-Money (surplus value) logic throughout each of its stages. With Fukuyama (1992) auguring the end of history with the instauration and consolidation of (neo)liberalism, and in a system marked by the aegis of liberalism, a techno-fixing of nature and a post-military complex and the control over populations through smart power (Mbembe, 2013; Han, 2017), it would not be correct to frame the whole of humanity as the cause of the Anthropocene. As Jonathan Crary postulates, neoliberal late-Capitalism is "inseparable from environmental catastrophe in its declaration of permanent expenditure, of endless wastefulness for its sustenance, in its terminal disruption of the cycles and seasons on which ecological integrity depends" (Crary 2013, 10). Although this essay will stick to the Anthropocene nomenclature for length and complexity purposes as this debate goes beyond the analysis we have at hand, it is crucial to acknowledge that this is in fact an epoch governed by the geological, political, ecological and cultural power of capitalist accumulation in which "capitalism leaves in its wake the disappearance of species, languages, cultures, and peoples. It seeks the planned obsolescence of all life. Extinction lies at the heart of capitalist accumulation" (McBrien 2016, 116).

Acknowledging the Anthropocene as an epoch governed by direct and indirect extinction through mass-accumulation calls for new materialism to analyze the crisis as a whole. Furthermore, the understanding of nature as an agent, dismantling the dialectic between Nature/Culture, also pushes theoreticians to stick to the Marxist meta-narrative while also acknowledging the post-humanist perspective the multispecies knots of life require us in order to come to terms with such uncanny emergency. As van Dooren et al. point out, "from the directed visual and scent markers with which a flower calls out to its pollinators, to canid play invitations with their complex modes of responsive etiquette, the world is a lively communicative matrix woven through with signs and wonders" (van Dooren et al. 2016, 2). That is, this crisis calls for a necessity to be analyzed through the humanities from a New Materialism and a Multispecies Studies perspective, taking up the understanding of our world, bringing diverse bodies of knowledge into conversation and steering them towards new directions, asking how human and non-human lives, lifeforms and accountabilities are pleaded into these entanglements (van Dooren et al., 2016).

With such a pressure crumbling down disciplines in which the future of human life and the way we live is under the entropy caused by the transgression of the Planetary Boundaries[1] (Rockström et al., 2009), and in which ontology and materialism have become front problems, provocatively aligning with New

Materialism can provide us with a theory and practice towards the issue at hand. What has brought the Earth to the Anthropocene has been the modification, colonization, destruction and pollution of the natural world through anthropogenic practices under the logic of capitalism. New materialism can, in turn, help us teeter from critical cultural materialism to an immersion within the milieus and the agents that live in such materialities, human and beyond-human.

Beyond the Holocene and the Terrestrial

The climate stability of the Holocene provided humanity with the conditions to establish long-lasting civilizations. All recorded history took place in the Holocene, and the conditions it had were pivotal for everything we know in terms of culture, history, politics, beauty or nature. With the Holocene gone and in the midst of the realization and disorientation of the Anthropocene, an epoch in which effects of humankind and mass-accumulation through the capitalist logic have escalated globally leading towards the non-human and human Sixth Mass Extinction, all these concepts need to be restructured, revised and re-mediated. With global climate departing from its natural behavior, the Anthropocene is part and perpetuator of the uncanny epoch of the end of nature, a time in which everything that once was "natural" (outside human culture) is now modified as humans have modified the atmosphere and, consequently, everything (McKibben, 1989). Therefore, all that once was outside human modification is now modified. In other words, as Ursula K. Heise (2016) postulated, the conception of nature that modern society conceived throughout years of cultural mediation in the Holocene as a domain apart from human intention is no longer existent. That is, the relationship between life forms and forms of life has turned into a liquid and turbulent realm (Helmreich, 2009). As Bastian & van Dooren (2017) shed light upon:

> this is a period in which relationships between life and death, creation and decay, have become uncanny; no longer entailing what was once taken for granted. Toxic legacies, mass extinction, climate change: all simultaneously

remake both temporal relations and possibilities for life and death. (Bastian & van Dooren 2017, 2)

In this light, the ocean is no longer the *aqua nullius*[2] realm as this process is already over. Human interaction and capitalist accumulation have colonized, directly or indirectly, the biggest part of our oceans and seas at the end of nature. As Elizabeth DeLoughrey highlighted, "the ocean is now understood in terms of its agency, its anthropogenic pollution and acidity, and its interspecies ontologies — all of which suggest that climate change is shaping new oceanic imaginaries" (DeLoughrey 2017, 34). Understanding that human culture is tuned in and connected to the physical world, affecting it and affected by it (Glotfelty & Fromm, 1996) calls for a dethroning of human perception towards an exploration of theoretical and mediation modes of coming to terms with non-human entities as constituted by infinite flows and forces (Alaimo, 2014). Therefore, to think ecologically is in fact "to situate the thinking body in an ecological field, being attentive to the myriad materialities running through and around it, constituting it and the thought that emerges in the relation between body and environment" (Hayes 2019, 21). Yet, these forces at the end of nature have been and are affected by capitalist practices and the logic of accumulation, leading to the transgression of the Planetary Boundaries which can be fatal for the planetary multispecies salon.

Within this paradigm, using what Jue (2020) coined as *milieu-specific analysis*[3] from a situated knowledge perspective (Haraway, 1988), this essay aims to develop how coral reefs "think" and how a beyond-human semiotics can help us understand both the specific milieu of the coral reef environments, and also the world-ecology in a planetary scale. By thinking, one should understand the ability to represent, produce and interpret signs and how all beings respond to these signs and adapt to these inputs. In other words, the whole world is made up of a semiotic lattice, in which everything is influenced, to a certain extent, by the acquisition and response to such signs (Kohn, 2013). In a sort of science fiction mediation, dislocating us from our familiarities towards our surroundings, this chapter tries to hold the tension between the milieu and semiotics of the coral reefs, and the terrestrial specificity of our natural environment. Moving beyond the *grounded* and terrestrial foundation of knowledge and using the Earth as a default start, this essay aims to challenge and expand culture and knowledge towards an amphibian, multispecies, plastic viewpoint. In the semiotic disorientation that both human rationale and reef ecology are immersed, a world is produced through the acknowledgement of the dependency it has to a cultural grid. As Martin & Rosello (2016) pointed out, when diverse discrepant possibilities arise within disorientation, disorientation becomes a cultural and political asset.

Acidic Milieus

As a continuous "deterioration of the chemical conditions needed for physiological and biogeochemical performance of the reef ecosystem" (McLeod et al. 2012, 21), Ocean Acidification (OA) is one of the Planetary Boundaries that can tear apart the synchronizations of the Earth and its myriads. The pH of the Earth oceans and seas has fallen from an 8.2 to an 8.1 since the beginning of industrialization and, in other words, the tipping point for worldwide capitalist expansion and fossil fuel usage. As Hayes points out, "given the logarithmic nature of pH, this drop represents a 25 percent increase in acidity over the past two centuries, thanks to the ocean's function as a giant sponge for the capture and storage of carbon dioxide (CO_2) released into the atmosphere" (Hayes 2019, 3). This, *a priori*, "small" change makes us go back 55 million years in order to find a comparable OA process (Hayes, 2019).

OA is a vivid example of what Rob Nixon coined as *Slow Violence*, a kind of violence "that occurs gradually and out of sight; a delayed destruction often dispersed across time and space" (Nixon 2011, 2). This violence is hardly ever perceived as violence. It is not a vivid, sensorial, immediate event such as an explosion or a tsunami. It gradually burns out the fuses of what is at hand. This connects to Povinelli's (2016) ideas on quasi-events, which happen and develop in a timespace beyond and under the natural perception humans have.

Through and because of OA amongst other causes such as sea-surface-temperature rises or oxygen depletion, coral reefs are suffering glowing and bleaching processes (De'ath et al., 2012). Defined as "a stress response that results in the loss of intracellular symbiotic dinoflagellates (Symbiodinium) and/or their photosynthetic pigments; on a broad spatial scale, bleaching results from extended warm periods" (Ainsworth et al. 2016, 338), bleaching events have damaged a big part of the Great Barrier Reef in Northern Queensland[4] and some reefs in Southeast Asia from 1998 up until now (Readfearn, 2020). These bleaching events, in turn, semiotically show us how slow violence comes into play in the Anthropocene and how, in turn, coral reefs receive, interpret and produce beyond-human semiotics and aesthetics of extinction.

In coral reef bleaching processes, it all starts with either (or both) sea-surface temperature rise and an acidic oceanic milieu. Corals live in a symbiotic relationship with zooxanthellae algae. The algae receive shelter, CO_2 and can nourish from the corals, while the corals gain photosynthetic products to fulfill their energy (Bollati et al., 2020). When this happens, the symbiotic relationship that corals have with the zooxanthellae algae that inhabit them, are their food source and give them their color, ends. The algae leave the coral tissue as it becomes stressed by the milieu in which the coral is immersed. This can, in turn, be catastrophic for the whole reef ecosystem and for the human and non-human livelihoods that depend on such reefs. Once the algae are gone, the white and pristine coral skeleton is exposed and in a matter of years, structures that have been constructed throughout millennia can be eroded and destroyed by its current acidic milieu, becoming a representative image of the Sixth Extinction (Bollati et al., 2020).

However, before jumping into bleaching, something uncannier can happen. Before the aesthetic death of the corals, massively mediated by documentaries such as *Chasing Coral* or *Blue Planet I* and *II*, some corals suffer glowing events. Described by the *Times Magazine* as "the most beautiful death," coral glowing involves a self-regulating mechanism, an optical loop that invokes both partners of the symbiosis while at the same time protecting the tissues from sun exposure. In healthy corals, sunlight is absorbed by the algae. Nonetheless, in corals facing bleaching, the sunlight bounces back and forth within the white skeleton; stressing the symbionts and making colors glow with higher intensity (Bollati et al., 2020). In other words, these events show how corals create both a sunscreen layer and a decoy for symbionts to return, brightening their colors as some sort of last push for their survival as subjects.

Glowing is a clear example of beyond-human semiotics and shows us how corals think, interpret their environment and aim for resilience in an acidic milieu. It puts, front and center, that in the paradigm of the Anthropocene, the exceptional status of humans in the world-system is not the framed scenario that rationalism has long extended (Haraway, 2008). It also shows how evolution and the interconnectivity of lifeforms are now under the anvil of the Anthropocene and the end of nature. Corals glow as a response to their milieu and the sensorial items this environment has. In turn, such corals produce signs in order to provoke a response to the symbionts that once inhabited them in evolutionary synchrony.

After glowing, the white death caused by bleaching leaves in front of us an eerie yet beautiful sea of skeletons. Similar in looks to the Thai Wat Rong Khun (วัดร่องขุ่น) temple yet with more dead bodies than probably every human graveyard, bleaching events leave in its wake the truth of the deathly motion and aesthetics of the Anthropocene; and how, due to an inability of semiotically engaging with the multispecies knots of life and the different timespaces, some of them so large and some of them so tiny, in which such knots are entangled. As Morton pointed out, we are "faced with the task of thinking at temporal and spatial scales that are unfamiliar, even monstrously gigantic" (Morton 2016, 25). With bleaching events, what is left before our eyes is the vast dimension of an underwater calamity. After bleaching events, the once living and bountiful ecosystem, whitens and, in a matter of weeks, all life is gone for good.

By 2050, 98% of the planet's coral reefs will be affected by bleaching-level thermal stress, as we enter in what is supposed to be the never-ending era of coral bleaching (Heron et al., 2016). The Great Barrier Reef would need between 10-15 years to start recovering from a single bleaching phenomenon (Holthaus, 2014). This seems rather unrealistic since bleaching events have started happening in a very high rate in the last years, having mass-bleaching events patterned from 2016 to 2020, with prediction to have more (Readfearn, 2020). That is why some voices have framed the Great Barrier Reef on a Terminal State (Jamail, 2016).

This, of course, has implications to both non-human and human ecosystems. In terms of semiosis, the symbiosis goes beyond algae and corals. Corals and fish depend on the well-being of each other, not only to feed and reproduce, but also to geolocate themselves. Coral reefs depend on young fish for the refilling of functional taxa. This process is at stake since many coral fish semiotically rely on acoustic cues to guide themselves in terms of habitat selection and settlement (Gordon et al., 2018). There is a tight link between reef degradation, fish larval preferences and juvenile settlement behavior as predegradation reefs were more appealing to fish than postdegradation ones (Gordon et al., 2018). That is, from a semiotics vantage point, the interpretation of signs that made both coral fish and coral reef thrive in harmony has been disrupted at the end of nature. This also reminds us that these sequences of lifeforms rely on "real embodied generations – ancestors and descendants – in rich but imperfect relationships of inheritance, nourishment and care" (van Dooren 2014, 27). In other words, "neither do synchronies and sequences occur in isolation; rather, multitudes of them bring together food and fed, pollinator and pollinated, traveller and medium travelled" (Bastian 2017, 151).

Coral reefs and ecosystems are creatures and agents that inhabit the narrative milieu coined as nature and, consequently, become pivotal in scientific tales about the past, present and future, shaped by historical and cultural contexts. Elements, such as the acidic particles of the ocean, microplastics, oil or atmosphere CO_2 become entangled, active and central actors rather than elements with no agency in the turmoil of the Anthropocene. To put it wholly, in the paradigm of the Anthropocene and the narratives it entails, agencies are distributed. That is, for instance, if we consider that the composition of the air we breathe depends on living beings such as coral reefs,[5] the atmosphere is no longer just a milieu apart from agents, but an agent itself. In other words, as Bruno Latour put it, "there are not organisms on one side and environment on the other, but a coproduction by both" (Latour 2018, 63).

Corals knots of life and the way they "think" are in an unparalleled situation in which they will not have time to modify and evolve. Darwinian evolution is at stake at the end of nature since agents beyond the rules of the natural world are gaining agency and, consequently, affecting the close-knit knots of life that have been perfected through imperfection during the history of the planet. In light of this, corals, deprived and left alone without any symbiotic connection, perish. The multispecies knots of time between coral reefs, evolution and humankind become disentangled and frayed. And thus, the way they "think" semiotically speaking is shaken to its core. Yet, what it is crucial to comprehend is that this disentanglement, this ecological crisis, is not something that clings to the mystical and magical agency that nature has been given throughout the ages from a romantic perspective. Understanding such semiotic relationships through New Materialism can help us grasp to a certain extent that the different human cultures and individuals of such cultures have fallen into blindness both physically and ontologically when it comes to comprehending the changing ecologies, bodies and lives of the Earth.

Through metaphorical lenses, coral reef glowing and bleaching processes can be an aesthetic device that embodies, through transmutation, the logic of the contemporary. In a world marked by external appearances, coral reef processes of glowing and bleaching embody external aesthetics and internal misery, in which humans in general have not found the real meaning beneath them. This relates to the politics of social media, such as Instagram, in which only the beautiful, the relatable, namely, the parts that want to be seen, are shown. This logic is also present in tangible policies such as Green Capitalism. To illustrate this shortly, as it goes beyond the scope of this chapter, capitalism is moving towards a shape in which the system presents itself as a "green" and "sustainable" alternative. This is done, of course, as long as its voracious logic is untouched and undisputed. This would perpetuate the inconsistencies and inequalities that lie at the heart of capitalism in each of its shapes. A beautiful, up-to-date outside with the same business-as-usual necrotic inside.

Thinking through and with coral reefs and the multispecies extinction they entail can help us, not only come to terms with the catastrophic situation that reefs are facing from an ecological, inclusive perspective, but also to grasp what is beyond coral reefs and which logics arise from the multispecies knots of life that are being frayed in such turmoil in a planetary scale. In addition, understanding the plight that reefs are facing from a milieu-specific analysis perspective, also portrays the paramount importance submerging into the realms of New Materialism has in order to grasp the vast, non-linear and multiple timespaces that are at stake at the end of nature in the Anthropocene.

The deathly processes that coral reefs are undergoing are affecting many human and non-human ecosystems. Their decline due to anthropogenic – and capitalogenic – causes is, as shown throughout this section, a vivid example of the reality of the Anthropocene and what is to come if the emergencies that the planetary boundaries illustrate for a sustainable life on Earth are not taken seriously enough. The Anthropocene, the Sixth Extinction and the way humanity is approaching such crisis reminds one about the Aesop Fable *The Tortoise and the Hare*. For many decades, scientists have put front and center what is at stake in terms of Climate Change and the effects it will have on the planet as a whole. Humankind, and especially the world superpowers, have implemented policies towards a business-as-usual model. Moreover, they have thought that they could win this stopwatch race against a changing world through business as usual, prioritizing monetary value and accumulation over the well-being and stability of the foundation of everything we know. In addition, "politicians, economists and even some natural scientists have tended to assume that tipping points in the Earth system – such as the loss of the Amazon rainforest or the West Antarctic ice sheet – are of low probability and little understood" (Lenton et al., 2019).

This is, namely, a very strange form of disinhibition in which scientific evidence has been systematically ignored (Latour, 2018). Now the time is up and the tortoise (climate change) that has been warning us for many decades is waiting for humanity from the finish line, taking its toll on the whole planet.

Furthermore, and connected to this argument, as Lenton et al. (2019) pointed out, within the planetary boundaries, we are reaching points of no-return[6] in certain sections of the world that, due to the planetary boundaries, are declining at an alarming rate, one of them being coral reefs, which would have tremendous consequences on the livelihoods of the whole planet, disrupting the multispecies knots of life as we know them. If palliative and/or radical measures are not implemented right now, coral reefs will decline by a 99% if the sea-surface-temperature increases over 2 degrees Celsius over its stable levels (Lenton et al., 2019). This would mean the perishing of uncountable non-human and human environments.

In this Titanic-like situation it seems, in a rather-apocalyptical fashion, that some elites are getting rid of the burdens of solidarity and have stopped pretending that they want to share the living space called "Earth" with the rest, dooming an unimaginable amount of human and non-human ecosystems (Latour, 2017). Nevertheless, that is why historical materialism and new materialism must fusion in order to come to terms with the political struggle the whole planet is facing between subjugators and subjugated both in human and non-human terms from a multispecies perspective. Thus, it is of paramount importance that we try to understand how non-human agents think and semiotically relate to each other.

Interdisciplinary Zoonosis

The white underwater graveyards after bleaching episodes are not something that appears out of the blue. They are the vivid representation of the "current inadequacy of the established science, policy and economics approaches" (Sörlin 2012, 788) to come to terms with the multispecies, multifocal crisis; together with a systematic ignorance of such sciences over monetary accumulation. Coral reef bleaching is pure materialism and calls for new materialist approaches. It belongs and is victim of a planetary system, a "capitalist realism" (Fisher, 2009) that we cannot get rid of. The planetary boundaries that have caused the coral reefs cataclysm have been pushed to their thresholds especially after the industrial revolution. They are, in turn, victims of the so-called modernity, framed within the expansion of capitalism to the world-system. Here, the belief that science *alone* can lead the Earth away from the planetary catastrophe it is actually facing is long gone in an emergency in which humanity and the agency it has through capitalist logic are the chief cause of the calamity at hand (Sörlin, 2012). Thus, the arts, humanities and social sciences embody an inevitable shift in order to center research on human societies as a focus and defy established truths. As Sörlin points out,

> Although ecologists and economists have put considerable hope over the last two decades into the idea that we may be able to defend ecosystem services by translating them into monetary terms, several humanities scholars (in alliance with many skeptical scientists) have presented fundamental criticism of this approach. (Sörlin 2012, 789)

That is, the current changing ecologies are calling for a reconfiguration of the humanities and the perception of what surrounds us. This reconfiguration needs to be recast beyond capitalist logic and through an ecological rationality. This, in turn, can only be done through a *specific-milieu analysis,* putting reason, mediations and the planet itself under New Materialism. What characterizes philosophy is in fact this swing between actuality and possibility, not accepting what exists, and its perception, as given (Žižek, 2006). This way, it can also help us go beyond human agents and, from an ecological perspective, come to terms with the different problematics that arise in the fraying of multispecies knots of life. Although controversial in approach, this suggests that analysts, theoreticians, and even scientists in different disciplines should immerse themselves into uncanny milieus, challenging Western models of rationality and objectivity to flesh out the issues at stake (Alaimo, 2016). This responsibility is yet a *pivotal* one, in the sense that responsibility can only become possible when responses are unclear, but we find ourselves with the urge of responding accordingly (Thiem, 2008). That is, thinking, writing, analyzing and coming to terms with the changing ecologies, the multispecies knots of life and the Sixth Extinction is a collective risk, and also a collective task towards responsibility and change (Rose, 2012). This has become even more present in the Coronavirus crisis, a symptom and cause of the broken relationship between human and non-human agents and inability to reconnect with it at the end of nature, which has been reported to be originated in a zoonosis event due to the degradation of ecosystems (Bonilla-Aldana et al., 2020).

Although the Coronavirus crisis has put emergency at the center of the debate, when it comes to the rest of the crises of the 21st Century (late-capitalism, climate change, neo-colonialism, alt-right populism, etc.), we seem to be living a Heideggerian lack of a sense of emergency (Heidegger, 1989). Here, self-certainty has become unsurpassable; where everything is held to be calculable and where human beings themselves seem to dominate everything themselves yet they are alienated blinded by the given systematic and imposed nature of being (Heidegger, 1989). Dragging Heidegger into the contemporary, even though the media apparatuses are bombarding societies with emergencies, the hegemonic conception over everyday lives in industrialized countries is "that nothing new happens: reality is fixed, stable and secured" (Zabala, 2017), ideologically framed and seen through an invisible infrastructure (Žižek, 2006).

Thus, it is not strange that four of the nine Planetary Boundaries have already been transgressed and that nine sections of the planet are facing no-return thresholds in the imminent future. In the understanding of the Earth as a complex, integrated network-system, as Zabala puts it, "the fact that these four boundaries have been crossed is an indication that the emergency they entail for our lives is hidden, absent" (Zabala 2017, 104). That is, climate scientists face the great challenge of demonstrating the magnitude of the ecological cataclysm to convince societies and politicians to take action to palliate the alarming outcomes of global warming (Zabala, 2017).

In light of this, as aforementioned, the arts and the humanities can play an important role in shaping emergencies beyond the given, addressing humanity itself and the hermeneutical ontological interpretations of these emergencies. These two disciplines can help us mediate and generate new perceptions of the world, creating a commitment to its transformation. They fall into the idea of "dissensus", which designates the agonistic struggle between what is seen and the way humans come to terms with it (Rancière, 2010). In other words, the arts and humanities, partnering with scientific data, can be crucial heuristics to reveal the emergencies the world is facing due to their ability to create intensity and depth, difficult to find in other disciplines (Zabala, 2017).

In the "hauntology" in which the future seems to be cancelled and in which we are unable to imagine, redefine and conceptualize new futures beyond the capitalist realism where we live (Fukuyama, 1992; Fisher, 2009), new modes of understanding need to arise in order to both come to terms with the current multispecies extinction we are facing and the inconsistencies of capitalism as a deathly system that is triggering such extinction. Artistic works and the humanities can be heuristics towards such change. In an *acid communism* fashion (Fisher, 2019), disciplines challenging the given must embrace a denaturalising and flowing multiplicity of perspectives while challenging, through new materialism the rational perceptions presented as the *real*. Rethinking the given, descending into the depths of a rationality that moves beyond the orthodox, immersing ourselves in unknown milieus surrounded by uncanny living and non-living agents that play their part in non-linear and uneven temporalities can be very useful and enlightening way to come to terms with the strangeness of the Anthropocene. Being more *reef-minded,* in other words, understanding that there is an interconnectedness between human and non-human agents that creates ecosystems in which agents engage with each other, representing and being victims of these engagements, can help humanity reconnect with an ecological rationality, understanding that, to a large extent, all agents on Earth belong to the same ecology.

Notes

1   The nine Planetary Boundaries are "the global biogeochemical cycles of nitrogen, phosphorus, carbon, and water; the major physical circulation systems of the planet (the climate, stratosphere, ocean systems); biophysical features of Earth that contribute to the underlying resilience of its self-regulatory capacity (marine and terrestrial biodiversity, land systems); and two critical features associated with anthropogenic global change (aerosol loading and chemical pollution)" (Rockström et al., 2009). Crossing one or more of these boundaries will trigger catastrophic consequences on a planetary scale.

2   Paraphrasing *Terra Nullius* as the land of none, concept appropriated during colonization processes, *Aqua Nullius* was the last stage of the oceans and seas before being absorbed by the omnipresence of humankind after the end of nature.

3   According to Melody Jue (2020), *Milieu-Specific Analysis* "acknowledges that specific thought forms emerge in relation to different environments, and that these environments are significant for how we form questions about the world, and how we imagine communication within it" (Jue 2020, 3). Furthermore, for Jue (2020), it is crucial to understand the ocean as a dynamic milieu "whose characteristics manifest by actively moving within it (as a human, octopus, plankton, or other) and through mediated forms of contact" (Jue 2020, 3).

4   Even though it is framed as one of the least threatened reefs, the Great Barrier Reef) has decreased its mean coral cover in a 50.7% between 1985 and 2012 due to mass-bleaching and OA due to pollution and coastal industries, Crown of thorns starfish blooms due to ecosystem shifts and climate change (De'ath et al, 2012).

5   Coral reefs generate half of the Earth's oxygen and absorb one third of carbon dioxide generated through anthropocentric livelihoods (Jamail, 2017). Thus, the invisibility of the loss of these corals is critical for both human and non-human ecosystems beyond the reef ecosystem itself. In a rather Actor-Network Theory fashion, if an ecosystem so diverse and pivotal for the Earth's stability perishes, the rest of the ecosystems will be gravely affected by its loss, modifying the Earth as a whole at the end of nature.

6   These nine non-return tipping points are: the Amazon Rainforest, the Arctic Sea Ice, Atlantic Circulation, the Boreal Forest, Coral Reefs, the Greenland Ice Sheet, Permafrost, the West Antarctic Ice Sheet and the Wilkes Basin (Lenton et al., 2019).

References

Ainsworth, Tracy D., Scott F. Heron, Juan Carlos Ortiz, Peter J. Mumby, Alana Grech, Daisie Ogawa, Mark Eakin and William Leggat. 2016. "Climate Change Disables Coral Bleaching Protection on the Great Barrier Reef". *Science* 253, no. 6283: pp. 338-342. DOI: 10.1126/science .aac7125.

Alaimo, Stacy. 2016. *Exposed: Environmental Politics and Pleasures in Posthuman Times*. Minneapolis: University of Minnesota Press.

_____. 2014. "Thinking as the Stuff of the World." *O-Zone: A Journal of Object-Oriented Studies*. 1: pp. 13-21.

Bastian, Michelle. 2017. "Encountering Leatherbacks in multispecies time knots." In *Extinction Studies: Stories of time, death and generations*, edited by Deborah Bird Rose, Thom van Dooren and Matthew Chrulew, 149-185. New York: Columbia University Press.

Bastian, Michelle, and Thom van Dooren. 2017. "Editorial Preface. The New Immortals: Immortality and infinitude in the Anthropocene". *Environmental Philosophy* 14, no. 1: pp. 1-9. DOI: 10.5840/envirophil 20171411.

Bollati, Elena, Cecilia D'Angelo, Rachel Alderdice, Morgan Pratchett, Maren Ziegler & Jörg Wiedenmann. 2020. "Optical Feedback Loop Involving Dinoflagellate Symbiont and Scleractinian Host Drives Colorful Coral Bleaching". *Current Biology* 30, no. 13: pp. 2433-2445. DOI: http://dx.doi.org/10.1016/j.cub.2020.04.055.

Bonilla-Aldana, Katterine, Wilmer E. Villamil-Gómez, Ali A. Rabaan & Alfonso J. Rodríguez-Morales. "A New Viral Zoonosis of Global Concern: Coronavirus COVID-19 Disease in 2019". *Iatreia* 33, no. 2: pp. 107-110.

Crary, Jonathan. 2013. *24/7: Late Capitalism and the Ends of Sleep*. London/New York: Verso Books.

De'ath, Gleen, Katharina E. Fabricius, Hugh Sweatman and Marji Puotinen. 2012. "The 27-Year Decline of Coral Cover on the Great Barrier Reef and its Causes". *PNAS* 109, no. 44: pp. 17995-17999. https://doi.org/10.1073/pnas.1208909109.

DeLoughrey, Elizabeth. 2017. "Submarine Futures of the Anthropocene." *ACLA Forum: Oceanic Routes, Comparative Literature* 69, no. 1: pp. 32-44.

Fothergill, Alastair. 2001. *The Blue Planet*. BBC One.

Glotfelty, Cheryll & Harold Fromm. 1996. *The Ecocriticism Reader: Landmarks in Literary Ecology*. Athens: University of Georgia Press.

Guattari, Félix. 2000. *The Three Ecologies*. First published in 1989. Translated by Ian Pundar and Paul Sutton. London/New Brunswick: The Athlone Press.

Gordon, Timothy, Harry R. Harding, Kathryn E. Wong, Nathan D. Merchant, Mark G. Meekan, Mark I. Cormick, Andrew N. Radford & Stephen D. Simpson. 2018. "Habitat Degradation Negatively Affects Auditory Settlement Behavior of Coral Reef Fishes". *PNAS* 115, no. 20: pp. 5193-5198. DOI: https://doi.org/10.1073/pnas.1719291115.

Fisher, Mark. 2019. *Acid Communism*. London: Repeater Books.

_____. 2009. *Capitalist Realism: Is There No Alternative?*. Hants: O Books.

Fukuyama, Francis. 1992. *The End of History and the Last Man*. New York: Free Press.

Han, Byung-Chul. 2017. *Psychopolitics: Neoliberalism and New Technologies of Power*. London: Verso Books.

Haraway, Donna J. 2008. *When Species Meet*. Minneapolis: University of Minnesota Press.

_____. 1988. "Situated Knowledges: The Science Question in Feminism and the Privilege of Partial Perspective." *Feminist Studies* 14, no. 3: pp. 575-599.

Hayes, Meghan. 2019. *An Oceanic Acid Trip: Forming Planetary Immersion*. MA Thesis. Amsterdam: University of Amsterdam.

Heidegger, Martin. 1989. *Contributions to Philosophy (Of the Event)*. Translated by Richard Rojcewicz & Daniela Vallega-Neu. Indianapolis: Indiana University Press.

Heise, Ursula K. 2016. *Imagining Extinction: The Cultural Meanings of Endangered Species*. Chicago: University of Chicago Press.

Helmreich, Stefan. 2009. *Alien Ocean: Anthropological Voyages in Microbial Seas*. Berkeley & Los Angeles: University of California Press.

Heron, Scott F., Jeffrey A. Maynard, Ruben van Hooidonk, C. Mark Eakin. 2016. "Warming Trends and Bleaching Stress of the World's Coral Reefs 1985-2012". *Scientific Reports* 6: 38402.

Holthaus, Eric. 2014. "Climate Change has 'Permanently' Changed the Great Barrier Reef". Pacific Standard. Accessed 30 January 2021. https://psmag.com/news/climate-change-has-permanently-chang ed-the-great-barrier-reef.

Honeyborne, James & Mark Brownlow. 2017. *Blue Planet II*. BBC One / BBC Earth.

Hughes, Terry P., Michelle L. Barnes, David R. Bellwood, Joshua E. Cinner, Graeme S. Cumming, Jeremy B.C. Jackson, Joanie Kleypas et al. 2017. "Coral Reefs in the Anthropocene". *Nature* 546: pp. 82-90. DOI: 10.1038/nature22901.

Jamail, Dahr. 2017. "Coral Reefs Could All Die Off by 2050". Ecowatch. Accessed 30 January 2021. https://www.ecowatch.com/coral-reef-bleaching-2408656490.html.

Jue, Melody. 2020. *Wild Blue Media: Thinking Through Seawater*. Durham: Duke University Press.

Kohn, Eduardo. 2013. *How Forests Think: Toward and Anthropology Beyond the Human*. Berkeley: University of California Press.

Latour, Bruno. 2018. *Down to Earth: Politics in the New Climatic Regime*. Cambridge: Polity Press.

Lenton, Timothy M., Johan Rockström, Owen Gaffney, Stefan Rahmstorf, Katherine Richardson, Will Steffen, Hans Joachim Schellnhuber. 2019. "Climate Tipping Points—Too Risky to Bet Against". *Nature* 575: pp. 592-595. DOI: https://doi.org/10.1038/d41586-019-03595-0.

Martin, Niall & Mireille Rosello. 2016. "Disorientation: An Introduction". Culture, Theory & Critique 57, no. 1: pp. 1-16. DOI: 10.1080/147357 84.2015.1128675.

Mbembe, Achilles. 2013. *Critique of Black Reason*. Durham: Duke University Press.

McBrien, Justin. 2016. "Accumulating Extinction: Planetary Catastrophism in the Necrocene." In *Anthropocene or Capitalocene?: Nature, History and the Crisis of Capitalism*, edited by Jason W. Moore, pp. 116-137. Oakland: PM Press.

McKibben, Bill. 1989. *The End of Nature*. New York: Random House.

McLeod, Elizabeth, Kenneth Anthony, Andreas Andersson, Roger Beeden, Yimnang Golbu, Joanie Kleypas, Kristy Kroeker et al. 2012. "Preparing to Manage Coral Reefs for Ocean Acidification: Lessons from Coral Bleaching". *Frontiers in Ecology and the Environment* 11, no. 1: pp. 20-27. DOI: https://doi.org/10.1890/110240.

Moore, Jason W. 2016. *Anthropocene or Capitalocene?: Nature, History and the Crisis of Capitalism*. Oakland: PM Press.

Morton, Timothy. 2016. *Dark Ecology: For a Logic of Future Coexistence*. New York: Columbia University Press.

Nixon, Rob. 2011. *Slow Violence and the Environmentalism of the Poor*. Cambridge: Harvard University Press.

Orlowski, Jeff and Larissa Rhodes. 2017. *Chasing Coral*. Netflix

Plumwood, Val. 2002. *Environmental Culture: The Ecological Crisis of Reason*. London/New York: Routledge.

Povinelli, Elizabeth A. 2016. *Geontologies: a Requiem to Late Liberalism*. Durham: Duke University Press.

Rancière, Jacques. 2010. *Dissensus: on Politics and Aesthetics*. London: Bloomsbury Academic.

Readfearn, Graham. 2020. "Great Barrier Reef's third mass bleaching in five years the most widespread yet". *The Guardian*. 6 April 2020. https://www.theguardian.com/environment/2020/apr/07/great-barrier-reefs-third-mass-bleaching-in-five-years-the-most-widespread-ever.

Rockström, Johan, Will Steffen, Kevin Noone, Asa Persson, Stuart III Chapin, Eric Lambin, Timothy M. Lenton et al. 2009. "Planetary Boundaries: Exploring the Safe Operating Space for Humanity". *Ecology and Society* 14, no. 2: 32. https://doi.org/10.5751/ES-03180-140232.

Rose, Deborah Bird. 2012. "Multispecies Knots of Ethical Time." *Environmental Philosophy* 9, no. 1: pp. 127–140. DOI: 10.5840/envirophil2012918.

Sörlin, Sverker. 2012. "Environmental Humanities: Why Should Biologists Interested in the Environment Take the Humanities Seriously?". *Bioscience* 62, no. 9: pp. 788-789. DOI: doi.org/10.1525/bio.2012.62.9.2.

Stockholm Resilience Center. "Planetary Boundaries: An Update". Accessed 15 January 2021. https://www.stockholmresilience.org/research/research-news/2015-01-15-planetary-boundaries---an-update.html.

Thiem, Annika. 2008. *Unbecoming Subjects: Judith Butler, Moral Philosophy and Responsibility*. New York: Fordham University Press.

van Dooren, Thom, Eben Kirksey, Ursula Münster. 2016. "Multispecies Studies: Cultivating Arts of Attentiveness". *Environmental Humanities* 8, no. 1: pp. 1-23.

_____. 2014. "Care". *Environmental Humanities* 5, no. 1: pp. 291-294.

Zabala, Santiago. 2017. *Why Only Art Can Save Us: Aesthetics and The Absence of Emergency*. New York: Columbia University Press.

Žižek, Slavoj. 2006. *The Parallax View*. Cambridge: MIT Press.

7

Asia and Asia*bodh*:
Historicality, Ethics and Jibanananda Das'
"Banalata Sen of Natore"

Jayjit Sarkar

> "Asia is a free-floating signifier."
> Kasian Tejapira, "Democracy"

~~Where~~ When is Asia in the "progressive" history of the World, which in a way also means, the history *of* Europe, the history as it unfurled before the eyes of those standing at the edge of the Eurasian plate and trying to look *afar*? Were they able to look far or is it that their "gaze" could not surpass the diaphragm of the Ural Mountains and the plateaus of Anatolia? The two "land mass" visible from Europe—which are also the immediate "others" of Europe—are the two continents, Asia and Africa: Asia to the east and Africa to the south. These two "land mass" have overwhelmingly shaped and constituted what we understand as Europe and also the way Europe understands itself. The latter's cultural biosphere contains, and sustains on, the "light" of Asia and the "dust" of Africa—where the word "Asia" comes from the Semitic *Asu* meaning "light" and "Africa" from the Phoenician *Afar* meaning "dust". The "light" and "dust" served as the necessary constructs for the so-called progressive movement of Europe from darkness to enlightenment and from barbarism to civilization. The word "Europe" comes from the Sumerian and Semitic *ereb* meaning "darkness". It became obligatory for the Europeans to invent and circulate the darkness and barbarism of these two land masses, Asia and Africa, and in a way "overdetermine" those elements incessantly so that their own bellicosity looks naïve, insignificant, and most importantly, just. How can we, therefore 'provincialize Asia' so that it no more turns again into a transcendental signifier for the world?

Is Asia, then, purely a European construct? The answer is both a "yes" and a "no". The idea of Asia constitutes far more complex phenomena than as it looks from a certain vantage point. On the one hand, Francois Godemont, a French scholar of Asia, refers Asia as "a fantasy seemingly woven from a Baudelaire poem, a melody by Ravel, a short story by Somerset Maugham and a James Ivory film" (Acharya 2010, 32) and on the other, there are thinkers like Okakura, Tagore, Gandhi, Nehru, Sun Yat-sen, Lee Kuan Yew, and many others from Asia who have played an important role in shaping and building different ideas of Asia, most of the time non-Eurocentric, over the course of the period. Their ideas were not necessarily "free of Europe", but rather predominantly different from the colonial "history", the history whose belongingness can be traced back to Europe. Europe, here, can be seen as a territory as well as a process of territorialization; the process of "territorialization" being similar to that of the "civilization" as a process. And then, more recently, there are "Asias" tinged with nationalist agendas and competitive market policies which together now look like a Möbius strip and a formidable "singular" force. This Janus-like Asia is a part of a global phenomenon and a new radical *turn* that the world has taken.

So, whose Asia is it anyway? Amitav Acharya in his "The Idea of Asia" points out not one, not two, but thirteen ways in which Asia can be understood: Asia, Asia-Pacific, Asia Pacific, Asia and the Pacific, Asia/Pacific, East Asia, Eastern Asia, Far East, Greater East Asia, Pacific, Pacific Asia, and goes on to highlight how "power, prosperity, and identity determine which of these names are in vogue" and how "hegemons are especially fond of naming regions after their own interests and spheres of influence" (Acharya 2010, 33). Acharya, in his other work "Asia is Not One" classifies Asia into imperialist Asia, nationalist Asia, universalist Asia, regionalist Asia, and exceptionalist Asia (Acharya 2010, 1002-03).

Many trace "the Asia consciousness" (Asia*bodh*) or the "awakening" of Asia back to the Russo-Japanese war of 1904-05 in which an Asian island country defeated a European giant. The military victory of Japan over Russia was in many ways comparable to that of the indigenous army of Ethiopia defeating Italy in the

Battle of Adwa (1896). This led to a surge of Asian-ism, the reverberation of which was felt throughout the continent and where, for the first time, people started associating themselves with their Asian identity. This also sowed the seed of a precarious and yet possible pan-Asia and paved the way for Japanese imperialism and Japan-centric Asian-ism. The latter propelled the idea of a Greater East Asia Co-Prosperity Sphere and led to catastrophic results like that of the formation of Manchukuo in China. If "Asia *is* One," then as Okakura Tenshin recommends, the underlying unitary principle of *that* Asia is Japan. This whole idea of Japan being the centre of Asia continued till the end of the Second World War, till Japan became the victim of its own aggressive policies in Asia-Pacific and was decimated. Nevertheless, Okakura was one of the first thinkers who believed firmly and concomitantly promoted a pan-Asia network. He begins his treatise *The Ideals of the East* with these now-famous lines:

> Asia is one. The Himalayas divide, only to accentuate, two mighty civilisations, the Chinese with its communism of Confucius, and the Indian with its individualism of the Vedas. But not even the snowy barriers can interrupt for one moment that broad expanse of love for the Ultimate and Universal, which is the common thought-inheritance of every Asiatic race, enabling them to produce all the great religions of the world, and distinguishing them from those maritime peoples of the Mediterranean and the Baltic, who love to dwell on the Particular, and to search out the means, not the end, of life. (Okakura 2012, 1)

But his thesis of "connecting Asia" was also proto-imperialist in nature as he went on to justify and explain Japan as "a museum of Asiatic civilization" and how "the history of Japanese art [...] becomes the history of Asiatic ideals — the beach where each successive wave of Eastern thought has left its sand ripple as it beat against the national consciousness" (3). Mark Ravinder Frost even points out how Sister Nivedita in her "Introduction" to *The Ideals of the East* "was at pains to balance Okakura's claim that Japan represented the perfection of Asian aesthetics..." (258). Japan bulldozing one South East Asian country after another was more in the line of the European *zeitgeist* and far from those Asian non-hegemonic ideals especially those propounded by Tagore and

Gandhi in the first half of the twentieth-century. Notwithstanding his Japan-centric discourses on Asia, it was, in fact, from Okakura, explains Tagore, that he comprehended the concept of the "Asiatic mind".

In Okakura, we find an anticolonial nationalism and a reverse imperialism which turned into an epidemic, especially in the case of Japan, in the first half of the twentieth-century. Such "strategic essentialism", to borrow a phrase from Gayatri Spivak, with turning the table upside down also reinforces and revitalizes the binaries of the colonial hegemons in the form of "new world" hegemonies — where the new order becomes merely a palindrome of the old order (where the n-e-w is merely a d-l-o). It becomes what it was not supposed to become; it turned what it started in the first-place resisting and revolting against. Such Asian-ism is a product of what Amartya Sen would call "dialectics of the captivated mind," here in case, anti-West/ West. Sen writes: "The dialectics of the captivated mind can lead to a deeply biased and parasitically reactive self-perception. Also, this singular mode of thinking can take the form of trying to 'get even'… and of seeking justice in the contemporary world by invoking the past and present offenses of the Western world" (Sen 2006, 91). Partha Chatterjee in his *The Nation and Its Fragments* also points out some of the fundamental predicaments of the anticolonial nationalism and reverse imperialism in the following manner:

> [It] creates its own domain of sovereignty within colonial society well before its political battle with the imperial power. It does this by dividing the world of social institutions and practices into two domains — the material and the spiritual. The material is domain of the "outside", of the economy and of statecraft, of science and technology, a domain where the West had proved its superiority and the East had succumbed. In this domain, then, Western superiority had to be acknowledged and its accomplishments carefully studied and replicated. The spiritual, on the other hand, is an "inner" domain bearing the "essential" marks of cultural identity. The greater one's success in imitating Western skills in the material domain, therefore, the greater the need to preserve the distinctiveness of one's spiritual culture. This formula is, I think, a fundamental feature of anticolonial nationalisms in Asia and Africa. (Chatterjee 1993, 6)

If, for Okakura, Asia stands for the Universal and the Ultimate, and Europe Particular, then for Swami Vivekananda, Asia stands for spirituality and Europe science (materiality). It is, again, the difference of the history of Asia from the seemingly linear and progressive history of Europe which makes Montesquieu to understand Europe as "progress" and Asia as "stagnation". Europe is too homogeneous and there has been too much of homogeneity within the (rival) discourses within the continent so much so that the episteme which came out of Europe and are distinguishably European, *a la* nationalism and racism, have always been meant for division and categorization — the main purpose was to establish the *differences*, epistemologically. Asia, on the other hand, has always been too heterogeneous and the discourses within Asia so varied that the main efforts have been to find commonalities: one such discourse being Asia is spiritual and the "Asian way" being the "Daoist" way. Since geologically there is not much of a difference between Europe and Asia as both are sitting on the same Eurasian plate, so it became almost a necessity for the Europeans to establish the cultural "otherity" of Asia and the difference of Asia from Europe; and vice-versa for the Asians in the twentieth-century. In the twenty-first century, the scenario has changed: the West is as much a market for Asia as Asia for the West.

"The need to differentiate from the West" as Amartya Sen diagnoses the essential problem with many of the "Asianisms", "is clearly visible in [the] postcolonial dialectic, and it is also easy to see the attraction for many Asians of the claim that Asia has something much better than Europe" (Sen 2006, 94). Tagore was always aware of this hermeneutical impasse. As early as 1908, he starts talking about what Sugata Bose calls "different universalism" which "shares significant common ground with the meaning of vernacular cosmopolitanism as evoked by Homi Bhabha or local cosmopolitanism as enunciated by Enseng Ho or rooted cosmopolitanism as described by Anthony Appiah [...]" (Bose 2010, 97-98). His idea of Asia was never at the cost of the other and had always been an integral part of his *Visvabodh* ("world consciousness"). In his treatise on Indian history and *Itihasbodh*, that is, historical consciousness, *BharaterItihas – Kader Itihas*, he even goes on to the extent of suggesting that "the English [like the Moslems] had become an inevitable part of this history and this country.... [T]hat India must, through greatness and the universality of her culture, make even the West a part of her civilization without being afraid of being absorbed by it" (Bose 2011, 122). This is Tagore's radical hospitality towards the other which is definitely not at the cost of the self. He acknowledges the historicity, the "strength, nature and need", of every country and how it deals with it, is different from others. But at the same time, he also envisions how "the lamp that they will each carry on their path to progress will converge to illuminate the common ray of knowledge...." (quoted in "Rabindranath Tagore and Asian Universalism", 1). He was also aware of the shadow of nationalism, the narrow domestic wall, lurking beneath the lamps: he was as much critical of the surge of nationalism in America as that of Japan. Japan's imperialistic desires and designs were antithetical to the "Asians values" which Tagore characterizes as "beautiful" and "delicious" (*madhur*).

The predominant discourses in the idea of Asia can be characterized in terms of three stages and two "shifts" over the course of the period: firstly, the imperialistic and nationalistic Asia (1905 onwards) which emerged in the first half of the twentieth-century with the imperialist tendencies of Japan and different anti-colonial movements throughout the continent; secondly, the Asia we find after the Colombo plan and the Bandung conference (1955) when the predominant strategy was how to survive the Cold War and how to deal with the existing power blocs; and thirdly, Asia in a post-globalised state where the general discourse is the "rise of Asia" or to be more exact, the so-called rise of Asian giants as market players: Asia has always been a potent market, but now the shift is towards Asia being potent enough to *create* a market.

Apart from these overwhelming modern ideas of Asia — that is, Asia of (anti)colonial and postcolonial times — Brij Tankha and Madhavi Thampi in their *Narratives in Asia: From India, Japan and China* also remind us of an "earlier genealogy", that is, Asia of the pre-colonial times which now finds hard to voice because of the overwhelming discourse that it is a colonial construct. The "earlier genealogy" of connecting-Asia entails the sacred geography of the continent and the inter-civilizational pilgrimages, trade routes on land and sea, the spread of Hinduism, later Buddhism and latest Islam, the ancient centres of learning and the scholarship exchanges between them, etcetera. In all these ancient and medieval phenomena too, we find an idea of Asia which is still pertinent today in our understanding of the region but are ignored unflinchingly under the guise of being archaic and not contemporary. Tankha and Thampi point out that the ideas of Asia are an eclectic mix, compound of developments both "premodern and modern." If we try to understand Asia majorly from the perspective of "modernity", especially in terms of capital and modern nation-state, we will be ignoring one of the most important dimensions of the idea of Asia which predates the advent of "modernity", that is, "traditional regional relations" amongst various parts: the deep sutures which are unlike anything globalization entails. This is the Ur-Asia—the "Asia" before Asia; the "Asia" before it was (re)constructed by the Western eyes. And this again, like sahitya, should not be misconstrued as another form of nativism but more in the form of "going back" which Ranajit Guha talks about while discussing Tagore's idea of historical consciousness in *History at the Limits of World History* as a "call for recognition by going back to the *suchana*, the obscure and yet undisclosed source where [the] experiences are still coiled in the incipience of sheer possibility" (Guha 2002, 78). The Ur-Asia is that Tagorean *suchana* and as that "sheer possibility".

While challenging and looking for other alternatives to the existing knowledge production and dissemination and its concomitant liaison with the geopolitical (re)formations and the hypothetical "indisputability of the historic-geopolitical pairing" of the world, Kuan-Hsing Chen proposes "Asia as method" as a critical arrangement, which he defines as:

> …using the idea of Asia as an imaginary anchoring point, societies in Asia can become each other's points of reference, so that the understanding of the self may be transformed, and subjectivity rebuilt. On this basis, the diverse historical experiences and rich social practices of Asia may be mobilized to

provide alternative horizons and perspectives. This method of engagement
... has the potential to advance a different understanding of world history.

At the same time, the formulation of Asia as method is also an attempt to
move forward on the tripartite problematic of decolonization,
deimperialization, and de-cold war. (Chen 2010, 212)

Kuan-Hsing Chen's "Asia as method", which uses Takeuchi
Yoshimi's article of the same title as a starting point, put forwards
the Asia of lived-experience as a new point of reference to
understand this part of the world which we call Asia. He draws on
"Asia" to comprehend different Asias and inter-Asias, and in doing
so, catapults Europe out from being a universal category — the
yardstick with which we understand everything — and being the
epitome against which we measure ourselves. He in a way also
impels and refuels Dipesh Chakraborty's project of
"provincializing" but with a subtle difference; as he himself points
out cynically, "after Europe is provincialized, can we directly talk
to each other, bypassing Europe and America? To provincialize
Europe is a process that will loosen but not change the structure of
the dialogue" and calls for a "more active process" (Chen 2010, 219).

Asia as method is self-reflexive in nature. It conceives Asia
with its historicality and facticity, away from the history which is
sipped in and understood through European modernity. The latter
is a tautology which behaves or rather is made to behave as the
great homogenizer, the universal background against which
different indigeneities across the world are analyzed and
understood. It is the universal and transcendental based on which
all other things are particularized. But the irony is, as Naoki Sakai
and later Dipesh Chakrabarty draw attention to, the fact that
Europe or the West is as particular, as provincial, and as a product
of historical processes as Asia is or as others are. The fact that the
West is the sole repository of modernity and all different
ramifications of modernity and the fact that the others are either
"below" or "lagging behind" or "shadow", were discursively
produced. The hegemony of the same has produced something
which Arif Dirlik calls "fatal distraction" where the West has
become over the years some sort of fetish for the non-West. "The

West" as Chen points out, "has become the object of both desire and resentment" (Chen 2010, 217). Asia as method is, at the same time, aware of the pitfalls of particularism. Sakai cites the example of Japanese uniqueness *nihonjin-ron* (the discourse of a particular Japanese-ness as depicted in Japanese historiography *kôkokushikan*) and states its fallacies: "Its insistence on Japan's peculiarity and difference from the West embodies a nagging urge to see the self from the viewpoint of the other. But this is nothing but the positing of Japan's identity in Western terms, which in return establishes the centrality of the West as the universal point of reference" (Sakai 1989, 105). Asia as method is conscious of the paradox that is universalism and particularism: as these do not form a cacophony but reciprocate in a fashion that strengthens each-other.

The Asia question is not free from the question of historiography. The "Asia", as we understand it today, is a result of narratological ploy: as it has been narrated *from* and narrated *by*, to us. "It has had", Ranajit Guha writes in the context of the Raj "the effect of replacing the indigenous narratologies of precolonial times by ones that are typically modern and western" (Guha 2002, 5). It becomes then an imperative, in Guha's own phrase, to look "over the fence" for other possible narratologies different from that of historiography and the way the latter arranges itself with historicality. And we argue here, like Guha, that one such alternative or possibility can be found in literary narratives. we also argue here, like Tagore, that it is the poet who can help us in our doing of history of Asia, significantly different from that of an *aitihasik pandit* ("academic historian"). It is the poet's *sense* of history which is going to give us a possible Asia — the poet's Asia — as it is lived: as an Asia we have been living and experiencing as an everyday reality. In our search for Asia as lived-experience in literature, we will look at a poem sipped in various and often contradictory experiences of being concrete and obscure, exotic and mundane, spatial and temporal, familiar and exotic, at the same time.

The following is one of the most popular poems in Bangla literature "Banalata Sen of Natore" by Jibanananda Das (1899-1954):

For aeons have I roamed the roads of the earth
From the seas of Ceylon to the straits of Malaya
I have journeyed, alone, in the enduring night,
And down the dark corridor of time I have walked
Through mist of Bimbisara, Asoka, darker Vidarbha.
Round my weary soul the angry waves still roar;
My only peace I knew with Banalata Sen of Natore.

Her hair was dark as night in Vidisha;
Her face the sculpture of Sravasti.
I saw her, as a sailor after the storm
Rudderless in the sea, spies of a sudden
The grass-green heart of the leafy island.
'Where were you so long?' she asked, and more
With her bird's-nest eyes, Banalata Sen of Natore.

As the footfalls of dew comes evening;
The raven wipes the smell of a warm sun
From its wings; the world's noises die.
And in the light of fireflies the manuscript
Prepares to weave the fables of night;
Every bird is home, every river reached the ocean.
Darkness remains; and time for Banalata Sen. (Das 2006, 1)

Published in 1942, the poem, quite succinctly presents a vast trajectory in terms of space and time — indicating the coalescence of the strange and the distant with the near and the familiar — as part of a single continuum. All history and all geography of the subcontinent, it seems, have led to this specific woman Banalata Sen from a very specific town in the erstwhile colonial Bengal "Natore". The poet has deliberately erased the personal whereabouts of this woman and discusses rather of how she is an embodiment of everything that has culminated so far over the course of the period across the length and breadth of mainly southern part of the continent. Jibanananda Das was famous for playing with proper nouns and the so-called Banalata Sen of this mofussil town called Natore (the then part of Rajshahi district of undivided Bengal) entails no exception. Such specificities in a way, as a reader is caught up in those specificities, make the poem more obscure. Banalata Sen is the metaphor for the end or the destination — a "home" for the birds and an "ocean" for the rivers — where all journeys end, and quite naturally, also where a new journey awaits.

The birds will take rest so that they can be ready for the next flight and the rivers will so that they become clouds. Is she then a microcosm of everything that has taken place in the past and everything that will take place in the future? She is not only the "latest" but also the "primal." She is a moment in time and a dot in map — a mere point in the endless series of points which stands for the end of all that has happened and the beginning of all that will happen.

The juxtaposition of the "here" with "there" and "now" with "then" and the acausal relationship which exists between them complicates the whole idea of microcosm and macrocosm, especially by blurring the boundary which exists between the two. The "time of Banalata Sen" — the "now" — is both primal and latest: it is something which the poet already "knew": "My only peace I knew with Banalata Sen of Natore"; she is the *already*, the primal, the source of/in all later experiences. She is, from where the poet departed and also later arrives at the end of the journey. The seed of this time-now was always, already there in the "aeons" of traversing. The traces of those "aeons" can also be found in, as it culminates into, the singularity of Banalata Sen of Natore. Similarly, all exotic and distant (read, precolonial and ancient) described in the poem leads the poet to something of which he was already familiar and vice-versa, that is, he could re-cognize the familiar only after reckoning with the strange and the sublime. This circuitous nature of the poem is more than just narratological; it is symptomatic of a fresh understanding of writing in general and history in particular. The precolonial and premodern sutures are invoked here in order to describe and highlight the locationality or, to be more exact historicality of Banalata Sen and her mofussil town of Natore which was only established during the colonial period, gives us a different approach to this telltale — a history different from the pages of historiography.

The "earlier genealogies", the primal sutures of ancient trade routes of/through Ceylon, Malaya and Vidisha and the spread of Buddhism — and the history and geography associated with such phenomena — with the help of which Das stitches the narrative of the poem gives us a different picture of Asia as different from the colonial (also modernity's) gaze. The history of that *time*, which includes Bimbisara, Asoka, Vidisha, the routes of Ceylon and Malaya, and the history of that *day*, which includes, the dew, the fireflies and the raven, find equal valency in the history which leads up to the modern incarnation called Banalata Sen of Natore. Something similar can be said of that of Asia. Of what constitutes Asia — of what makes Asia, Asia — are not only the happenings of that time but also of that day (read, every day) or as what Tagore would call the latter: *sedinkar itihas*. A pundit of history would be concerned about the former and would gladly ignore the latter. A poet, on the other, is constituted by "a matter of seeing in a way... [which the poet can] claim to have been uniquely his own" (Guha 2002, 77), the large part of what constitutes *sedin karitihas* ("the history of that day") — the history as it unfurls before *my* eyes — the history which *I am* also a part of.

There are two Asias: one, the history of which the historians have recorded and now narrate at ease and, two the historicality of "what is unknown or not quite explicit" (77). The first is something we get hold of through historiography in its various forms, whereas the second, stands out as "the incipience of sheer possibility" (78). The latter, as Guha points out "requires no evidence of actualization, nor even of a beginning, but simply the recognition of something yet to be" (78). He illustrates:

> What does a possibility that is merely incipient amount to? It amounts in this instance to tracing the formation of a creative individuality [different from that of an academic historian] back to its roots in a region of primal experience. But that experience, however primal, is by no means inert. It has a life of its own and a movement characterized by a certain towardness, although towards what is not yet clear. It is, in short, a tendency that does not know where it is going. However, insofar as it is going somewhere at all, it is a movement in time. It is thus a tendency already informed by historicality. (79)

Das' "Banalata Sen of Natore" traces back Asia to its *suchana* when it was a mere possibility — the Asia-as-sheer-possiblity; when and where the "experience" we now call Asia was "still coiled in the incipience of sheer possibility" (78). All historical objects in the poem have a name but peculiarly enough are all encircled with a halo of mystery, vagueness and obscurity and more than just mere being "exotic", it signifies "a certain towardness, although towards what is not clear" (79). How the gray world of Bimbisara and Asoka, the elusive cities of Vidisha and Vidharba, of Sravasti and of the cinnamon island and the maritime adventures hinted in the poem end up being mysteriously at the doorstep of Natore's Banalata Sen is not clear. Even how the "non-historical" phenomena in the poem relate themselves to her, is not clear. These, as it appears, are "sources" (Tagorean *suchana*) not "causes" and as these phenomena are not following the logic of causality, they possess a historicality which is different from that of historiography — a historicality which is "ontologically totally different from factual occurrence[s]" (quoted in Guha 2002, 79). It is the history of a being "with the being of those beings which it encounters within its own world" (79). This is the lived-history, the history of Asia as it was experienced — as it was lived by those who lived in it; something which is *beyond* and can never be accomplished by "Asia-as-object" historiography.

There is a sense of *mineness* in the way the poet has roamed, saw, and experienced across different mythistorical phenomena being unfurled before his eyes. There is a sense of *mineness* in his weariness — the weariness with which he has looked at those phenomena. He has experienced and understood the factuality of the "object-historical" with the weariness and fatigue of a traveler traveling for long. The experiences of that day, which includes experiencing the sound of the dew, a raven scrubbing off the heat of the sun from the wings, the colour of the fireflies in dark et al have a particular way of "seeing it as mine" and in this poet's mineness, there are "the images that will be distinguish its vision from that of others, the words that will be recognizably different from those produced by other voices" (81). By the same token, quite appropriately, it also provides us with the material for creatively writing itself into the "history which we ourselves are" (quoted in Guha 2002, 81). The factuality of the object-historical conventions of history of Asia then, as Guha points out while taking a cue from Heidegger, is different from facticity of being-in-the-world, that is, being of Asia as experienced by the beings (of the Asians) involved with it.

Jibanananda Das' "Banalata Sen of Natore," thus, presents us with an Asia*bodh* or Asia consciousness which is ontologically different from the "Asia" we find in historiography—an Asia as lived-experience—as we have been living for aeons and will do so for aeons. This is different from the Asia in academic histories—histories which were written when we were "inside" that histories. This is the being-in-the-asia and being-with-the-asia which becomes fundamental here and need to be taken into consideration in any possible discussion on the idea of Asia, whether modern or pre-/post-modern, whether colonial or pre-/post-colonial, whether historical or pre-/post-historical. But since these categories are characteristically European and reinforces the discursive practices of Eurocentrism as a form of universalism, can we do away with these practices altogether? In doing so, we need to challenge and seek alternatives to the current episteme.

References

Acharya, Amitav. 2010. "Asia is not One." *The Journal of Asian Studies* 69, no. 4: pp. 1001-1013.

_____. 2010. "The Idea of Asia." *Asia Policy*, no. 9: pp. 32-39.

Bose, Sugata. 2010. "Different Universalisms, Colorful Cosmopolitanisms: The Global Imagination of the Colonized." In *Cosmopolitan Thought Zones: South Asia and the Global Circulation of Ideas*, edited by Sugata Bose & Kris Manjapra. UK: Palgrave Macmillan.

_____. "Rabindranath Tagore and Asian Universalism." Accessed on 22 March 2021. http://research.gold.ac.uk/id/eprint/20908/23/Rabin dranath%20Tagore%20and%20Asian%20Universalism.pdf.

Bose, Sugata and Ira Pande. 2011. "Tagorean Universalism and Cosmopolitanism." *India International Centre Quarterly* 38, no.1: pp. 2-17. https://www.jstor.org/stable/44733613.

Chatterjee, Partha. 1993. *The Nation and Its Fragments: Colonial and Postcolonial Histories*. New Jersey: Princeton University Press.

Chen, Kuan-hsing. 2010. *Asia as Method: Toward Deimperialization*. Durham: Duke University Press.

Das, Jibanananda. 2006. *Jibanananda Das: Selected Poems*. Translated by C. D. Gupta. Gurgaon: Penguin Books.

Frost, Mark R. 2010. "That Great Ocean of Idealism: Calcutta, the Tagore Circle, and the Idea of Asia, 1900-1920." In *Indian Ocean Studies: Cultural, Social, and Political* Perspectives, edited by Shanti Moorthy and Ashraf Jamal. London: Routledge.

Guha, Ranajit. 2002. *History at the Limit of World History*. New York: Columbia University Press.

Okakura, Kakuzo. 2012. *The Ideals of the East: With Special Reference to the Art of Japan*. Tokyo: Tuttle Publishing.

Sakai, Naoki. 1989. "Modernity and Its Critique: The Problem of Universalism and Particularism." In *Post-Contemporary Interventions: Postmodernism and Japan*, edited by Masao Miyoshi & Harry Harootunian. Durham: Duke University Press.

Sen, Amartya. 2006. *Identity and Violence: The Illusion of Destiny*. London: Penguin Books.

Tankha Brij and Madhavi Thampi. 2005. *Narratives of Asia: From India, Japan and China*. New Delhi: Sampark.

8

Filling the "Empty" Space between the Natural World and Humans: Environmentalism, Non-Human Animal Rights, and Broken Promises in *Holes*

Rachel L. Carazo

Children's and young adult literature often provide social commentary about a range of important topics, including race, gender, ethnicity, and environmental issues. In particular, and of interest to this essay, are critical discourses about the natural world, which require more nuanced contemporary evaluations, as many studies on children's learning and exposure to print and digital media demonstrate, since these processes emphasize "the importance of children's literature in the assimilation of values and instilling of an ideological infrastructure which will become a way of life."[1] Yet the progression of interest in environmental studies, while growing in complexity, have often focused on trajectories that are human-centered and lacking of the interdisciplinary nature that Timothy Clark finds to be so important in contemporary environmental studies, especially since "[m]ost criticism today is contextual, aiming to situate a text in a cultural or cultural-historical context"[2] rather than using multiple theoretical perspectives.

Nevertheless, the kinds of integral interrelationships, especially interspecies and inter-object relationships, that appear in one late-twentieth-century novel—Louis Sachar's Newbery Medal winning work, *Holes* (1998)—allow for an interdisciplinary look at environmental theories in context. In the work, a group of boys, which includes Stanley Yelnats (whose nickname is Caveman) and Zero (whose full name is Hector Zeroni), finds itself digging holes and looking for, as they only discover later, a lost treasure. As these young men learn how to get along with one another and rediscover the meaning of family, the truth about what happened to the environment begins to emerge. Specifically, only once a respect for the environment as well as nonhuman others emerges in (Camp) Green Lake can the landscape heal. Yet this regeneration is not accomplished simply through Stanley's negation of the curse brought down upon his ancestor, Elya Yelnats, but through his recognition of and interrelationships with the environment that are required during the process.

Thus, simply perceiving Stanley and Zero as the heroes is not enough; neither is it enough to deem Kate, who becomes the anti-heroine Kissin' Kate Barlow as she avenges the murders of Sam and Mary Lou (a donkey), as the primary (human) way in which vengeance can be taken on humans who have broken their promises and caused destruction: instead, the environmental boundaries, formations, and nonhuman entities (both living and inanimate) take similar actions. In fact, the environment enacts vengeance as well as offers avenues for healing, both of which are necessary for the process to turn out so well, for, as the landscape around (Camp) Green Lake has already demonstrated, it *can* and *will* punish human errors against it and innocent others.

There are few published studies on Sachar's award-winning novel: Annette Wannamaker (2006) focuses on masculinity, finding that *Holes* "often treats feminine traits, symbols, and characters as frightening, disgusting, or excessive aspects — like the gaping holes in the landscape or the cruel Warden — that need to be filled in, covered over, silenced, or expelled;"[3] Pat Pinsent (2002) focuses on fairy tale motifs in the novel, finding that the narrative's mix of "fantasy and realism [...] does not overtax the reader's credulity, but rather endows the novel with a positive message about the qualities of the human spirit,"[4] thus, like Wannamaker, taking a human-centered approach. Kirsten Møllegaard (2010) maintains this anthropocentric theme with her essay, "Haunting and History in Louis Sachar's *Holes*," but she does bring in some aspects of place that account for her analysis, which finds that *Holes* "simultaneously deconstructs and infuses the notoriously 'empty' landscapes of the West with specters of racial violence, rebellious women, and Wild West legends."[5]

However, these essays do not focus on environmental theories in great detail; neither do they give much agency to the environment and entities that exist within it in their own right, instead perceiving that "[t]he earth has no cultural meaning in itself, however many forms of politics—romantic, totalitarian, conservative, anarchist—may be projected upon it."[6] Thus, examining the novel based on three primary characteristics—(1) the symbolism of feet and promises, (2) violence against the 'Romantic' environment, which consists of interracial and interspecies love, and (3) issues of environmental 'consumption,' which is connected to the themes of onions and yellow-spotted lizards—and how these aspects intersect with multiple environmental theories, gives a degree of agency back to the landscape. Moreover, through the effort, a new, posthuman interpretation of the narrative emerges that credits the landscape and non-human animals as well as the humans in resolving the story's conflicts. Consequently, whether the (Camp) Green Lake is marked by greenery or holes, it still maintains its agential integrity even though the humans toiling within it have different experiences. And only when the interrelationships between humans, nonhumans, *and* the environment are re-aligned does the landscape "recover," making the environment a prominent and unyielding character throughout the work.

An Overview of Environmental Scholarship in Context

As studies about the environment have become more and more popular, many writers and scientists have relied heavily on labeling as a way to convey how the natural world can or should be viewed as well as what trajectories scholars should take when evaluating literature, non-human animals, and human relations with the natural world. In the case of *Holes*, the most prominent examples of ecocritical themes include Romanticism, ecological justice, non-human animal rights, and issues of consumption as they relate to the natural world.

Romanticism

First, there is the importance of Romanticism. As a theory exemplified by writers and artists like William Wordsworth, William Blake, Samuel Taylor Coleridge, and Caspar David Friedrich, Romanticism functions based on the idea that individuals, their emotions, and their creative impulses serve as central human experiences.[7] In addition, children/youth are important figures in this perspective, since, as Dobrin and Kidd reminds readers, "there is the belief that children are innocent and/or virtuous."[8] Thus, when applied to the environment, Romanticism can give the natural world an innocent, surreal quality that nevertheless maintains its "self-organising, dynamic, creative, vital, organic and or a living whole."[9] As a result, the environment is an integral force in and of itself as well as in relation to the living beings and inanimate objects that comprise it.

Moreover, the link between the figure of the boy (i.e. Romantic child) and the mature adult also features as an aspect of Romanticism. In *Holes*, Stanley is this "boy-child" who is innocent of the crime regarding the shoes, but nevertheless "guilty" in terms of the family curse. Thus, his lack of self-confidence and directionless trajectory are eventually reconciled with his growth, which parallels Roger Cox's idea that "Romanticism sought to heal the relationship between child and adult—that is to say the relationship between the child we were and the adult we have become—which the Romantics believed had been broken by the modernising drive of industrial capitalism."[10] Stanley's victimization by shoes (which are, as he learns much later, thrown by Zero), symbols of modern capitalism, can therefore be seen as the impetus that allows for his connection between his youth, which continues despite his maturation, and the breaking of the curse. A similar assessment can also be made of Zero, who has stolen, but who remains a figure of innocence due to his separation from his mother and his good personality.

Lastly, the idea of romantic love cannot be removed from the discussion since the primary (and tragic) relationship between (Kissin') Kate Barlow and (Onion) Sam is, indeed, a romantic, sensualized one. Their love for each other is presented as being natural and true. They are both good-hearted people, whose love is foiled by the depicted evils of consumerist society, which is embodied in Trout Walker, the rich resident of Green Lake who can buy modern gadgets and always flaunts them. Moreover, the fact that Walker's family curse, like the Yelnats and Zeroni ones, continues through to the Warden, reminds readers that, like everlasting love, the "the aesthetic richness of our Romantic past shapes art and culture today,"[11] for the remnants of Kate and Sam's romance continue to persist in material forms throughout the contemporary sections of the novel.

Ecological Justice

A second important ecocritical perspective that intertwines with the Romantic in *Holes* is the idea of ecological justice, which *The Environmental Justice Reader* (2002) defines as "the right of all people to share equally in the benefits bestowed by a healthy environment [...] the places in which we live, work, play, and worship."[12] Thus, according to this definition, the humans in an environment should be able to benefit from and live well within the setting that comprises the natural and surrounding world. Nevertheless, the political or organizational goals in the environment are also comprised in this theory since, as Freeland and Gordon explain, "it reflects the absolute goals of achieving a sustainable environment which addresses both primary and secondary concerns (human and general environment)."[13] As a result, these "goals" appear to exist outside of simply human concerns, making it a stronger case for humans to have a better relationship with the environment and all living beings within it.

The reality in *Holes* that Stanley, Zero, and his fellow diggers are plagued by a harsh environment; must depend on the "hierarchy" of the Warden, Mr. Sir, and Mr. Pendanski to bring them water in the middle of the day; and find that "ownership" of certain spaces — for example, "[t]he Warden owns the shade"[14] — is unequal indicates that ecocritical justice does not exist in Camp Green Lake. Moreover, in Elya's storyline, his mobility gives him control over natural resources from which Madame Zeroni cannot benefit because she is missing a foot. Access is therefore limited by concepts of ableism. Thus, only certain characters appear to control natural resources, which makes environmental justice a critical paradigm to consider.

The intergenerational nature of the families in the novel also fits with this concept of equality and equal usage of natural resources. According to Clark, in many cultures, there is the idea that "if full environmental justice requires that a duty to future generations and to non-human life informs contemporary decision-making, then the conception of those 'rights' held by living people must shift accordingly."[15] Therefore, justice is not conceived of in terms of *one* generation of a family; it is conceived of as concerning *multiple* generations.[16] As a result, the curses that affect the Yelnats, Zeroni, and Walker families, which are propagated in particular by Elya Yelnats and Trout Walker, are indicators of injustices against the natural world, and they must be, in terms of the novel, propitiated.

Nevertheless, many of these definitions of ecocritical justice are human-focused, which is problematic in Sachar's novel. In the perspective of some scholars, "nature is not an agent, a being able to act with the reciprocity one would expect of an alter ego. Law is always for men, and it is for men that trees or whales can become objects of a form of respect tied to legislation – not the reverse."[17] Considerations that the environment has no agency, cannot find ways to correct the missteps of humans, and does not perceive any kind of "law" remains an dysfunctional idea in *Holes*, in which the very *nature* of the story includes the opposite notion: the environment, which includes humans, nonhumans, and objects, can and does exert a corrective force resembling justice and the law on several occasions.

Nonhuman Rights

The term "environment" often refers to the landscape or vegetation in many theories, thus leaving out or, at least, rendering invisible the nonhuman animals that are present in the space and dependent on ideas of justice and ethics that affect the rest of the natural world. Yet Peter Singer's seminal work, *Animal Liberation: The Definitive Classic of the Animal Movement* (1975), emphasizes how nonhuman animals should be offered equal consideration as humans when their lives and wellbeing are under discussion. Moreover, based on Arne Naess's deep ecology, "to kill another creature is in some sense an act of violence against oneself."[18] These ideas therefore indicate that the treatment of nonhuman animals is and always should be an inherent factor when considering the environment in a narrative.

Thus, the treatment of nonhuman animals in *Holes*, such as Mary Lou (Sam's donkey), Elya's pig, and the yellow-spotted lizards, provides evidence that this theory, among the others, remains a relevant paradigm functioning in the novel that cannot be overlooked. Mary Lou is given equal consideration by Kate when Kate feeds her; according to the narrator, "Whenever [...Kate] bought onions, she always bought an extra one or two and would let Mary Lou eat them out of her hand."[19] Also, Sam's common refusal of a tip permits the 'extra' money to be used to buy onions for Mary Lou. Sam tells Mrs. Tennyson, a woman whom he has assisted, "I don't take charity [...] [b]ut if you want to buy a few extra onions for Mary Lou, I'm sure she'd appreciate it,"[20] highlighting how this theory functions at its best in the novel. Nevertheless, equal consideration, for example, has a darker side when Trout Walker has Sam killed. Because Mary Lou is Sam's constant companion and apparent equal, the donkey is also killed at the same time, indicating that she is as strong of a representative of Kate's love toward Sam and equally important when Walker intends to hurt Kate.

There are also examples of mistreatment or neglect of nonhumans that factor into Sachar's novel; and, most importantly in the context of the story, the way in which humans treat other people appears to be the way in which they treat nonhumans. For example, Elya does the wrong thing with Madame Zeroni less from malice than from a sense of distraction and neglect. He treats his pig in a similar way; even though he invested his time and effort toward the pig's growth, he abandons it just as easily to its fate with

Myra's father and Igor Barkov, Myra's suitor, as he does Madame Zeroni. On the other hand, the Warden and Mr. Sir, who do not treat other people very well, also kill and shoot at nonhumans, especially the yellow-spotted lizards. Thus, nonhuman animal rights and issues of mistreatment and neglect are important signs about the nature of the characters involved and the strength of the bonds that exist between them: characters, like Kate and Sam, as well as Stanley and Zero, have more respect for nonhumans than other characters, thus making their bonds stronger, more equal, and more tolerant.

Anthropomorphism

Another issue that can be connected to nonhuman animal rights involves uses of anthropomorphism, which is "the attribution of human qualities or characteristics to nonhuman entities."[21] Generally, animal studies scholars support viewing the expressions and activities of nonhuman animals through their own subjectivities, rather than through human ones.[22] Nevertheless, in literature, there are times when the device is used to make a point in the narrative or to highlight the good or bad aspects of someone's character. Thus, at the beginning of *Holes*, when Stanley explains how humans have inaccurately described and perceived certain aspects of the yellow-spotted lizards, he is addressing a degree of anthropomorphism, which inherently indicates his good character.[23] Such a tactic fits with Kim-Pong Tam's (2014) "findings [that] highlight the potency of anthropomorphism in mobilizing conservation efforts, and the role of efficacy in how people respond to other global, modern crises."[24] As a result, anthropomorphism, while widely seen as a detriment to nonhuman entities since it imposes human agency and emotions upon their own, nevertheless has wider uses that can indicate the closeness or respect that particular humans have for the natural world.

Consumption

The last concern connected with environmentalism and ecocriticism is consumption. As the material needs of people increase, grow more complex, and depend more on technological processes that often infuse the natural world with toxins and refuse, the field of ecocriticism and ecocritical narratives appear to grow in response "in strength and character."[25] In fact, all these concerns appear in *Holes*. For example, having the biggest or best of some "thing" starts with Elya's bid to have the biggest pig to offer Mr. Menke. Then, in Stanley's case, the worth of the pair of shoes as well as the technological and often controversial business processes that sports shoes represent in developing nations—for of the many careers that cause negative mental and physical health effects, "[m]ost at risk are miners, farmers, fishermen, loggers, workers in the clothing manufacturing industry and health sector employees"[26]– add to the consumerist concerns of the novel. Moreover, the most covetous person (and family) depicted in the family is Trout Walker. He believes that Kate should marry him because "[h]e was the son of the richest man in the county."[27] He also shows off his consumerist goods, buying a new motorboat to speed across Green Lake as a symbol of his status. Yet the fact that he and his family are especially seen as villains indicates that this kind of consumption is not only morally questionably but also a significant causal factor for the desertification of the environment around the lake.

Nevertheless, such a clear-cut evaluation becomes complicated by the same notions that allow for the morally good characters to cross boundaries of race, class, and species with their love: in the end, Stanley does not forgo consumption as he helps bridge the rift between families, stories, and the environment. He actually consumes parts of nature and its related products, albeit in a manner different from the others, in particular the Walkers. And this capacity stems back to Kate and Sam's story, for the Sploosh that makes his father famous smells like peaches[28]—the same peaches that Kate made to show her love for Sam and the same peaches that show Kate's good stewardship and interaction with the natural world.

The Yelnats' partnership with Clyde Livingston, who endorses the product on television and has now forgiven both Stanley and Zero for their involvement in the "theft" of his donated sneakers is a form of consumption that serves a positive function in society: it uses "natural ingredients"[29] to help eliminate odor, thus spreading the effect of Kate's peaches to the world and allowing for a mass consumption of her environmental capacities.

As a result, while depictions of consumption in the novel are often seen as morally wrong, there is no clear cut priced as that functions in regard to the environment. Yet what is clear is that rather choose only one side of the argument, environmentalism, like *Holes*, must engage with issues of consumption in order to find A way for all stakeholders to exist equity in the contemporary world, this making Sachar's novel innovative in children's and young adult literature in this respect.

A Summation of the Theories

Through a review of these theories it becomes evident that even though environmental studies and criticism began with a smaller scope, the influence of posthumanism has steadily made environmental studies more interdisciplinary and conscious of the relationships between species and other, non-human entities, such as rocks, vegetations, and the atmosphere.[30] These changes, which move beyond seeing the human as the center of scholarship and life, in general,[31] and which recognize that the shared spaces and experiences of humans with different species of nonhumans create contact zones[32] and isopraxis,[33] cannot be overlooked. Deleuze and Guattari built on this idea in *A Thousand Plateaus: Capitalism and Schizophrenia* (1987) as well with the notion of "becoming-animal;"[34] yet the reality that 'becoming' can affect and be affected by vegetal and objects—which, for Jane Bennett exert their own agency[35]— changes the way that relations between living and nonliving entities are enacted in the environment.

As a result, Clark's comment urge to have environmental studies include multiple and diverse trajectories has become more and more important: and some of the latest environmental trends can be applied to literary case studies. Instead of evaluating the appearance of birds or, in the case of *Holes*, yellow-spotted lizards in one particular way, it is possible to apply multiple ecocritical trends to one work, not only highlighting the ways in which each idea draws out particular truths about human and nonhuman interrelationships,[36] but also how the combination of these theoretical principles results in a posthuman rendering of options that once seemed strict and bounded by their own characteristics. Thus, in the context of *Holes*, by approaching the interconnections of (a) a broken promise with feet and nonhuman entities; (b) a sense of ecological justice with the way the environment reacts to the victimized interracial and interspecies love between Kate, Sam, and Mary Lou; and (c) the anthropocentric view with which the yellow-spotted lizards are often treated despite the manner in which they ultimately aid the innocent human protagonists as well as indicate that not all instances of human consumption are bad for the natural world, a posthuman intertwining of bounded theories can be applied to *Holes* in a fruitful and thought-provoking way, thus allow *Holes*, to "challeng[e] dominant conceptions of the human."[37]

Redefining the Environment in *Holes*

Even though the starkest examples of the environment in *Holes* center on the desert landscape of Camp Green Lake and its backstory, in which it was a green, lake-filled, and thriving town—as its name suggests—there are nevertheless other living and nonliving entities, including symbols, that function within the novel's setting. Three important ones—on which this essay will concentrate—involve broken promises and feet; the romantic nature of interracial and interspecies love; and issues connected to environmental consumption, as symbolized most by the yellow-spotted lizards and the onions/sploosh.

Broken Promises/Broken Feet:
Betraying the Bounty of the Earth

The promise the Elya Yelnats makes to Madame Zeroni serves as the initial symbol of interracial friendship and respect for the environment in the novel. Elya has his heart set on marrying Myra Menke even though Madame Zeroni, "an old Egyptian woman who lived on the edge of town"[38] who serves as his friend confidante, warns him that "Myra's head is as empty as a flowerpot."[39] Yet when Elya persists, indicating that Myra's father will choose the man who has the most wealth to offer — in the form of "a fat pig"[40]– Madame Zeroni agrees to help him. She reveals that he should take her runt pig "every day to the top of the mountain and let it drink from the stream" that has "water run[ning] uphill,"[41] a clear reference to a Romantic view of nature since "non-human 'nature' also acquires connotations of the untouched, the pure, the sacral."[42] Elya should also sing to the pig as he does so, creating a bond between them and creating a moral separation between how Elya interacts with non-humans compared to the purely transactional nature that Myra's father uses, highlighting the idea that "[a] history of ways of conceiving and treating the forest is thus one of different conceptions of being human."[43] However, in return, Elya must promise to carry and sing to Madame Zeroni the same way as well so she can "drink from the stream" before she dies.[44] If he does not uphold his part of the bargain, "Madame Zeroni warned that [...] he and his descendants would be doomed for all eternity."[45]

On the surface, this failed exchange and subsequent curse resembles many of the other curses that are brought down upon characters in children's literature. Nevertheless, the racial characteristics of the characters as well as the interspecies connection between humans, nonhumans (the pigs), and the environment, as represented by the spring, create a more complex, *companion species* pattern that follows the posthuman complexities of Donna Haraway[46] and breaks the dualistic binaries that Rosi Braidotti often attributes to human-centered society.[47]

The fact that Elya breaks a promise *is* a big deal. Yet because he breaks a promise to members of minority ethnic, racial, and nonhuman groups, the effects of the curse affect more than just him. They remain intergenerational, reacting negatively not just upon one family, but upon *all* of them. Once Elya realizes that Myra is indeed "empty headed," he abandons her, the pig, the up-flowing spring, and Madame Zeroni. Instead, he ventures to America, allowing his interracial and inter-generational friendship to fall apart; allowing the runt pig to be slaughtered and treated as Myra's family pleases; and permitting Madame Zeroni to die without being able to reach the spring on her own because "[s]he was sitting in a homemade wheelchair. She had no left foot. Her leg stopped at the ankle."[48] Like the stream that runs uphill (up from the metaphorical foot and leg of the mountain), this magical and restorative natural setting can only be reached through a *group* effort and a growth in maturity that is embodied in these collective interactions and promises to one another. Yet once these promises are broken, the landscape responds, first by preventing the good luck and actualization of the entire Yelnats family.

Even Stanley's supposed crime of stealing Clyde Livingston's (a basketball player) shoes is one involving setting and the apparent agency of nonhuman entities[49] even though it becomes evident at the end of the novel that Zero was the one who stole the sneakers and then threw them from an overpass. Yet the connection between the environment, feet, and interracial friendships remains crucial to this scene when Stanley "had just walked out from under a freeway overpass when the shoe hit him on the head."[50] Moreover, Stanley's father is also obsessed with feet since he is "trying to invent a way to recycle old sneakers."[51] Thus, the lack of luck involving feet and shoes, which plagues Stanley's father and the causes him to get sent to Camp Green Lake, serves as a stark reminder of Madame Zeroni's missing foot and inability to climb on her own. Furthermore, the nature of feet, which connects humans and nonhumans to the natural world, brings the curse full circle. Since Madame Zeroni is denied her wish to be carried by her friend to the spring, Elya's future relatives are plagued by issues regarding feet until the curse is lifted and until these symbols become fully functional once more.

The Murder of "Romantic" Nature: Crimes against Racial and Interspecies Love

The next crime, which is against interracial love (between Kate Barlow and Onion Sam) and interspecies love (their love for the donkey Mary Lou, their skills with growing onions and preserving peaches), though, becomes the most violent, resulting in a similar destruction of the town and its natural life. Kate Barlow is a school teacher in Green Lake who loves "Onion" Sam, a young Black man with "big strong arms" and an even bigger heart for the townspeople,[52] and his donkey, Mary Lou, to whom Sam attributes old age—"Sam claimed that Mary Lou was almost fifty years old, which was, and still is, extraordinarily old for a donkey."[53] The pair spend a lot of time together in the schoolhouse as Sam repairs the building and uses his love as a way to help the entire town grow and prosper. However, when Kate and Sam share a fateful kiss in the rain—a life-giving energy that subsequently stops afterward, leaving the land dry and marked by holes—Sam is murdered on the lake and Mary Lou is shot. Due to her fury, Kate becomes an outlaw, Kissin' Kate Barlow, and only her death at the hands of a spotted lizard defeats her.

The interconnections between this romance and the natural world serve as the starkest reminders in the novel that love between races/ethnicities as well as between humans and nonhumans—both animals and plants—aids in the continuance of life and the natural environment in which it occurs. The healing nature of Sam's onions remains one critical example of this connection. Even though there is a doctor (Doc Hawthorn) in the town, "[t]he folks in Green Lake were afraid to take chances. They would get regular medicine from Doc Hawthorn and onion concoctions from Sam."[54] Moreover. Kate's peaches are famous, and they remain an aspect shared between Kate and Sam that indicates their compatibility. Sam's love for her peaches is a way to express his love for her since the society in which they live does not support their union.

The endurance of the peaches, which Zero finds in the overturned boat called *Mary Lou* near the end of the novel also indicates how it is the love and caring for nature that endures. Even though the "sploosh," as Zero calls it makes him sick and "lay on his side, with his knees pulled up to his chest,"[55] it has nevertheless existed in these jars for a long time. Stanley surmises that "[w]hatever it was [...] it must have been in the boat when the boat sank. That meant it was probably over a hundred years old."[56] Most emphatically, the sploosh that semi-sustains them is under the nonhuman symbol of Mary Lou—a boat named after her, thus allowing for a posthuman stance since "it does not take the human cultural sphere as its sole point of reference and context."[57] Thus, these representations of the environment—as cared for and loved by Kate and Sam—survive through the drought that has descended upon Green Lake and remind Zero and Stanley of the important aspects of life—such as Madame Zeroni's stories and song and like the history of Kissin' Kate—which can endure beyond one lifespan (and generation).

The manner in which Mary Lou serves as a conduit between Kate and Sam also highlights the important of nonhuman animals in creating a link between humans and the landscape. Just like caring for the pig provides Elya with a way to grow stronger and serve as a protector of a nonhuman, Sam's love and companionship with Mary Lou allows for him to remain close to the earth and its magical bounty of onions. Later, when Sam and Zero are hiding under the boat, which is called *Mary Lou*, Zero even surmises that "I bet she was pretty [...] Somebody must have loved her a lot, to name a boat after her,"[58] indicating that beauty is not bounded by species: Mary Lou is beautiful in any form, whether it is as the long-lived donkey, the boat, or the symbolic name spoken by humans to represent these entities. The fact that Mary Lou also survives because of these onions, as Sam claims by emphasizing her age,[59] underlines that an interconnected relationship between different races, species, and nonhuman entities is crucial for the happiness of everyone and that "the 'self' is understood as 'local, fluid, contingent, and as contesting and rending the hierarchal binaries of nature/culture, self/other, male/female, human/nonhuman'."[60]

That Kate and Sam are as happy as they are — with Mary Lou, their onions, and their peaches — is undeniable. It is only when hatred, greed, and intolerance predominate that Kate, Sam, and Mary Lou suffer.

Lizards Don't Like Onions, or Environmental "Consumption"

Even though the desert landscape that transforms Green Lake after the death of Sam and the retribution that Kissin' Kate occurs over many years, it remains the starkest sign that the environment reacts to the crimes enacted against it and the innocents who live(d) on it. Moreover, the yellow-spotted lizards serve as the most dangerous living beings that inhabit this desert space, and, according to Stanley,

> Each lizard has exactly eleven yellow spots, but the spots are hard to see on its yellow-green body. The lizard is from six to ten inches long and has big red eyes. In truth, its eyes are yellow, and it is the skin around the eyes which is red, but everyone always speaks of its red eyes. It also has black teeth and a milky white tongue.[61]

From this description, an important point is that people who see the lizard (i.e. the environment and its aspects) do not actually see it and judge it the way that it actually is. Instead, the lizards are named for spots that are barely visible and considered red-eyed when, in fact, they are not. Thus, the lizards remain symbols of the manner in which humans often anthropomorphize nature in a way that is not real or relevant. In the context of *Holes*, this connection remains important for two reasons: first, the environment is providing the residents of Camp Green Lake with everything that they need to possibly resolve the curse, if they would only look closer; second, the lizards, while dangerous, nevertheless appear to help when good-hearted people are in need.

It is evident through the stories about Kissin' Kate, the remnants of her life left behind (the lipstick case, the *Mary Lou*), and the topography (God's Thumb) of the camp, that taking a closer look at the natural world, as Stanley eventually does, give the environment of Camp Green Lake more value than other characters realize. Even though the landscape appears to be empty and dead, it is full of everything that Stanley needs to repair the curses that have been inflicted on the area. Moreover, the reality that the lizards, while surely deadly, for anyone bitten by them "will die a slow and painful death. Always,"[62] does not detract from the fact that they appear and engage with good-hearted people at crucial moments in the narrative. When Kate Barlow reaches the end of her story—with Trout and Linda Walker attempting to torture her in order to find the location of the treasure—a "lizard landed on Kate's bare ankle. Its sharp black teeth bit into her leg. Its white tongue lapped up the droplets of blood that leaked out of the wound."[63] Yet Kate "die[s] laughing"[64] and unafraid of her fate, because, unlike the Walkers—who were always 'digging holes' and ignorant of the bounty of the natural world—she could see the landscape as it was and how it mattered: through the vision of Sam and her memories of him and Mary Lou that accompany her through her last moments.

The Warden, who is a descendant of the Walkers, still sees the holes—the empty spaces around her—that she thinks that these holes can only be filled with treasure. Stanley and Zero see holes in their environment at first as well, which their names indicate since Stanley "is given the nonsense nickname "Caveman," as though he were himself a vacancy, and his best friend is nicknamed Zero."[65] However, when Stanley finally decides to dig his last hole after carrying Zero (Hector Zeroni) up and down God's Thumb, he finds that lizards surround them and the briefcase that contains the belongings of a relative also named Stanley Yelnats. As he stands in the hole with Zero, with the Warden, Mr. Sir, and Mr. Pendanski looking down at them, "[h]e could see six lizards. There were three on the ground, two on his left leg, and one on his right sneaker."[66] Yet the lizards never bite them. Because he and Zero had been living off of Sam's onions on God's Thumb, they smelled like onions. And in this moment, Sam's past advice to a client—"It's very important you drink a bottle tonight. You got to get it into your bloodstream. The lizards don't like onion blood"[67]—and Stanley and Zero's plight connect. The lizards do not like onions in someone's blood because onions are connected to a love and respect for the environment, which Sam and Stanley share through this crop. Instead, the lizards attempt to harass the Warden and her followers, for, unlike Stanley and Zero, the landscape for them is made only for holes and emptiness instead of the full potentials that others see.

From these examples it is evident that while the lizards (the environment) have deadly capabilities, they can also protect those who are connected to the environment to the point that, like the onions, it is in someone's blood. Thus, where people who do not know how to read the environment see only death in the yellow-spotted lizards, they will also see holes in the natural world. Yet when people like Stanley can consider the paradoxes of how people see living beings and the larger world, they can begin to fill the holes with something more real and valuable.

Healing the Landscape and Disseminating Environmental Awareness

Just as the environment becomes cursed and unproductive in Green Lake after the murder of Sam and Mary Lou because of Kate's love for them, the Yelnats family continues to struggle and face bad luck until Stanley reconnects human and nonhuman love by carrying Zero up God's Thumb and allowing him to eat Sam's onions, the primary vegetal/food element in this part of the story. Yet the carrying, both literally and symbolically, of interracial and interspecies love are the critical components that heal the desert landscape. Just like Madame Zeroni explains, "Every day you will carry the pig up the mountain. It will get a little bigger, but you will get a little stronger,"[68] this maturation of carrying a love for different races, different nonhumans, and the larger environment up to "God," as represented by the peak allows for the regeneration of all life affected by the curse.

Once Stanley and Zero return to dig their last hole, the curse is broken: Stanley and Zero find the former Stanley Yelnats' suitcase, they are protected from the yellow-spotted lizards, and a lawyer comes to take Stanley, and, at Stanley's urging, Zero away from the camp. This rescue is possible because, "Stanley's father invented his cure for foot odor the day after the great-great-grandson of Elya Yelnats carried the great-great-great-grandson of Madame Zeroni up the mountain."[69] In fact, the manner in which Stanley's father invents how to deodorize shoes is a concoction much like the sploosh that Zero and Stanley found in the upturned *Mary Lou*, bringing the importance of the two storylines back together and emphasizing how race, nonhuman-ness, and even the symbol of feet all collide to protected the landscape, for, most importantly for Green Lake, "the first time in over a hundred years, a drop of rain fell into the empty lake."[70]

Moreover, the notion of feet becomes more positive in its renewed contact with the world. During his confession, Zero admits that "I didn't know they were his. I just thought they were somebody's old shoes. It was better to take someone's old shoes, I thought, than steal a pair of new ones."[71] Thus, Zero thought that old, worn-down shoes (and previous forms of contact with the environment) was better than a new start; yet in addition to the attention that the shoes' disappearance causes, there is the reality that "they smelled really bad,"[72] which justified his disposal of them — and thus his disposal of this old perspective. Nevertheless, taking new shoes rather than earning them, which mirrors developing an environmental relationship instead of taking one — becomes emphasized by the divine nature of Stanley and Zero's time spent on God's Thumb that reflects religious stewardship models toward the environment rather than a sense of colonialism.[73] Even though Zero seems to think that having stinky shoes (and hence the cursed connection to humans and nonhumans) seems enviable, stating, "I ended up getting arrested the next day when I tried to walk out of a shoe store with a new pair of sneakers. If I had just kept those old smelly sneakers, then neither of us would be here right now,"[74] it becomes evident that the reality is much different. Zero's life improves only once he becomes a steward of the natural world and Stanley though the growth of their perspectives *together*. Thus, "[a]s Stanley stared at the glittering night sky, he thought there was no place he would rather be. He was glad Zero put the shoes on the parked car. He was glad they fell from the overpass and hit him on the head,"[75] for all of these apparent mischances had final taught him that working together with the landscape, nonhumans, and his friends as well as learning how forgive were the real successes of his experiences at the camp.

Then, Clyde Livingston, whose name could be seen as *Living Ston[e]* in a connection to the dry environment that has now become regenerated and whose shoes Stanley was once accused of stealing, now advertises the Sploosh and reveals, "everyone around here calls me 'Sweet Feet'."[76] Through this improvement with his connection to the natural world, even though his case is more consumer-oriented than Stanley's and Zero's, Livingston nonetheless creates a situation in which a new environmental awareness can be shared and even consumed in the modern world. As a result, the lessons of (Camp) Green Lake continue to resonate into the characters' future as media and business processes show the capacity to be affected by and to disseminate this same environmental awareness.

Through this examination of the three important environmental elements in Louis Sachar's *Holes* — broken promises and feet; the romantic nature of interracial and interspecies love; and issues connected to environmental consumption, as symbolized predominantly by the yellow-spotted lizards and the onions/sploosh — the relevance of the novel to the geography and agency of the landscape becomes critical to understanding the merit of the novel. Moreover, the fact that multiple environmental theories intertwine in the narrative provides an interdisciplinary and hybrid approach to evaluating the work that is often neglected.[77] Consequently, through this lens, the novel, as a significant and award winning text of youth literature, emphasizes not only how children's and young adult literature can address critical issues of the contemporary world, but also how reconsiderations of how humans can consume the environment in a more sustainable way are possible.

Notes

1   Lea Baratz and Hanna Abu Hazeira, "Children's Literature as an Important Tool for Education of Sustainability and the Environment," *International Electronic Journal of Environmental Education* 2, no. (Jan 2012): 35.

2   Timothy Clark, *The Cambridge Introduction to Literature and the Environment* (Cambridge: Cambridge University Press, 2011), 4.

3   Annette Wannamaker, "Reading in the Gaps and Lacks: (De)Constructing Masculinity in Louis Sachar's *Holes*," *Children's Literature in Education* 37, no. 1 (March 2006): 15. doi: 10.1007/s10583-005-9452-4

4   Pat Pinsent, "Fate and Fortune in a Modern Fairy Tale: Louis Sachar's *Holes*," *Children's Literature in Education* 33, no. 3 (September 2002): 203.

5   Kirsten Møllegaard, "Haunting and History in Louis Sachar's *Holes*," *Western American Literature* 45, no. 2 (Summer 2010): 139.

6   Clark, *The Cambridge Introduction*, 59.

7   Stephen Prickett, *European Romanticism: A Reader* (London: Bloomsbury, 2014), 3.

8   Sidney I. Dobrin and Kenneth B. Kidd, "Introduction: Into the Wild." In *Wild Things: Children's Culture and Ecocriticism*, edited by Sidney I. Dobrin and Kenneth B. Kidd (Detroit: Wayne State University Press, 2004), 5.

9   Alison Stone, *Nature: Ethics and Gender in German Romanticism and Idealism* (London: Rowman & Littlefield, 2018), 2.

10   Roger Cox, "The Child of Romanticism I: The Noble Savage and Romantic Naturalism." In *Shaping Childhood: Themes of Uncertainty in the History of Adult-Child Relationships*, edited by Roger Cox (London: Taylor & Francis Ltd, 1996): 77.

11   Claudia Moscovici, *Romanticism and Postromanticism* (Lanham, MD: Lexington Books, 2007), 5.

12   Clark, *The Cambridge Introduction*, 88.

13   Gregory Freeland, and Frederick D. Gordon. "Introduction." In *International Environmental Justice: Competing Claims and Perspectives*. Edited by Gregory Freeland and Frederick D. Gordon, 1-20 (Porters Woods, UK: ILM Publications, 2012), 2.

14   Louis Sachar, *Holes* (New York: Scholastic Paperbacks, 1998), 3.

15   Clark, *The Cambridge Introduction*, 128.

16   Henry Shue, *Climate Justice: Vulnerability and Protection* (Oxford: Oxford University Press, 2014), 234.

17   Clark, *The Cambridge Introduction*, 188.

18   Clark, *The Cambridge Introduction*, 23.

19   Sachar, *Holes*, 109.

20   Sachar, *Holes*, 179.

21   Cathryn Bailey, "Anthropomorphism." In *Encyclopedia of Environmental Ethics and Philosophy*, edited by J. Baird Callicott and Robert Frodeman, 62-64. Vol. 1. Detroit, MI: Macmillan Reference USA, 2009. *Gale eBooks* (accessed January 7, 2021), 62. https://link. gale.com/apps/doc/CX3234100028/GVRL?u=nhc_main&sid=GVRL&xid=7a87000d.

22   Richie Nimmo, "Animal Cultures, Subjectivity, and Knowledge: Symmetrical

Reflections beyond the Great Divide," *Society & Animals* 20 (2012): 173. doi: 10.1163/156853012X631379.

23   Sachar, *Holes*, 41.

24   Kim-Pong Tam, "Anthropomorphism of Nature and Efficacy in Coping with the Environmental Crisis," *Social Cognition* 32, no. 3 (2014): 276. doi: 101521soco2014323276.

25   Simon C. Estok, "The Urgency of Ecocriticism and European Scholarship," *CLCWeb: Comparative Literature and Culture* 16, no. 4 (2014): 2. Gale Academic OneFile (accessed January 14, 2021). https://link.gale.com/apps/doc/A4034 48970/AONE?u=nhc_main&sid=AONE&xid=dde1e2c0.

26   Khue Pham Minh, "Work-Related Depression and Associated Factors in a Shoe Manufacturing Factory in Haiphong City, Vietnam," *International Journal of Occupational Medicine and Environmental Health* 27, no. 6 (2014): 950-951.

27   Sachar, *Holes*, 102.

28   Sachar, *Holes*, 226.

29   Sachar, *Holes*, 231.

30   Clark, *The Cambridge Introduction*, 4.

31   Rosi Braidotti, *The Posthuman* (Cambridge: Polity Press, 2013), 25.

32   Donna Haraway, *When Species Meet* (Minneapolis: University of Minnesota Press, 2007), 4.

33   Haraway, *When Species Meet*, 229.

34   Gilles Deleuze and Félix Guattari, *A Thousand Plateaus: Capitalism and Schizophrenia* (University of Minnesota Press, 1987), 260.

35   Jane Bennett, *Vibrant Matter: A Political Ecology of Things* (Durham, N.C.: Duke University Press, 2010), vii.

36   Haraway, *When Species Meet*, 207.

37   Clark, *The Cambridge Introduction*, 64.

38   Sachar, *Holes*, 28.

39   Sachar, *Holes*, 30.

40   Sachar, *Holes*, 28.

41   Sachar, *Holes*, 30.

42   Clark, *The Cambridge Introduction*, 7.

43   Clark, *The Cambridge Introduction*, 61.

44   Sachar, *Holes*, 31.

45   Sachar, *Holes*, 31.

46   Haraway, *When Species Meet*, 4.

47   Braidotti, *The Posthuman*, 3.

48   Sachar, *Holes*, 28.

49   Bennett, *Vibrant Matter*, vii.

50   Sachar, *Holes*, 24.

51   Sachar, *Holes*, 9.

52   Sachar, *Holes*, 107.

53   Sachar, *Holes*, 107.

54   Sachar, *Holes*, 108.

55   Sachar, *Holes*, 158.

56   Sachar, *Holes*, 157.

57   Clark, *The Cambridge Introduction*, 6.

58   Sachar, *Holes*, 161.

59   Sachar, *Holes*, 107.

60   Clark, *The Cambridge Introduction*, 66.

61   Sachar, *Holes*, 41.

62   Sachar, *Holes*, 4.

63   Sachar, *Holes*, 124.

64   Sachar, *Holes*, 124.

65   Stephanie Yearwood, "Popular Postmodernism for Young Adult Readers: *Walk Two Moons, Holes,* and *Monster,*" *ALAN Review* 29, no. 3 (2002): 52. https://doi-org.ezproxy.snhu.edu/10.21061/alan.v29i3.a.11.

66   Sachar, *Holes*, 205.

67   Sachar, *Holes*, 224.

68   Sachar, *Holes*, 31.

69   Sachar, *Holes*, 229.

70   Sachar, *Holes*, 226.

71   Sachar, *Holes*, 184.

72   Sachar, *Holes*, 184.

73   Todd LeVasseur, *Religious Agrarianism and the Return of Place: From Values to Practice in Sustainable Agriculture* (Albany, NY: SUNY Press, 2017), Location 220.

74   Sachar, *Holes*, 184.

75   Sachar, *Holes*, 187.

76   Sachar, *Holes*, 231.

77   Clark, *The Cambridge Introduction*, 4.

Bibliography

Bailey, Cathryn. "Anthropomorphism." In *Encyclopedia of Environmental Ethics and Philosophy*, edited by J. Baird Callicott and Robert Frodeman, pp. 62-64. Vol. 1. Detroit, MI: Macmillan Reference USA, 2009. *Gale eBooks*. Accessed 7 January 2021. https://link.gale.com/apps/doc/CX3234100028/GVRL?u=nhc_main&sid=GVRL&xid=7a87000d.

Baratz, Lea and Hanna Abu Hazeira. "Children's Literature as an Important Tool for Education of Sustainability and the Environment." *International Electronic Journal of Environmental Education* 2 (Jan 2012): pp. 31-36.

Bennet, Jane. *Vibrant Matter: A Political Ecology of Things*. Durham, N.C.: Duke University Press, 2010.

Braidotti, Rosi. *The Posthuman*. Cambridge: Polity Press, 2013.

Clark, Timothy. *The Cambridge Introduction to Literature and the Environment*. Cambridge: Cambridge University Press, 2011.

Cox, Roger. "The Child of Romanticism I: The Noble Savage and Romantic Naturalism." In *Shaping Childhood: Themes of Uncertainty in the History of Adult-Child Relationships*, edited by Roger Cox, pp. 76-98. London: Taylor & Francis Ltd, 1996.

Deleuze, Gilles, and Félix Guattari. *A Thousand Plateaus: Capitalism and Schizophrenia*. University of Minnesota Press, 1987.

Dobrin, Sidney I., and Kenneth B. Kidd. "Introduction: Into the Wild." In *Wild Things: Children's Culture and Ecocriticism*, edited by Sidney I. Dobrin and Kenneth B. Kidd, pp. 1-15. Detroit: Wayne State University Press, 2004.

Estok, Simon C. "The Urgency of Ecocriticism and European Scholarship." *CLCWeb: Comparative Literature and Culture* 16, no. 4, 2014. Gale Academic OneFile. Accessed 14 January 2021. https://link.gale.com/apps/doc/A403448970/AONE?u=nhc_main&sid=AONE&xid=dde1e2c0.

Freeland, Gregory, and Frederick D. Gordon. "Introduction." In *International Environmental Justice: Competing Claims and Perspectives*, edited by Gregory Freeland and Frederick D. Gordon, pp. 1-20. Porters Woods, UK: ILM Publications, 2012.

Haraway, Donna. *When Species Meet*. Minneapolis: University of Minnesota Press, 2007.

LeVasseur, Todd. *Religious Agrarianism and the Return of Place: From Values to Practice in Sustainable Agriculture*. Albany, NY: SUNY Press, 2017.

Minh, Khue Pham. "Work-Related Depression and Associated Factors in a Shoe Manufacturing Factory in Haiphong City, Vietnam." *International Journal of Occupational Medicine and Environmental Health* 27, no. 6 (2014): pp. 950-958.

Møllegaard, Kirsten. "Haunting and History in Louis Sachar's *Holes*." *Western American Literature* 45, no. 2 (Summer 2010): pp. 139-161.

Moscovici, Claudia. *Romanticism and Postromanticism*. Lanham, MD: Lexington Books, 2007.

Nimmo, Richie. "Animal Cultures, Subjectivity, and Knowledge: Symmetrical Reflections beyond the Great Divide." *Society & Animals* 20 (2012): pp. 173-192. doi: 10.1163/156853012X631379.

Pinsent, Pat. "Fate and Fortune in a Modern Fairy Tale: Louis Sachar's *Holes*." *Children's Literature in Education* 33, no. 3 (September 2002): pp. 203-212.

Prickett, Stephen. *European Romanticism: A Reader*. London: Bloomsbury, 2014.

Sachar, Louis. *Holes*. New York: Scholastic Paperbacks, 1998.

Stone, Alison. *Nature: Ethics and Gender in German Romanticism and Idealism*. London: Rowman & Littlefield, 2018.

Shue, Henry. *Climate Justice: Vulnerability and Protection*. Oxford: Oxford University Press, 2014.

Tam, Kim-Pong. "Anthropomorphism of Nature and Efficacy in Coping with the Environmental Crisis." *Social Cognition* 32, no. 3 (2014): pp. 276–296. doi:101521soco2014323276

Wannamaker, Annette. "Reading in the Gaps and Lacks: (De)Constructing Masculinity in Louis Sachar's *Holes*." *Children's Literature in Education* 37, no. 1 (March 2006): pp. 15-33. doi: 10.1007/s10583-005-9452-4

Yearwood, Stephanie. "Popular Postmodernism for Young Adult Readers: *Walk Two Moons*, *Holes*, and *Monster*." *ALAN Review* 29, no. 3 (2002): pp. 50-53. https://doi-org.ezproxy.snhu.edu/10.21061/alan.v29i3.a.11

9

The Adventures of Tintin in Heterotopia

Debnita Chakravarti

The world is a book, and we travel our planet mostly through pages. For many of us, one of the earliest passports to the remotest corners of the world – and even beyond, to the moon – has been the Tintin albums. Their creator, the Belgian artist Georges Remi or Hergé, took his young journalist and his little dog Snowy on adventures to faraway exotic places, and for the last nine decades readers from seven to seventy have been accompanying him in rapt delight.

The *Tintin in* … format of many of the album titles signals their strong connect with particular places. Starting from his first foray in 1930 – *The Adventures of Tintin in the Land of the Soviets* – the Belgian boy reporter has found himself all over the world. His escapades take him to countries as varied as Scotland and Saudi Arabia, Iceland and Italy, several parts of the two Americas, not to mention fictitious nations like Syldavia and Borduria. He finds himself shipwrecked on seas ranging from the Arctic to the Arabian, and stranded in all kinds of varied and extreme locales such as Saharan deserts and Amazonian rainforests. He even travels to the moon and gets hijacked by aliens into outer space.

The locations serve several functions apart from furnishing fascinating settings. One reason for the abiding popularity of the series has been Hergé's ability to reflect the socio-political milieu of the places his protagonist visits through the meticulous research that he brought to his craft. His lifelong interest in politics and governance ensured that the albums were always more than exciting adventures for children. They held their readers' fascination equally when they grew up, allowing them to discover new facets and layers in the same narratives they had loved with the uncomplicated innocence of childhood. Critics have for long commended the depth of understanding about local issues and intricacies of international relations that the series has unfailingly demonstrated.

The myriad settings have additionally provided a rich gallery of characters who have peopled the books and inhabited the readers' imagination over the years. For a little-travelled artist in Belgium, Hergé has managed to bring to life an astonishing assortment of fictional figures from all over the world, complete with their national traits and individual idiosyncrasies. Very few comparable works can boast a range of dramatis personae as distinctive and disparate as Sophocles Sarcophagus and Ivan Ivanovitch Sakharine, General Alcazar and the Maharaja of Gaipajama, Jolyon Wagg and Igor Wagner, Ben Kalish Ezab and Bianca Castafiore.

The different locales have also been important for character development. Hergé uses Captain Haddock as the very human, very volatile embodiment of extreme emotions and passionate reactions against which the younger protagonist Tintin can be portrayed as the infinitely more composed and level-headed role model. The retired seaman provides exaggerated — and often very entertaining responses to the new places, people and customs he encounters, giving the perfectly-poised Tintin a chance to enlighten him about life in other parts of the world (and the readers as well), in a tone of acceptance and empathy for the other. Apprising himself quickly of the political, social and economic dynamics of the new place he finds himself in, Tintin wastes no time in joining the side of the oppressed and the underdog against the machinations of villainous adversaries like Rstapopoulos and Dr Müller.

But even in a series where the settings of the tales have prominent roles to play rather than being mere exotic backdrops, there is one album where the site of the narrative is of particular importance. The twentieth adventure that Tintin embarks on is like no other before or after it. It is famously called "the white Tintin" because of its strikingly stark cover page. It was reportedly the album that was Hergé's favourite, and by his own admission the most personal of all his books.[1] Tintin scholars have noted its multiple points of divergence from others in the series. For both the artist and his protagonist, this particular volume in the series stood out as being uncharacteristically intimate and poignant, emotional and introspective, unsettling and therapeutic.

This chapter participates in the Tintinology scholarship that has accrued around this particular volume, using an approach that has never been brought to the series before. It offers a Foucauldian reading of *Tintin in Tibet*, arguing that the Himalayan terrain that forms the backdrop of this album may be analysed as a heterotopia, following the French thinker's theory of space.

In "Des Espaces Autres" (Of Other Spaces), a lecture that Michel Foucault gave in 1967, he introduces the concept of "heterotopia." He designates our era to be engaged with space, contrasting it to the nineteenth century's obsession with time. Talking about the relationship of our lives to the spaces that they are lived in, he focuses on "those which are endowed with the curious property of being in relation with all the others, but in such a way as to suspend, neutralize, or invert the set of relationships designed, reflected, or mirrored by themselves. These spaces, … are in rapport in some way with all the others, and yet contradict them."[2]

He categorises them into two general types: utopias, and heterotopias. As opposed to the first, which are "fundamentally unreal", the latter he calls "real and effective spaces", which are "absolutely other" to the places they represent. He formulates heterotopia as the spatial articulation of a discursive order that refracts or disturbs prevailing paradigms. They are, in his words, "effectively realised utopias", outlined in the very institution of society, but constituting in actuality a "counter" to the real social procedures and actions. He emphasises that these are places which represent, challenge and overturn social orders and hierarchies, which lies outside society even while being a part of it. They are both mythical and real simultaneously, and may be found in every culture in the world, a "constant feature of all human groups."[3] They are everywhere and nowhere.

Foucault uses the mirror as his first example. In it one sees oneself where one is actually not located, opening up an unreal space beyond the surface of the reflecting glass. But the mirror also has a solid "real" existence, helping the subject to locate oneself in an actual contextualised space. He then offers a "heterotopology", the "study, analysis, description, and 'reading'" of these different spaces (hetero = different, topos = space). Heterotopias may assume myriad forms, Foucault notes, and goes on to classify heterotopias into those of crisis, ritual, purification, deviation and compensation. As examples of heterotopias of crisis he names boarding schools or military academies where male sexuality can be explored, the honeymoon suite where the defloration of the bride can take place, special areas for menstruating female or women in labour, places which are sacred or privileged in some way, reserved for individuals in a state of "crisis" of some kind, and forbidden for the ordinary members of society. This first kind of heterotopia, that of crisis, Foucault believed, was being replaced by the second "which could be described as heterotopias of deviance, occupied by individuals whose behaviour deviates from the current average or standard. They are the rest homes, psychiatric clinics, and …prisons."[4]

The chapter considers the Tibetan highlands, where Tintin is compelled to travel in this volume, as unique among all the spaces into which the intrepid boy reporter has ever ventured. The tale begins with the young journalist holidaying in the Swiss Alps with his elderly companion Captain Haddock. He receives a redirected letter from his Chinese friend Chang (who was introduced in *The Blue Lotus*) announcing his trip to Europe. But the happiness at this visit is soon clouded over by the newspaper report of Chang's airplane having crashed in Tibet, leaving no survivors. Amidst the news of this tragedy, Tintin has a vivid dream where he sees Chang in a snowy wasteland, calling out to him for help. This unusual vision convinces Tintin that his young friend is alive and in dire need of his assistance. He sets out to search for the plane wrecked boy against all advice, accompanied by a vocally reluctant Captain Haddock who feels that Tintin is being completely irrational. This view is iterated at every step of the duo's journey to India and subsequently to Tibet, where everyone from the airport manager to the locals emphasise the impossibility of anyone surviving the terrible air crash on the Tibetan Himalayas, and even in the slim possibility of that miracle, subsequently managing to stay alive in that extremely harsh terrain.

In what is undoubtedly his most difficult expedition ever, Tintin finds himself in a landscape more desolate than even the barren surface of the moon. This is a rare episode in his eventful life when the amicable young man is not surrounded by his usual coterie of friends and acquaintances. The uniquely eccentric, colourful and comical personages instantly recognisable to readers of the series who make regular appearances are missing here. Professor Calculus makes a brief appearance only at the beginning, and the Thom(p)sons, who managed to hitch an inadvertent ride even to the moon, are conspicuously absent. Bianca Castafiore makes a fleeting disembodied appearance when her famous jewel song from *Faust* is heard over the radio at the Himalayan base camp where the search party halts for the night. Only Captain Haddock and the ever-faithful Snowy — Tintin's inseparable shadow — accompany him on this particular adventure. The progressive distancing from the protagonist's comfort zone that the adventure entails is emphasised by the imposing peaks of the Tibetan Himalayas in stark contrast to the gently rolling Alpine slopes where Tintin was enjoying his Alpine vacation when this story began. As he travels farther away from his known context into an unfamiliar oriental culture and subsequently begins his ascent away from locality into the vast uncharted ice fields of the Himalayan foothills, the young Belgian finds his entourage of coolies and guides diminishing steadily until he is left only with Haddock and Snowy for company. And at more than one point of the expedition, Tintin finds himself completely alone.

Like every other location that he chose to set his stories in, Hergé recreates the mountains of Tibet with meticulous care and precision. Intense research ensures that every last geographical detail of this volume is accurate, just as the minute touches of the brief Indian stopover or the unique culture of Tibet's inhabitants. The artist who methodically maintained files all through his life, which enabled him to present every vehicle and every weapon with admirable accuracy all through the series, made sure to represent the remote and exotic country of Tibet with his characteristic fidelity to details. Just like the colourful stopovers at India and Nepal, the Tibetan vistas come alive in graphic virtuosity. His subscription of the *National Geographic* came in handy in ensuring that the mountaineering minutiae — from the ice axes and spikes to the various climbing techniques were faultless.

But beyond the geographic fidelity the Tibetan mountains in this book take on a heterotopic function. They serve as an example of what Foucault categorises as a heterotopia of crisis. They provide the young Belgian reporter with a site where he must test the limits of his commitment to friendship. His intuition that Chang is alive and is stranded in the mountains waiting for help to arrive is met at every step with the sharp resistance of reason. He is told repeatedly that this is an impossibility, a mere fancy that he chooses to indulge in order to avoid accepting the bitter truth of his dear friend's demise. Tintin's real bond with Chang must be tested through the imagined vision that Tintin experiences, and the entire narrative plays upon this duality of the actual and the virtual, which Foucault designated as a dynamic of his heterotopias.

It is fitting that an adventure that hinges on the unproved and unprovable premise of a flimsy impulse goes on to use other metaphysical and mythological elements. Building on his interest in extra-sensory perception, which Hergé shared with his soon-to-be second wife Fanny Vlaminck, the rational reporter who always works with detached precision through material clues and hard evidence now embarks upon an emotional personal journey fuelled solely by an illogical whim. In a series which is unfailingly scientific in spirit and deductive in process, this particular volume stands as an extraordinary exception celebrating the controversial and the improbable, the unconfirmed and the incredible. Apart from the episode of the aliens in *Flight 747*, no other Tintin adventure banks so much on conjecture, making use of dubious subjects that are debatable at best for the mainstay of its plot. Even the two moon adventures, published a good nineteen years before man first walked there, were based on much firmer ground. This is because in his Tibetan trip Tintin must disprove the charges of evasion and resolve the crisis of his own baseless belief. In order to do this, he is compelled to explore the depths of his commitment to the very idea of friendship.

The Tibetan highland is invested with an added layer of enigmatic aura through the trance-vision of a monk and the introduction of the mythical and controversial Yeti. The physicality of the landform is imbued with a metaphysical dimension that is a characteristic of the Foucauldian heterotopias that enclose within themselves a symbolic charge that is more than the sum total of its physical parts. The notable Tibetologist Alexandra David-Neel provided him with details about the monastic mores and mysticism, including the levitation, trance and prescience that the monk Blessed Lightning provides as points of plot progression.[5] The other more significant element was the Yeti. Hergé had followed very closely the interest in the western newspapers in the 1950s about the possible existence of the Abominable Snowman. The book *On the Track of Unknown Animals* (1955) by his friend Bernard Heivelmans and the first-hand accounts of the mountaineer Maurice Herzog helped him to structure these conjectures and present the most ambitious and extensive portrayal of this intriguing creature in any literary work. The Tintin series is a veritable zoo of diverse fauna from all around the globe, and their treatment would be a fitting subject of a very interesting study. But from his Milou (the original French name for Snowy) to the Migou (the local Tibetan name for the Yeti) Hergé takes the greatest leap of imagination. It might be argued that the diverse animal life of the Tintin series is bracketed within these two extremes of the most familiar and the least known, the comfortingly every day and the terrifyingly exotic, the Snowy of Marlinspike Hall and the Abominable Snowman of the Himalayan snow peaks.

The Himalayan peaks where the search for Chang is conducted becomes a heterotopia of crisis for the protagonist. Tintin's search for Chang is as much his quest for the foundations of his own self as that for his missing friend. The severity of the snow-capped peaks throws into stark relief the very sense of identity of the usually-confident Belgian reporter. Before he can discover any sign, which prove that Chang is still alive, he needs to ascertain the cornerstones of his own commitment. And before he starts to climb up the peaks towards his friend, Tintin needs to touch the depths of doubt in a journey inwards into his soul.

Two incidents in the book are significant in this travel within Tintin's own self. The usually circumspect adventurer uncharacteristically gets lost in a Himalayan snowstorm and is forced to make a stop in his onward march. This is a juncture in the expedition where the rescuer needs to be rescued himself. He finds himself as lost in the directionless snow as the hapless Chang in his vision. This is a fate that would ordinarily befall the perpetually confused Thom(p)son twins or the befuddled Captain Haddock, who would then be retrieved in time from their quandary by their enterprising young friend. But in this icy topography that freezes the most purposeful resolutions into inaction, Tintin faces a serious setback. A similar low-point, both literal and figurative, occurs when he falls into an abyss as he negotiates his unsure way over the tricky terrain and vanishes from the pages for several panels. Hergé is here charting the entire range of emotional heights and depths as he makes fruitful use of his precipitous setting, using it heterotopically even as the graphic artist in him reproduces the mountains in all their awful majesty. As Tintin progresses in his journey, the landscape becomes more and more surreal, at once a real place and a metaphorical space—an-other topos, as Foucault called it, simultaneously the setting of a journey as well as a challenge to it, real and symbolic at the same time. The iconic cover, where a set of mysterious footprints proceed diagonally into the whiteness of the unknown terrain, draws both the protagonist and the reader into this mysterious world.

Hergé expands on the theme of friendship through two other relationships in this narrative—that between Chang and the Yeti, and between Tintin and Captain Haddock. The first one is an act of conjecture, imagining a creature whose existence has never been proven to be humane and capable of compassion, not the monster that it is made out to be by popular belief and local folklore. Not only does Hergé declare his support for those who believe in the creature's existence by drawing him into the reality of his narrative, he succeeds in making his readers sympathise with the Yeti at the end of the book, sharing his sorrow at losing the boy he had saved from certain death, cared for and grown to love.

The other, and perhaps more significant tie of friendship that is brought to crisis is that between Tintin and his older companion Captain Haddock. Tintinologists and casual readers have mused for long on the real nature of the unlikely and very close relationship between the retired marine and the young reporter. The two men with their diametrically opposite personalities are one of the most recognisable pairs in literature symbolising friendship. Most of the books in the series feature episodes where one comes to the other's aid, very often saving his life, ever since Haddock made his memorable appearance in *The Crab with the Golden Claws*. But it is in this volume that their bond undergoes a crucial test, and emerges stronger for it.

Nearing their destination Tintin and Haddock start scaling the highest peaks, a project so fraught with danger that even their guide Tharkey refuses to continue further. The Belgian reporter and the older seaman tread their perilous path over boulders and crags, tied to each other by mountaineering ropes. Coincidentally this is reminiscent of the rope that had brought Tintin into the Captain's cabin on the ship Karaboudjan where they had first met. Several adventures later, Hergé once again uses the rope as the symbol of the ties between the two unlikely companions. As was the situation earlier, this time too, the rope is a lifeline in inimical conditions. But unlike in *The Crab with the Golden Claws*, here there are no gun toting villains. Tintin in Tibet is one of the rare albums where there is no real antagonist, the other being *The Castafiore Emerald*. Instead of the machinations of gangsters and conspiracies of dictators, Tintin and Haddock find themselves at the mercy of the elements. Haddock slips and dangles from the end of the rope, unable to regain his foothold on the precarious rocks. Perched overhead, Tintin can barely support the weight of the much heavier man as the rope keeps cutting painfully into him. When Haddock realises the hopelessness of the situation, he insists on cutting himself off with his knife, choosing to sacrifice himself rather than consigning his young friend also to certain death. When Tintin realises Haddock's suicidal intentions, he pleads desperately with the Captain not to cut through the rope. He is ready to die together rather than live at the expense of losing his friend. The crisis is resolved with Hergé's trademark penchant for humour by putting Haddock's characteristic clumsiness to good use; his knife slips and hits the retreating Tharkey who gauges the emergency and comes to assist the duo. But this incident marks a poignant point in the relationship of these two men. Their relationship is intensified—cleansed and sanctified, as it were—in this snow-white heterotopia of purgation. Personal bonds are appraised and moral fibre tested as one's existence hangs precariously over ravines as unplumbed as one's doubts. Hergé chose his topography well; the bleak barren severity of the Tibetan cliffs and crags present the perfect heterotopic setting for the journey into one's soul.

The chapter examines how Tibet functions as a heterotopia of crisis for both Tintin and his creator. The twentieth in a set of twenty-four (if one considers the incomplete *Tintin and Alph-Art*), this is one of the later albums. It was written in 1958-59 against Hergé's personal problems which found resolution in creating this "white volume", a description evident from the cover of this entry in the series that stands out from the other very colourful ones. Georges Remi experienced persistent nightmares around the year 1958. He describes several of them in detail, where snow features prominently, what he called "the beauty and cruelty of white."[6] He consulted the Swiss psychoanalyst Ricklin, a pupil of Carl Jung, in April 1959 after one of his most terrifying drowning dreams. He was diagnosed with emotional and professional stress and advised to stop working on his ongoing project. He chose to tackle his fears instead in the way he knew best—by drawing them out (pun intended) on the page of the new Tintin adventure. The location that Hergé chooses for his new book also functions as a heterotopia of deviation for himself. Tintin had achieved unimaginable fame worldwide, and increasingly the burden of this success was weighing his creator down. He was tempted several times to desert his teenage hero and devote his attention to more abstract art forms, but his Catholic sense of morality and his Boy Scout ethos of "never give up" did not allow him to desert his protagonist. The snow-capped Himalayan peaks become the walls of the Foucauldian prison that he deconstructs as a heterotopia of deviation, where one must be incarcerated for a certain duration in order to discipline oneself.

The importance of the location in this Tintin volume becomes clearer if one knows how difficult it was for the author to arrive at it. After considering several possible narrative strains, even a return to the cowboys of America which was his favourite boyhood subject, Hergé finally decided on his protagonist's latest adventure and where to set it. An important factor was Chang Chon-Ren, the Chinese student at the Brussels Palace of Fine Arts who had inspired *The Blue Lotus*, the fifth volume in the series that Hergé was justifiably proud of. In the course of his regulation research on China in writing that story, Hergé made the acquaintance of this young foreigner who influenced him deeply. Apart from teaching him Chinese calligraphy and giving him tips on painting, Chang impressed upon Hergé the importance of meticulously researching his material before reproducing it in graphic art. It was through their animated interactions that the armchair artist developed an informed perspective on the politics of the Far East. During his weekly visits to his Belgian friend, Chang spoke of "history, anecdotes, costumes, poetry, art," among other things.[7] The two collaborated closely on both the drawings and the text of that volume. Hergé returned the favour by immortalising Chang as a central character in the story, a young orphan who becomes Tintin's guide and companion in the new country. If the fictional Chang becomes like a brother, not only from another mother but a completely different culture as well, to his alter-ego Tintin, his real-life counterpart was no less for Hergé. Chang returned to Shanghai, and in the intervening years events in China and later the war disrupted contact between the two friends. Twenty-five years later, encountering an artistic block with his personal life in turmoil, Hergé thought about his dear friend achingly and channelised him creatively for a second time.

Tintin in Tibet takes its lead from the last scene of *The Blue Lotus*, where Tintin parts tearfully from his Chinese friend and his adoptive family. In this new album he learns about his friend's plane crashing on the slopes of the Himalayas and breaks down emotionally. Incidentally, Chang is the only character in the entire series for whom the normally poised reporter who faces the most dangerous challenges with intrepidity is shown weeping. His supposed untimely death as a result of an unfortunate accident on the remote Tibetan highlands provides Hergé with a space that Foucault would have identified as a heterotopia of purgation, allowing a cathartic cleansing of his repressed yearning for his long-estranged friend. There is often a sense of purgation, of ridding oneself of impurities and undergoing a process of purification in heterotopias, allowing in someone in a state of deviance to render him fit once more before being let out into society. Thus, they might be spaces of rehabilitation and regeneration of both body and mind. Hergé's psychoanalytic therapy, his snow-drowned nightmares, his failing marriage and his lost liaisons all find poignant representation in the unremitting blanched expanse of this extraordinary text.

Foucault mentions that heterotopias often presuppose a system of opening and closing that isolates them into controlled, contained spaces. One might need permission to enter, or might be forced to enter, such a space, as in a prison. He adds that one must sometimes perform certain designated gestures or procedures in order to gain admittance to one of these spaces, like a Middle Eastern hammam, a communal bath house. Tintin's ability to gain access to the slopes where the accident occurred is met with several points of resistance. The narrative is clearly marked in its stages as the protagonist struggles to progress to the next level. The coolies and the guide urge him and his companions to imitate several ritualistic gestures and heed their many proscriptions as they negotiate the mountain tracks.

Foucault talks about the quality of heterochronicity that might be found in these other spaces, combining within themselves mutually incompatible slices of time, both real and imagined. The slopes of the Tibetan Himalayas dovetail into their physical terrain the present expedition of hope as well as the recent site of tragic despair and death. The Western visitors move forward in a purposeful onslaught in a land replete with Oriental tradition and superstition. The incident of the *chorten*, the holy monument preserving the ashes of the lamas, which according to local custom must never be crossed from the right, is an example of the local age-old wisdom coming in contact with foreign disdain of superstition. There is a sense of immeasurable time lying undisturbed for centuries between the impregnable peaks that are now accessed by two white men and a white dog, who stand incongruous against this all-white landscape. The unhurried way of life at the monastery, reflected in the periphrastic manner of speech employed by the monks, is a continuation of the traditional past. It marks a sharp contrast with the planned schedule of the western visitors whose speech is clipped, matter-of-fact, prosaic and of the present. Like many of the albums in the series, *Tintin in Tibet* explores the interesting interface as the protagonist and his older companion encounter other cultures. But here additionally, there is the distinct sense of the past and the present interlocking into each other as the central characters make their way through the Himalayan highlands. The multilayered temporality fragments the Tibetan slopes into an-other spatial dimension apart from its physical literality.

The spatial turn has gathered momentum in the humanities and social sciences since the last two decades of the twentieth century in the works of thinkers like Adrian Soja, Leven De Cauter, Michael Dehaene, Barney Warf and Santa Arias. As part of this discourse the concept of heterotopia finds increasingly extended critical appeal not only in literary departments but across disciplines as varied as cultural geography and visual studies, making its presence felt in architectural theory and urban activism with equal relevance. Real and imagined spaces from Melville's *Pequod* to the Kowloon Walled City have been embraced into the discourse of divergent domains and subversive spaces. This chapter participates in this project of parsing alternative arenas by offering an "other" reading of one of the most abiding icons of popular culture in the world. And in doing so, it provides a uniquely "grounded" perspective never before accorded to the Tintin comic series, a work otherwise the subject of such "mountainous" commentary.

Notes

1   Farr, *Companion*, 161.
2   Foucault, "Of Other Spaces," 332.
3   Ibid., 333.
4   Ibid., 334.
5   Sadoul, *Entretiens*, 177.
6   Ibid., 58.
7   Thompson, *Tintin*, 77-78.

Bibliography

Apostolidès, Jean-Marie. *The Metamorphoses of Tintin, Or, Tintin for Adults*. Stanford: Stanford University Press, 2010.

Assouline, Pierre and Charles Ruas. *Hergé: The Man who Created Tintin*. Oxford: Oxford University Press, 2009.

Daubert, Michel. *Tintin: The Art of Hergé*. Brussels: Museum Hergé, 2013.

Farr, Michael. *Tintin: The Complete Companion*. London: Egmont, 2011.

Foucault, Michel. "Of Other Spaces: Utopias and Heterotopias." In *Rethinking Architecture: A Reader in Cultural Theory*, edited by Neil Leach. Abingdon: Routledge, 1997.

McCarthy, Tom. *Tintin and the Secret of Literature*. London: Granta Books, 2011.

Sadoul, Numa. *Entretiens avec Hergé: Tintin et Moi*. Paris: Casterman, 1983.

Sterckx, Pierre. *Tintin: Hergé's Masterpiece*. Paris: Rizzoli, 2015.

Thompson, Harry. *Tintin: Hergé and His Creation*. London: John Murray, 2011.

Tisseron, Serge. *Tintin Chez le Psychanalyste*. Paris: Calmann-Lévy, 1985.

_____. *Tintin et les Secrets de Famille*. Paris: Séguier, 1990.

Notes on Contributors

1. Jayson Althofer is an independent researcher based in Toowoomba, Australia. His recent and forthcoming publications include: "Friedrich Engels and Gothic Marxism: A Fairy-Tale Introduction," *Critical Imprints* VIII: The Supernatural in Literature (December 2020); "'A ghost-ship in fog': Alexander Trocchi's *Détournement* of Gothic Literature in *Cain's Book* (1960)," in *Gothic Mash-Ups: Hybridity, Appropriation, and Intertextuality in Gothic Storytelling*, ed. Natalie Neill (forthcoming from Lexington Books); and, co-written with Brian Musgrove, "Capital of Dreadful Light: Marx, Engels and Diabolic Enlightenment," in *Gothic Dreams/Nightmares*, ed. Carol M. Davison (forthcoming from Manchester University Press).

2. Mario Bosincu is Lecturer in German Studies at the University of Sassari (Italy). His research focuses on Ernst Jünger, the German tradition of cultural criticism, and Romanticism. He is member of the Italian Association for German Studies and co-editor of the *Giornale critico di storia delle idee*. His publications include: *Autorschaft als Widerstand gegen die Moderne. Über die Wende Ernst Jüngers* (Königshausen & Neumann, 2013), *Sulle posizioni perdute. Forme della soggettività moderna dall'anticapitalismo romantic a Ernst Jünger* (Ipoc, 2014).

3. Ratul Nandi is an Assistant Professor of English in Siliguri College, West Bengal, India. He has published several research papers and articles in Journals, Edited volumes and News Papers. His current research interest includes Animal Studies, Anthropocene and Climate Change, Ecocriticism, Romanticism, Literary Theory and Continental Philosophy.

4. Pavlína Flajšarová, Ph.D, is an Associate Professor in the Department of English and American Studies, Faculty of Arts, Palacký University Olomouc, Czech Republic. In 1999–2000,

she was a Fulbright visiting researcher at The Catholic University of America in Washington, D.C. She has published four scholarly monographs, *The Bridge and the Eclipse: Metaphor in The Poetry of Samuel Taylor Coleridge* (Palacký University Press, 2004), *Poetry in Great Britain and Northern Ireland after 1945* (Uniprint, 2007), *Diaspora in the Fiction of Andrea Levy* (Palacký University Press, 2014), and *Grace Nichols Universal and Diverse: Ethnicity in the Poetry and Fiction of Grace Nichols* (Palacký University Press, 2016). Her early publications focused on the topic of nature and natural sensitivity in the works of British Romantic poets Samuel Taylor Coleridge and William Wordsworth. She has also presented many papers on anglophone poetry and fiction in International conferences, published numerous articles in peer-reviewed journals, and contributed several entries into *The Greenwood Encyclopedia of American Poets and Poetry* (Greenwood Press, 2005). Recently, she co-authored three monographs on Scottish contemporary fiction and a volume of Canadian literary history, all by Palacký University Press. Her current research interest is in British ethnic and diasporic literature. At present, she serves as the Vice-dean of International Relations at the Faculty of Arts, Palacký University.

5. Oriol Batalla completed his MA in Comparative Literature and Cultural Analysis from the University of Amsterdam, Netherlands. His research interest includes Critical Theory, Cultural Analysis, Environmental Humanities, Extinction Studies, Historical and New Materialism, Political Ecology and Political Philosophy.

6. Ankita Sharma is currently pursuing her Ph.D from the Department of English, GGS Indraprastha University, New Delhi, India. Her research interests include Memory Studies, Affect Studies, Contemporary autobiographical fiction, War literature, Science fiction and Creative writing. She holds a Master's degree in English literature from the University of Delhi, India.

7. Jayjit Sarkar is Assistant Professor in the Department of English, Raiganj University, India. He is the author of *Illness as Method: Beckett, Kafka, Mann, Woolf and Eliot* (Wilmington, DE: Vernon Press, 2019) and the co-editor of *Border and Bordering: Politics, Poetics, Precariousness* (Stuttgart: ibidem Press, 2020); *The Portrait of an Artist as a Pathographer: On Writing Illnesses and Illnesses in Writing* (Wilmington, DE: Vernon Press, 2021) and *The Films of Apichatpong Weerasethakul* (Liverpool: Liverpool University Press, forthcoming, 2021).

8. Rachel L. Carazo is an Ed.D. at St. Thomas University and MLIS at the University of Southern Mississippi, USA. She has a graduate degree (M.A, English) from Northwestern State University. She is currently editing several collections on *Gladiator*, mythological equines, and dragons.

9. Debnita Chakravarti is Associate Professor in the Department of English, Shri Shikshayatan College, India. She has a doctoral degree from the University of Reading and a postdoctoral fellowship from the University of Southampton, UK. Alongside Romanticism, Dr. Chakravarti's research interests include popular culture, leading to chapters on Disney heroines, *Broadchurch*, *Friends*, the films of Zoya Akhtar and Rituparno Ghosh. She has been published by Routledge, Pearson, Ashgate, McFarland (essays in edited books) besides several peer-reviewed journals. She is a regular literary conversationalist at the Kolkata Literary Meet.

Index